ALTERNATIVE SCHOOLING
IN AMERICAN EDUCATION

Pygmalion *or* Frankenstein?

Edited by
John C. Carr
Jean Dresden Grambs
E.G. Campbell
University of Maryland, College Park

ADDISON-WESLEY PUBLISHING COMPANY, INC.
Reading, Massachusetts • Menlo Park, California
London • Amsterdam • Don Mills, Ontario • Sydney

LIBRARY
The University of Texas
At San Antonio

ISBN 0-201-00898-X
ABCDEFGHIJ-AL-79876

Preface

The myth of Pygmalion and the story of Frankenstein provide appropriate symbols through which the question of the effectiveness of schooling may be examined. The sculptor Pygmalion molded Galatea, a creature of beauty, while Dr. Frankenstein, the mad scientist, manufactured a monster. In their efforts to create an educated society through either a continuance of traditional schooling or through newer and different content and methods, have the schools breathed life into a Galatea or have they assembled a dangerous, lumbering creature—a monster operating out of control?

These questions are particularly pertinent now. Many attempts have been made to reform the schools in the United States in the twentieth century. The array of experiments in schooling styles during the last fifteen years has left many educators frustrated and confused, some productive and content, and most ambivalent, not sure what the efforts have been for or the degree to which success or failure can be gauged.

As "alternative" becomes an accepted term for schooling in this country, issues about the purpose of formal education and how it may be achieved take on new urgency. As alternative schools—both liberal and conservative—become optional throughout the country, an understanding of what such schools are (or can be) is important if wise decisions are to be made about support and funding, organization and administration, and teaching and learning.

In three sections centering around the issues of "What is needed?", "What has been tried?", and "Was it worthwhile?", *Pygmalion or Frankenstein: Alternative Schooling in American Education* attempts to help readers determine where on a scale ranging from Beauty to Monster alternative choices lie.

Special gratitude is extended to Larry Glaser and Cheryl Faraone for their assistance in preparing the manuscript.

College Park, Maryland   JCC
June 1976   JDG
    EGC

Contents

VS.

...with marvelous artistry Pygmalion carved a snowy ivory statue which he named Galatea....

...and the statue came to life...and she was beautiful....

from the myth of "Pygmalion and Galatea"

...A new species would bless me as its creator and source; many happy and excellent natures would owe their being to me....

...I beheld the wretch—the miserable monster whom I had created....He muttered some inarticulate sounds, while a grin wrinkled his cheeks....

...Alas! I had turned loose into the world a depraved wretch....

from Frankenstein *by Mary Wollstonecraft Shelley*

My Galatea, Your Monster, or Why Don't We Do It My Way? An Introductory Essay

Mark Twain contended that "Soap and education are not as sudden as a massacre, but they are more deadly in the long run." Soap aside, he might well have been expressing the point of view of all critics of American education since World War II.

Debate that had principally centered around the emergence of ideas fashioned on John Dewey's philosophy of education was exacerbated by the mid-1940s as Americans reconsidered the future of their society. Recognition of teaching-learning experiences in the military, exposure to worldwide cultures, and an awareness of the possibilities that technology made possible caused many educators and laypersons to align themselves clearly in either the camp of "classicism" or in the camp of "life adjustment." On the one hand, salvation was seen residing in the traditions of Western civilization; on the other, in the realities and human interactions of the present. It was perhaps in this period—which coincided with the development of cybernetics—that the notion of public education as Pygmalion's beautiful Galatea or Frankenstein's monster emerged. Of course, spokespersons for both camps likened their philosophy of education to Galatea and their opponent's to the monster.

Since the end of World War II, American society has undergone many changes, among the most significant for public education being desegregation, decentralization of cities, exploration of space, community control of schools, growing behavioral permissiveness, disenchantment with the political and social establishment, student unrest, and growing militancy within the teaching profession. Regardless of philosophical orientation, most Americans by the 1960s came to believe that "...schools no longer appear to mean what most of us hoped they would mean in American society."[1]

With the changes in society came pressures—both direct and indirect—for changes in the schools, and with the demands for change came reaction to those demands. And so the polarities of "beautiful" and "monstrous" became more firmly established. As the staggering events of the sixties generated intense controversy over America's values and vision, schools became increasingly difficult places in which to learn and to work. Almost as a kind of release valve, various kinds of alternative approaches to schooling developed and with them an even sharper delineation about the work of educational Pygmalions and Frankensteins.

The notion of schooling as something beautiful or monstrous has roots that extend beyond the American experience to the beginnings of civilization itself. The central issue, finally, echoes the "art for art's sake" debate raised in the philosophy of art: Does formal education (by which we mean "schooling") exist for intrinsic or instrumental reasons? Should education be its own reward—enriching, fulfilling, and answering only to itself? Or should formal education prepare people for competitive survival in society, concerning itself with practical, saleable skills? What methods of instruction can best achieve educational goals?

As with Galatea versus the monster, these are extremes, but they do describe the backboards against which the time-honored arguments have bounced. While large numbers of graduates of American schools have been able to function fairly adequately, the issues remain: What is schooling for and how can we best achieve its objective? Or, as many believe, ". . . the most compelling problem confronting secondary education is the issue of what the high schools should be about."[2] In addition, there is the question: ". . . who is to make what decisions for whom? That question is probably the most pressing educational question both today and tomorrow. It is at the core of current discussions of accountability, voucher systems and the like in schooling. It is at the core of any minority group demands for self-determination and equality. Ultimately, it brings us into the matter of who owns the child and who is to determine his freedom."[3]

These concerns, as indicated earlier, are not new. Such concerns and the criticisms into which they naturally evolved have beset American schools from the beginning. Demands for reform came shortly after the founding of the first public schools in Massachusetts in the middle of the seventeenth century—and demands for change have come when and wherever there have been concerned citizens. Content and methodology remained essentially the same in the schools—fixed at all levels—until the end of the nineteenth century when a new kind of secondary school developed. It has been in the twentieth century, during which time public education as we know it evolved, that rancorous divisions over substance and approach have occurred.

One of the difficulties in creating schooling satisfactory to all stems from efforts to ensure that American schools provide educational opportunities unparalleled in other nations and other times. American schools are now characterized by universality, compulsory attendance, public support, nonsectarianism, equal opportunity, and a single-ladder organization. Together these constitute a massive requirement and generate complication upon complication for day-to-day implementation.

Add to this the fact that, prior to fifty years ago, the majority of adolescents did not go beyond the elementary-school level. The most recent estimated statistics of the Office of Education, Department of Health, Education, and Welfare indicate that approximately 51,300,000 students are enrolled in public and private schools in the fifty states. The range of capabilities, interests, and needs of these students is great; coupled with shifting societal expectations and the adjustments required by rapid technological change, it seems inevitable that schools as they have existed are "damned if they do and damned if they don't."

The very fact that public schools are publicly controlled attracts the interest of utopian thinkers to them as a means of bringing about social change. Consequently, the schools are frequently torn between two poles. As the purveyor of the nation's cultural heritage, they are inevitably conservative; but as a potential instrument of social betterment, they are under constant pressure to improve the society around them.

When other educational institutions fail, Americans turn almost instinctively to the schools. The typical urban public school today is expected to perform the role of social worker, parent, physician, minister, policeman, drug counselor, human relations counselor, and employment agency.[4]

Because the greatest number of us have been exposed to formal education of some sort and approximately two-thirds of the American adult population has graduated high school, we all believe we know something about what schooling should and should not be. "If only things had been different when I was in school" seems to be a common plaint; experience has made every citizen a friendly or antagonistic critic of the formal learning process. We are not satisfied with the realization that as creations of human beings, schools cannot be perfect.

As pointed out by a committee of the Association for Supervision and Curriculum Development:

The bulk of criticism has been of five kinds: (a) schools are inefficient; (b) schools are socially and technically inadequate; (c) schools are inhumane; (d) schools are culturally inauthentic; and (e) schools are culturally authentic in maintaining the social-economic status quo of powerless groups in our society. The criticism of the schools in terms of what is wrong with society has appeared variously as Social Reconstructionism, Romantic Radicalism, and Political-Cultural Radicalism.[5]

Essential to the argument over whether schooling is Galatea-like or monsterlike is the question of achievement in cognitive skills. Arguments from the fifties forward have dealt with this concern, as the writings of Daniel Bell, Mortimer Smith, Robert Lynd, Arthur Bestor, Paul Woodring, Max Rafferty, and Hyman Rickover attest. A primary assumption of these writers is the notion that schools have as their major responsibility the development of the cognitive domain and that results should be judged primarily by the curriculum which already exists and the methods of teaching that implement that already-existing curriculum. Standard measures of growth are determined through I.Q. and achievement tests.

While not rejecting cognitive skills, those educators labeled progressive/liberal see school as having certain other responsibilities. In the twentieth century, writers of this persuasion include John Dewey, William Heard Kilpatrick, Harold Rugg, Jules Henry, and more recently Edgar Friedenberg, Paul Goodman, Charles Silberman, John Holt, Jonathan Kozol, James Herndon, and Ivan Illich. Basic to the thinking of this group is the idea that new educational designs will nurture an equitable environment in which all people can fulfill their potential, not equally but individually.

Working from opposing philosophical and practical points of view, both camps, one perceived as philosophical (in the traditional sense) and the other perceived as scientific, probably agree—some semantic differences aside—that Robert Hutchins, former president of the University of Chicago, is correct in his observation that the schools "...may do many things for the young: they may amuse them, comfort them, look after their health, and keep them off the street. But they are not public schools unless they start their pupils toward an understanding of what it means to be a self-governing citizen of a self-governing political community."[6]

And there, as Hamlet observed, is the rub. Through what study and what way can students be brought to this stage of awareness? Is the proper course through the channels of tradition and what its proponents identify as "academic respectability"? Or through those of "humanistic liberalism"? Such questions of value remain unresolved in the largest democratic school system in the world.

Since the beginning of the 1960s, efforts to reform the schools have manifested themselves principally through experimentation with alternative styles of education. Proposals and efforts to abolish schools, to create schools outside the system, to establish other equally accepted schools within the system, and to provide for differences of approach within individual schools, have met with varying success. Under many names and guises, formal educational experiences designed for change have come to be identified principally under the labels of "open," "free," and "alternative."

Regardless of designation, the National Alternative School Program, a clearinghouse at the University of Massachusetts, estimated in August 1975 that approximately 1000 alternative schools were operating nationwide.* According to the Clearinghouse, about half of the schools are in suburban communities. (In addition to the locales mentioned below, some others are Great Neck, New York; Webster Grove, Missouri; and Beverly Hills, California.)

Among the kinds of alternative schools which came into existence during the late 1960s and the early 1970s are:

Schools without walls or satellite schools in which students work in many parts of the community: businesses, galleries, health-care units, as well as other agencies of society outside the school building. The Parkway School, Philadelphia, is perhaps the best-known example. Other cities such as Washington, D.C., Baltimore, Chicago, Boston, and Madison, Wisconsin have hosted such schools.

---

*Until recently, "alternative" referred to schooling that was different from traditional content and method. Recent efforts, as explained later in this article, have pressed for what might be called an "alternative to alternatives."

Open Schools, usually for able students, in which individualized study and self-direction are the order of the day. St. Paul's Open School, St. Paul, Minnesota, and the Newton High School, Newton, Massachusetts are principal examples.

Ethnic/racial schools, whose concern has been the development of group and individual pride and the development of basic skills. Examples are Black House and Casa de la Raza, for Mexican-American students, both in Berkeley, California. (It is interesting to note that both schools have been challenged by the United States Department of Health, Education and Welfare on the grounds of discrimination.)

Dropout centers/street academies, where basic educational and vocational skills are offered. Cities that have offered such programs are New York, Washington, D.C., and Chicago.

Special problem schools, where students with severe academic or emotional difficulties, or special concerns (such as pregnancy) are able to pursue some aspect of secondary-school education. Louisville, Kentucky and Grand Rapids, Michigan have been in the forefront of providing such alternative schools.

Mini-schools or schools-within-schools, in which entire school populations (or parts of them) group in smaller segments to focus on special interests or problems. Berkeley High School, Berkeley, California and several schools in New York City have attempted this approach.

Free schools established outside of the school system by parents or other interested individuals. Free schools, which typically operate in a permissive fashion, are supported by parents and other interested people. Free schools have appeared in almost all parts of the country, notably in California and in the suburban areas of large cities.

With the appearance of each new approach to schooling the issue of Pygmalion versus Frankenstein again arose. The fundamental questions discussed earlier were raised. In addition, and at a specific level, recurring criticisms marked the efforts of these schools: too much free time, insufficient attention to the basics, improper attention to significant goals, and a lack of intellectual vigor. The argument also has been offered that adolescents do not possess sufficient maturity to assume the responsibilities that alternative schools require.

In fascinating contrast to the development of the kinds of alternative schools described above is the new "basics alternative" option, gaining ground in many places throughout the United States. B. Frank Brown's observation that "...nonformal education and nontraditional learning are the wave of the future"[7] is being met by demands for schooling that ensures tradition, "basics," and discipline. Conservatives argue that the day of "permissive education" is on the wane and American public schools now face a return to basics in reading, writing, arithmetic, and behavior.

The demand in recent years for innovation and for alternative schools has resulted in an ironic and unforeseen development in public education. . . . There is a strong and spreading movement to include among the alternatives the kinds of schools that the alternative approach repudiates. In other words, the old-fashioned academic school has suddenly become a novel experiment. In towns and cities where the open classroom concept or some other variation of neo-progressivism has been introduced, the advocates of strong academic schools have made an interesting strategic move. They have argued before school boards that if experiments in free and unstructured programs are permitted then experiments in the traditional academic approach should also be permitted. And in many places they are winning the argument.[8]

Lending support to Mortimer Smith's comments are those of Charles Silberman, author of *Crisis in the Classroom*, the study that popularized many of the innovations of the 1960s:

A lot of people tried what they call open classrooms.... They literally broke down walls out of a mistaken idea that 'open' means 'open space.' The noise level got so high that nobody knew what he was doing. They used programmed instruction which is not individual in the real sense. And they did it all without teacher training. It was chaos, and kids didn't learn a goddam thing.[9]

Alternatives to traditional schooling, alternatives to alternative schooling—on what swing of the pendulum are we floating? Toward Pygmalion's Galatea or Frankenstein's monster? John I. Goodlad observes, "Other generations believed that they had the luxury of preparing their children to live in a society similar to their own. Ours in the first generation to have achieved the Socratic widsom of knowing that we do not know the world in which our children will live."[10]

How can we prepare young people for that world?

As we begin to discern a context for the educational innovation of the 1960s forward, we gain the impression of great school reform. Closer examination suggests that much of what seemed revolutionary has proved ephemeral. Changes in the organization of schools, and specifically the classroom, and changes in both teaching approaches and aspects of the curriculum (especially mathematics, science, foreign languages, and social studies) have disappeared or become muted. Many observers believe that the schools, as agents of society, are essentially the same as before. The old curriculum is intact, they argue, and the textbook has regained supremacy. The College Entrance Examinations hover in the wings, more menacing than ever.

A Ford Foundation study makes it increasingly clear that the decade of change and innovation has had no lasting effect in either changing the schools or improving the quality of teaching and learning. "Perhaps the most significant outcome of this period of experimentation is the realization that realignment of the time in class, allowing students to learn at their own rate, teaching by computers, knocking down walls, and teaming teachers are not the significant variables.''[11]

Fred Hechinger seems more optimistic when he comments, ''The extreme turn to open education as an 'alternative school' may no longer be in the forefront of reform; but the virtues of more informal teaching, with greater attention to children's individual needs, have been given new recognition and impetus.''[12]

Cautioning us to see things in the broader context, Hechinger continues, ''American school reform moves not in a straight line, but in spirals. Wasteful as those circuitous movements may seem, they may well offer greater safety than a rigid commitment to an approved and accepted course. Whatever their shortcomings, these gyrations reflect the way American society moves.''[13]

In a free society, alternatives of all kinds seem appropriate. Perhaps the question of whether schools and schooling are beautiful like Galatea or monstrous like Dr. Frankenstein's creation can be resolved by the existence of alternative schools of every kind. Perhaps the question—or the high emotion associated with it—is an important factor only when no alternatives exist. Mario Fantini suggests that the establishment of all kinds of schools for all kinds of people is a solution vocal parents can bring about by forcing their local school systems to be truly accountable for the education of all students.[14]

This text is organized into three sections. Section One, ''The Need to Create Something Different,'' is concerned with some fundamental issues about schooling and how effective education can be achieved. Articles in this section, as in the others, are intended to raise for the reader concerns that may be grasped more clearly by thinking of them in a polar fashion. Section Two, ''Starting New or Piecing Together,'' explores not only how alternative schools work, but also presents reports of many efforts to make contemporary schools viable—either in new or traditional ways. Section Three, ''Judgments: Galatea or the Monster,'' presents critical commentary by a variety of educational experts who speak directly to the question of whether school reform, as represented through alternative schools, has achieved its objective.

All articles are followed by questions and suggestions intended to assist the individual reader to probe, independently or in conjunction with others, issues he or she may face as a teacher, administrator, or parent.

Each of the three sections of *Pygmalion or Frankenstein?* is preceded by a *Versus* section, which presents in succinct fashion timely expressions of concern about the issue raised in the section. Each section is also introduced by comments from the editors.

The first page of each article in the book contains three items of material that should prove helpful to teachers and students. First, a provocative, capsulizing quotation from the article itself; second, suggested comparisons or contrasts to other articles in the book; and third, a biographical sketch of the author(s).

NOTES

1. James B. Macdonald and Esther Zaret, eds., *Schools in Search of Meaning, 1975 Yearbook* (Washington, D.C.: Association for Supervision and Curriculum Development, 1975), p. 1.

2. B. Frank Brown, "The Reform of Secondary Education," *National Association of Secondary School Principals Bulletin* **58**, no. 382 (May 1974), p. 48.

3. John I. Goodlad, ed., "Working Paper for the White House Conference on Children," excerpted in *The Washington Post*, 13 December 1970.

4. Diane Ravitch, "The Public School's Tasks and How They Grew," *The New York Times*, 16 November 1975. © 1975 by The New York Times Company. Reprinted by permission.

5. Ibid.

6. Robert Hutchins, quoted in Ravitch, "The Public School's Tasks and How They Grew," *The New York Times*, 16 November 1975.

7. B. Frank Brown, "The Reform of Secondary Education," *National Association of Secondary School Principals Bulletin* **58**, no. 382 (May 1974), p. 54.

8. Mortimer Smith, "Another New 'Back to Basics' School," *Council for Basic Education Bulletin* **19**, no. 2 (October 1974). Reprinted by permission.

9. Charles Silberman, quoted in "Back to Basics in the Schools," *Newsweek,* 21 October 1974. Copyright 1974 by Newsweek, Inc. All rights reserved. Reprinted by permission.

10. John I. Goodlad, ed., "Working Paper for the White House Conference on Children," excerpted in *The Washington Post*, 13 December 1970.

11. B. Frank Brown, "The Reform of Secondary Education," *National Association of Secondary School Principals Bulletin* **58**, no. 382 (May 1974), p. 47.

12. Fred Hechinger, "Where Have All the Innovations Gone?" *The New York Times*, 16 November 1975.

13. Ibid.

14. Mario Fantini, *Public Schools of Choice* (New York: Simon and Schuster), 1974.

VS.

Man can't live without Utopian visions.[1]

The goal of humanistic education must be to prepare people for dealing humanely with the unexpected situations with which our rapidly changing world is going to confront us. Who is naive enough to believe that any information, or any skills, will be relevant in ten or even five years? Education must become then learning about learning, learning how to deal with the unexpected, with new situations. In short, education requires the changing of sensibilities and mental processes so that the student knows how to learn, not what to learn.[2]

...A primary task for the reformer is to help educators realize that there is no middle ground; either they work to make education, schooling, and social reform one, or they function as agents of a vastly inequitable and repressive society.[3]

1. Panaceas sold to the public rarely work in practice.
2. Educational panaceas, in particular, win widespread laudatory publicity before they have demonstrated their true worth.
3. Evidence of the failure of educational panaceas is rarely reported in the mass media.[4]

I have discovered it is not enough to act on the premise that if you merely expose a child to enough of those ideas that make up our culture, he will make good use of the exposure. There is such a strong drift away from the passing-on of the traditional culture that it is quite easy for a child to avoid absorbing even the best of it, and I find it patronizing for an educator to assume that children should be 'reached' largely through material relevant to the present, and through the kid culture of rock music and slogan politics.[5]

Tne broadened curriculum. Among the courses offered at the Ravenswood High School in East Palo Alto (Calif.) are the following: Non-Verbal Communication, Reading Classified Ads, the Con Game, Life Styles, Games and Gaming, History of American Athletes, How to Beat the Achievement Tests, and something called, rather mysteriously, Bicycle Writing.[6]

SOURCES FOR VERSUS

1. Michael Harrington, quoted in *Cacotopias and Utopias* (New York: The Fund for the Republic, Center for the Study of Democratic Institutions, 1965).

2. Ted Perry, "Core What?" *American Film Institute Education Newsletter*, No. 1, 1972.

3. James J. Shields, Jr., "Educational Alternatives: A Postscript—Social Reform as Educational Policy", *Foundations of Education: Dissenting Views*, eds. James J. Sheilds, Jr. and Colin Greer (New York: Wiley, 1974), p. 187.

4. Albert Shanker, "Where We Stand", *The New York Times*, 1 December 1974.

5. Margot Hentoff, "Schools We Want: A Family Dialog," *The Saturday Review*, 19 September 1970.

6. "Trivia of the Month," *Council on Basic Education Bulletin*, May 1972, p. 15

SECTION ONE
Issues: The Need to Create
Something Different

Arguments about education appear to be almost as old as written language. Who should go to school? What kind of schooling is best? What should be taught in school? How should it be taught?

The public debate over education, its processes and promises, has been especially lively and vocal during the last thirty years. Although before this time educational issues occasionally made front-page news, the average person usually encountered public education via the sports page or through his or her own children's progress. Several events have changed the American perspective: the seeming Soviet scientific excellence, court-ordered school desegregation, and the controversy over the Vietnam war. These events, although not central to the basic mission of the schools to provide general education for children and youth, presented severe challenges to existing school programs and patterns of school organization.

As one might expect, the rediscovery of the schools by many nonschool individuals produced a rash of remarkable critical responses. Educators who were in policymaking positions during the 1950s and 1960s felt buffeted by articulate speakers and writers who, although they may have had only minimal contact with contemporary American public education, spoke passionately about all the deficits therein. Desegregation revealed the incredible inequality which separate-but-equal had masked for so long, dooming generations of black students to grossly inferior education with resultant low achievement, and creating an almost permanent poverty subclass. The unpopular Vietnam war, with the threat of the draft hanging over the lives and futures of millions of young people, moved a generation of college students to unprecedented revolt against the status quo. Most directly affected were those agencies of society closely concerned with youth—the schools. Some institutions were paralyzed with confusion and fear while others became hyperactive in efforts to "be with it."

Other societal pressures, both direct and indirect, caused Americans to question, deeply and anxiously, their values and how those values were determining ways of living and learning. As experiments with alternative life styles came into existence, so, naturally, did experiments with alternative learning styles. Almost every form of educational experience in history was re-examined. Ferment became foment and, by 1975, the concept of alternative schooling—in both the private and public sector—had become an accepted premise. But as the troubled sixties recede in memory and the latter part of the seventies generates some reaction to the previous chaos, both parents and students seek direction about what schooling is best for their needs.

In this first section, it is clear that both conservatives and liberals perceive the beauty of Galatea in their own persuasion and the ugliness of the monster in opposing ones. On the one hand, Alvin Toffler, in the opening article, alerts us to future unknowns while others "... are reaching back, back for things that maybe never existed. They want some kind of basic teaching for their children."*

Articles in this section are preceded by a *Versus* page which presents contrasting points of view. The *Versus* items might be examined separately or together; they may serve as the basis for initial or summary debate; they may also be examined and discussed in relation to the other *Versus* pages at the beginnings of Sections Two and Three.

As you read Section One, make comparisons and contrasts among articles and in relation to issues raised on the *Versus* pages (and elsewhere in the book where you may have read). It is also important to relate what you read to immediate educational developments in your community. How would the citizens of your community react to the various criticisms and suggestions made in this section? To what extent do you and your fellow students or faculty agree that there is a "need to create something different"? Can you agree—some, a little—on how things should be different? The annotated bibliography at the end of the section suggests additional readings that may help you obtain the information and insight needed to answer these questions and be persuasive about your beliefs.

Some specific questions to keep in mind as you read are:

- What assumptions about "good schooling" can be derived from reading these critical reviews?
- Do the individuals appear to speak from an elitist or antielitist position? Is "good education" to be reserved for the few who can most benefit or should it be available to all?
- What reasons are given to account for the current deep dissatisfaction with the schools?
- Which of these criticisms match your own experience? With which criticisms are you most in sympathy?
- Are there some criticisms of the schools you would add to the ones that follow?

---

*John Sullivan, quoted in Donnel Nunes, "Some Schools in Area Returning to 3R's," *The Washington Post*, 7 September 1975.

"The ultimate purpose of futurism in education is...to help learners cope with real-life crises, opportunities, and perils...."

Compare Toffler's remarks with those of Max Rafferty in "American Education: 1975–2000" and with the National Commission's "Recommendations for Improving Secondary Education" (both in Section One).

The Psychology of the Future

Alvin Toffler

All education springs from some image of the future. If the image of the future held by a society is grossly inaccurate, its education system will betray its youth.

Imagine an Indian tribe which for centuries has sailed its dugouts on the river at its doorstep. During all this time the economy and culture of the tribe have depended upon fishing, preparing and cooking the products of the river, growing food in soil fertilized by the river, building boats and appropriate tools. So long as the rate of technological change in such a community stays slow, so long as no wars, invasions, epidemics or other natural disasters upset the even rhythm of life, it is simple for the tribe to formulate a workable image of its own future, since tomorrow merely repeats yesterday.

It is from this image that education flows. Schools may not even exist in the tribe; yet there is a curriculum—a cluster of skills, values and rituals to be learn-

Alvin Toffler, "The Role of the Future in Education," in *Learning for Tomorrow*, ed. Alvin Toffler (New York: Random House, 1974). Copyright © 1974 by Alvin Toffler. Reprinted by permission of Random House, Inc.

Alvin Toffler is best known for his book *Future Shock*, in which he raised fundamental issues about contemporary society's ability to cope with the forces of technological change. He is author of *The Culture Consumers* and editor of *The Schoolhouse in the City*. Mr. Toffler is a former editor of *Fortune* magazine. He has taught at the New York School for Social Research (New York) and has been a consultant to the Rockefeller Brothers Fund and to corporations and educational institutions.

ed. Boys are taught to scrape bark and hollow out trees, just as their ancestors did before them. The teacher in such a system knows what he is doing, secure in the knowledge that tradition—the past—will work in the future.

What happens to such a tribe, however, when it pursues its traditional methods unaware that five hundred miles upstream men are constructing a gigantic dam that will dry up their branch of the river? Suddenly the tribe's image of the future, the set of assumptions on which its members base their present behavior, becomes dangerously misleading. Tomorrow will not replicate today. The tribal investment in preparing its children to live in a riverine culture becomes a pointless and potentially tragic waste. A false image of the future destroys the relevance of the education effort.

This is our situation today—only it is we, ironically, not some distant strangers—who are building the dam that will annihilate the culture of the present. Never before has any culture subjected itself to so intense and prolonged a bombardment of technological, social, and info-psychological change. This change is accelerating and we witness everywhere in the high-technology societies evidence that the old industrial-era structures can no longer carry out their functions.

Yet our political leaders for the most part propagate (and believe) the myth that industrial society is destined to perpetuate itself indefinitely. Like the elders of the tribe living on the riverbank, they blindly assume that the main features of the present social system will extend indefinitely into the future. And most educators, including most of those who regard themselves as agents of change, unthinkingly accept this myth.

They fail to recognize that the acceleration of change—in technology, in family structure, marriage and divorce patterns, mobility rates, division of labor, in urbanization, ethnic and subcultural conflict and international relations—means, by definition, the swift arrival of a future that is radically *different* from the present. They have never tried to imagine what a super-industrial civilization might look like, and what this might mean for their students. And so, most schools, colleges and universities base their teaching on the usually tacit notion that tomorrow's world will be basically familiar: the present writ large. Nothing, I believe, could be more profoundly deceptive.

I would contend, in fact, that no educational institution today can set sensible goals or do an effective job until its members—from chancellor or principal down to the newest faculty recruit, not to mention its students—subject their own assumptions about tomorrow to critical analysis. For their shared or collective image of the future dominates the decisions made in the institution.

The primitive father teaching his son how to carve a canoe had in mind an image of the future his son would inhabit. Since he assumed that the future would replicate the present, just as the present replicated the past, his image of the future was just as rich, detailed, comprehensive and structured as his image of the present. It *was* his image of the present. Yet when change struck, his imagery proved not merely obsolete but anti-adaptive because it left out the possibility of radical change.

Like our distant ancestor, educators, too, need an image of tomorrow's society. But this image must include the possibility—indeed, the high likelihood—of radical change. This image need not be "correct" or "final"; it cannot be. There are no certainties, and any picture of a foreseeable society that depicts it as static or stable is probably delusory. Thus, to design educational systems for tomorrow (or even for today) we need not images of a future frozen in amber, as it were, but something far more complicated: sets of images of successive and alternative futures, each one tentative and different from the next.

SCENARIO IN THE CLASSROOM

What applies to the educator and the institution applies even more strongly to the learner. Just as all social groups and institutions have, in effect, collectively shared images of the future, each individual also has, in his or her cranium, a set of assumptions, an architecture of premises, about events to come. The child, almost from birth, begins to build up a set of expectations from its daily experience. Later these expectations become more complexly organized, and they begin to encompass more and more distant reaches of future time. Each person's private image of the future shapes his or her decision-making in crucial ways.

Students today receive a vast amount of undigested information and misinformation from newspapers, records, TV, movies, radio and other sources. As a result, they are aware of the rapidity with which the world is changing. But if many young people are prepared to contemplate the idea of radical change in the real world, this does not mean that they have the slightest idea about the implications of high-speed change for their own lives.

Some time ago I performed an unusual and confessedly nonscientific experiment with thirty-three high-school students, mainly fifteen- and sixteen-year olds. I asked each of them to help formulate a collective image of the future by writing down on a slip of paper seven events he or she thought likely to occur in the future, and to then date these events. I avoided saying anything that would restrict the *kind* of events or their *distance* into the future. The class threw itself enthusiastically into the exercise, and in a few minutes I had collected from them 193 forecast events, each of them duly dated. The results indicated that these urban, middle-class, rather sophisticated teenagers had accumulated many notions about the world of tomorrow.

From their forecasts there emerged, for example, a terrifying future for the United States in which, presumably, they would live out at least a part of their lives. The class scenario begins peacefully enough with predictions that the Vietnam War would end and United States relations with China would improve, both in 1972. (The exercise was run a year earlier, in 1971.) But soon events become more turbulent. New York City breaks away to become a state in 1973, and 1974 is a bad year characterized by race riots in June and a United States pullout from the United Nations. While both marijuana and prostitution are legalized, internal political events must be bleak because 1975 sees a political revolution in the United States.

In 1976 the value of the dollar declines, other nations ostracize the United States, and gas masks are distributed, presumably because of pollution. By 1977 the space program has ended and United States citizens are under constant surveillance in streets and homes. Senator Kennedy emerges somehow as President in 1978 (a special election?), but a major financial crisis occurs, and the following year, 1979, we break off relations with Europe. We learn to cure cancer, but by then pollution has become irreversible and we are highly dependent upon the oceans for food. All this, however, is merely a prelude to a cataclysmic year, 1980. That year can be described in a burst of screaming headlines:

AMERICAN REVOLUTION OVERTHROWS PRESENT GOVERNMENT
CULTURAL AND POLITICAL REVOLUTION BREAKS OUT IN U.S.
MAJOR RIVERS AND STREAMS DIE
NATURAL DISASTER WIPES OUT MANY PEOPLE
FAMILY SIZE LIMITED
MARS LANDING
COLONY PLANTED ON MARS
NUCLEAR WAR BREAKS OUT!

America's time of troubles is far from over. In 1981, Richard Nixon is assassinated, and while race relations take a turn for the better, and the renewed space program results in new missions to the planets, by 1983 we have a military dictatorship ruling the nation. Now the Soviet Union joins with the United States in a war against China (this is, after all, 1984 by now). Scientific progress continues and the rate of change accelerates further—indeed, embryos now take only six hours, instead of nine months, to gestate. But science is of no help when California, hit, one assumes, by an earthquake, slips into the Pacific Ocean in 1986. We are beginning to colonize the moon, while population on earth reaches a crisis point, and the dollar is now worth only 25 percent of its 1971 value.

As the 1990s open, the Russo-Chinese War is still on, but things begin to improve. Peace among the great powers becomes more likely. Nuclear energy, especially in the form of fusion reactors, is widely in use, and a three-day work week is initiated. Our ecological problems are still extremely pressing, but solutions are at least in sight. In fact, 1995 looks like a good year. The government changes, the space effort expands once more, we finally develop a "more organized system" of education, and, apparently, young people are making their political weight felt, for we elect a new President who is only twenty years old. (Scoffers might note that William Pitt became prime minister of Britain at twenty-four.) We are now also experiencing zero population growth.

I will not go on to describe their forecasts after 2000 A.D., but there is enough here presumably to suggest that at least this group of teenagers do not look forward to a stable world, or one progressing smoothly along well-worn grooves. They look forward to high turbulence for at least the next two decades.

THE FUTURE-SCANNING TALENT

It is perfectly astonishing, once we stop to consider it, that we are able, out of the stuff of everyday experience, to conjure up dreams, visions, forecasts and prophecies of events yet to come. Scientists marvel at the body's machinery for sensing the environment and for converting its impressions into concepts, ideas, symbols and logic. Yet our talent for projecting images of the future is even more remarkable. In fact, though educators have scarcely noticed it, this "future-scanning" talent is the basis for learning, itself.

If we could not form anticipatory mental pictures of the future, if we could not match these against emergent realities and then correct them, we could not—except in the narrowest sense—learn at all.

All of us project an ever-changing image of the future on the screen of consciousness. Our heads teem with assumptions about the future. These assumptions can be very short-term and practical. I may do no more than assume, for example, that the postman will arrive in the morning or even that the cup of tea will still be there, an instant from now, when my fingers close around it. On the other hand, the assumptions may be very long-range and impersonal. I may envision a world racial conflict in 1985, the emergence of Japan as the world's chief industrial power by 1990, or a meeting with extraterrestrials in the year 2000. The assumptions may be correct or incorrect, consistent or inconsistent, slowly changing or turning over rapidly. But whatever the case, taken together, they constitute my image of the future.

This invisible architecture of assumptions shapes my personality and lends consistency to my behavior. These assumptions, in fact, make it possible for the individual to survive in varied and fast-changing environments. For it is precisely this ability to visualize futures, to generate and discard thousands upon thousands of assumptions about events that have not yet—and may never—become reality, that makes man the most adaptive of animals. It is a prime task of education to enhance this ability, to help make the individual more sensitively responsive to change. We must, therefore, redefine learning, itself. Put simply, a significant part of education must be seen as the process by which we enlarge, enrich, and improve the individual's image of the future.

ACTION AND IMAGERY

Education, however, is not just something that happens in the head. It involves our muscles, our senses, our hormonal defenses, our total biochemistry. Nor does it occur solely *within* the individual. Education springs from the interplay between the individual and a changing environment. The movement to heighten future-consciousness in education, therefore, must be seen as one step toward a deep restructuring of the links between schools, colleges, universities and the communities that surround them.

The ultimate purpose of futurism in education is not to create elegantly complex, well-ordered, accurate images of the future, but to help learners cope with real-life crises, opportunities and perils. It is to strengthen the individual's practical ability to anticipate and adapt to change, whether through invention, informed acquiescence, or through intelligent resistance.

To function well in a fast-shifting environment, the learner must have the opportunity to do more than receive and store data; she or he must have the opportunity to *make change* or to fail in the attempt. This implies a basic modification of the relationship between educational theory and practice.

High-speed change means that the reality described by the teacher in the classroom is, even as the lesson proceeds, undergoing transformation. Generalizations uttered by the textbook or the teacher may be accurate at the beginning of a lesson, but incorrect or irrelevant by the end. Insights, highly useful at one time, become invalid under the new conditions. The instinctive recognition of this by young people has been one of the key factors behind the collapse of teacher authority.

In the past, one assumed that one's elders "knew" how things were. Yet if the reality is changing, then their knowledge of it is not necessarily trustworthy any longer, and, significantly, they, too, must become learners.

When we introduce change and, therefore, higher levels of novelty into the environment, we create a totally new relationship between the limited reality of the classroom and the larger reality of life. Abstractions are symbolic reflections of aspects of reality. As the rate of change alters technological, social and moral realities, we are compelled to do more than revise our abstractions: we are also forced to *test* them more frequently against the realities they are supposed to represent or explain.

Those who conduct opinion surveys know that the more variation there is in a population to be sampled, the larger the sample required to get an information-rich result. The same is true with respect to variation through time. The more rapid the pace of change, the more novelty-filled our environment, the more often it becomes necessary to "sample reality"—to check our abstractions.

Thus learning under conditions of high novelty requires us to move back and forth between theory and practice, between classroom and community, faster and more frequently than ever before. Failure to measure our abstractions often against reality increases the likelihood that they will be false. But the university and the lower schools, as organized today, are designed to construct or transmit abstractions, not to test them.

This is why we need to accelerate the trend in many colleges and universities to offer credit for action-learning done off-campus through participation in real work, in business, in community political organizing, in pollution-control projects, or other activities. Many of these efforts today are badly organized, ill-thought-through, and regarded by the university as basically insignificant—concessions to the restlessness of students who no longer want to remain cooped up in the classroom. I would argue that such efforts not only must be continued, but must be radically expanded, must be linked more imaginatively to the formal learning process, must be extended downward to younger and younger students in the secondary schools and even, through adaptation of the idea, to primary-school children. Indeed, for older students, this action-learning ought to become the dominant form of learning, with classroom learning seen as a support rather than as the central element in education. Such experiments as the University Without Walls are primitive prototypes of what is possible.

Students learn best when they are highly motivated to do so, and despite a great deal of mythology to the contrary, this motivation rarely comes from "inspired teachers" or "well-designed texts" alone. So long as students are cut off from the productive work of the surrounding society and kept in an interminably prolonged adolescence, many—if not most—are de-motivated. Teachers, parents and other adults may shower them with flowery rhetoric about how today's youth will be the leaders and decision-makers of tomorrow. But the rhetoric is contradicted by a reality that actively deprives the young of participation either in significant community decision-making or in socially approved productive work. Beneath the rhetoric lies a contempt summarized in the twin terms "parasites" and "investments." Conservatives tend to look upon students as parasites, eating up community resources without contributing anything productive in return. Liberals leap to defend the youth by terming them "investments" in the future. Both notions are insulting.

The secret message communicated to most young people today by the society around them is that they are not needed, that the society will run itself quite nicely until they—at some distant point in the future—take over the reins. Yet the fact is that the society is not running itself nicely, and, indeed, there may be little of value left for them to take over in the future, unless we reconceptualize the role of youth in the social order. Not because young people will necessarily tear down the social order, but because the rest of us *need* all the energy, brains, imagination and talent that young people can bring to bear on our difficulties. For the society to attempt to solve its desperate problems without the full participation of even very young people is imbecile.

My father worked at twelve or thirteen. Most children in the past—and most children in the less affluent nations today—were and are needed for their productive contribution. It is a dangerous myth of the twentieth-century rich that our children are *not* needed, that they can be kept in artificial environments called schools and universities, incubating until they are twenty-one or even thirty, before being expected to participate in the everyday affairs of the society.

In the United States we herd 8,000,000 university students and some 51,000,000 younger children into educational institutions, assuring them all the while that it is for their own future benefit. It is all done with the best of intentions. It keeps them out of the labor force and, for a while, off the streets.

This policy, however, is based on a perilously faulty image of the future. By maintaining the false distinction between work and learning, and between school and community, we not only divorce theory from practice and deprive ourselves of enormous energies that might be channeled into socially useful action, we also infantilize the young and rob them of the motivation to learn.

On the other hand, by linking learning to action—whether that takes the form of constructing buildings on campus, or measuring traffic flow at an intersection and designing an overpass, or campaigning for environmental legislation, or interning at city hall, or helping to police a high-crime area, or serving as sanitation and health aides, or building a stage set, or doing research for a trade union, or working out a marketing problem for a corporation—we change the source of motivation.

The motive to learn is no longer the fear of a teacher's power to grade or the displeasure of the parent, but the desire to do something useful, productive and respected—to change the community, to make a dent, if even a small one, on reality. This desire to leave a dent, to make an impact, today fuels a wide range of antisocial activity from spray-painting graffiti on a public wall or vandalizing a school building to committing murder. It is not unrelated to the fact that most crime is the work of the young.

Only by recognizing the urgency of this desire to make a mark (and thereby to clarify or establish one's own identity) and by reconceptualizing the role of youth with respect to work and social needs can the education system become effective.

Today, unfortunately, most action-learning programs scarcely begin to take advantage of their full potentials. For example, most are seen as forms of independent study. For many students, they might be far more effective as group ventures. The organization of groups of students (self-organization would be better) into problem-solving or work teams makes it possible to design additional learning—learning about organization and group dynamics—into the situation. By consciously including people of varied ages in such teams, it becomes possible to provide "generational bridges"—a way of breaking down some of the trained incapacity of different age groups to talk to one another.

Through focusing on some sharply defined external objective or desired change, the group develops a degree of shared intimacy and attacks the prevailing sense of loneliness and isolation felt by so many students even on small campuses. Most important, however, the motivation for learning changes. The group itself generates internal social reinforcements for learning, and the nature of the problem being attacked defines the nature of the learning required, so that the definition of relevance is created by the real situation rather than by the say-so of a teacher.

Members of a small group working to bring about some change in the ecological condition of their community, for example, will find they must learn something about science, economics, sociology and politics, as well as the communicative skills required to define the difficulties, outline alternative solutions, and persuade others.

In the meantime, decision-making, so crucial to coping with change, becomes, itself, a subject of the learning process. Most students in most schools and universities seldom participate in group decision-making. While they .may be asked to make decisions about themselves—such as which courses to take (and even this is restricted at the lower levels)—they are seldom called upon to make personal decisions *that affect the work or performance of others.* The decisions they are characteristically called upon to make have little or no impact on anyone's life but their own. In this sense, they "don't count." They are isolates. Attempting to solve real-life problems, action-learning done in the context of a goal-sharing group, trains the participants in decisional skills and begins to develop an understanding that their decisions do count—that personal decisions can have important consequences.

It is precisely at this point that action learning converges with future-consciousness. For, when we speak of an image of the future, we are speaking of the ramified consequences of present-day decisions, whether public or personal. Action-learning, particularly when carried out by groups, is a useful tool for demonstrating the necessity for a future-orientation—the need to study alternatives, to develop long-range plans, to think in terms of contingencies—and especially to think through the *consequences*, including second- and third-order consequences, of action.

This emphasis on the future can, furthermore, be applied not merely to group issues, but to the development of generalized, tentative life-plans for the individual participants as well—plans which the learner is, of course, free to change at will, but which, by their very existence, help orient the individual in the midst of hurricaning change. In this way, the future becomes intensely personal, instead of remote.

In turn, the development of group or personal plans, however tentative, immediately forces the question of values into the foreground. For plans have to do with our images of preferred futures, as distinct from those that are merely possible or probable. No problem in education has been more disgracefully neglected in recent years. The attempt to avoid ancient orthodoxies having led to the myth of a value-free education, we now find millions of young people moving through the educational sausage-grinder who have never once been encouraged to question their own personal values or to make them explicit. In the face of a rapidly shifting, choice-filled environment, one which demands decision after adaptive decision from the individual, this neglect of value questions is crippling.

Action-learning creates opportunities for students to move from the field back to the classroom or lounge or living room not merely for analytic discussion of their strategies for change, but for probing exploration of the personal and public values that underlie their successes and failures. This process of value clarification is a vital part of any education designed to help people cope with "over-choice."

In short, the combination of action-learning with academic work, and both of these with a future orientation, creates a powerfully motivating and powerfully personal learning situation. It helps close the gap between change occurring "out there" and change occurring within the individual, so that learners no longer regard the world as divorced from themselves, and themselves as immune to (and perhaps incapable of) change. In a turbulent, high-change environment, it is only through the development of a "psychology of the future" that education can come to terms with learning.

■   Toffler claims that education always springs from some view of the future. Other commentators about education state that education is basically conservative and historical—rather than being future-oriented, the school is past-oriented. What do you conclude about the probable future direction of education from reading Toffler?

■   Discuss: How would education *about* the future change education? *Should* education about the future change education?

■   Is education about the future an appropriate topic in elementary school? Junior high school? High school? College? Does a person's view of the future determine to some extent how much he or she might see implications for education? Explain.

■   Examine the predictions made by the high-school students mentioned in Toffler's article. To what degree have their predictions been validated? How reasonable do they seem in light of recent events? What predictions can you add to the list of these young people?

> *"Describing the look of things up ahead on the school front for the next thirty years has always been like charting the course of an Alpine glacier during the same period of time: infinitely slow, completely predictable, and very, very dull."*

Examine Rafferty's remarks alongside those of Mortimer Smith in "The Reforms Most Needed in Education" (Section One).

American Education: 1975–2000

Max Rafferty

Aside from the perhaps legendary figures of Mother Shipton and old Nostradamus, the most uncannily accurate prophet since Biblical days just has to be the late H. G. Wells. Long before any of them were even a gleam in their creators' eyes, Wells was accurately predicting the invention of the airplane, the development of the tank, the explosion of the first atomic bomb, the use of poison gas, and the discovery of the laser.

On a somewhat more modest scale, meteorologists can forecast future weather for as much as a week ahead, although most of them carry umbrellas to picnics just like the rest of us. And of course there are always the economists, who for three years running have been predicting a runaway boom on the American industrial front which presumably will get here sooner or later.

So you see it's possible to foretell the future, at least in some areas and within relatively narrow frames of reference. Education, however, has always been another breed of cats altogether, defying all predictions of meaningful change for

Max Rafferty, "American Education: 1975–2000," in *The Future of Education: 1975–2000,* ed. Theodore W. Hipple (Pacific Palisades, California: Goodyear, 1974), pp. 161–80. Reprinted by permission.

Max Rafferty is Dean of the School of Education, Troy State University, Troy, Alabama. One of the leading exponents of traditional education, Dr. Rafferty is the former Superintendent of Instruction for the State of California. His articles have appeared widely, and he is the author of *What They Are Doing to Your Children* and *Suffer, Little Children.*

the simple reason that it just never changed very much. Describing the look of things up ahead on the school front for the next thirty years has always been like charting the course of an Alpine glacier during the same period of time: infinitely slow, completely predictable, and very, very dull.

There are some indications that this immemorial state of affairs may now be changing. But before I try to anticipate what lies ahead for education, it will be necessary to do two things: (1) define education, and (2) dispose of some false premises which have grown up around it in recent years like so many tares and thistles.

If you will grant me my own definition, namely that education is learning to use the intellectual tools which the human race, over the centuries, has found to be indispensable in the pursuit of truth, then it follows that the following assumptions about education—though widely held for more than a generation now—are as preposterous as a Russian peace plan:

PHONY ASSUMPTION #1: That the schools exist to adjust pupils to their environment, or to make pupils accepted easily, comfortably, and happily by their peer group, or to enable them to practice togetherness, or to promote on-going, forward-looking relevance.   Schools exist to do none of these things; they exist to make pupils learned. Period.

PHONY ASSUMPTION #2: That in education there are no positive and eternal verities, no absolutes—everything is relative.   If this should by some remote and unlikely chance turn out to be true, then we teachers would be automatically unemployed, just as a minister of the gospel would be out of work if God indeed should turn out to be dead.

PHONY ASSUMPTION #3: That the school curriculum should be based on the immediate interests and the felt needs of the pupils.   A child's "felt needs" differ both widely and wildly from child to child and from year to year, indeed almost from day to day. A curriculum built upon such shifting sands would be a fragile edifice indeed.

These first three phonies are, I regret to say, the philosophical underpinnings of modern American education, and they go a long way toward explaining why the schools of the future are going to have to give John Dewey's pragmatism, utilitarianism, or what-have-you the old heave-ho if they are not to be engulfed in a deepening pool of bland, unctuous, cloying, sentimental slop.

Try a few more of the education establishment's phonies on for size:

PHONY ASSUMPTION #4: That a big school is better than a small one.   Not necessarily. Not any more than a big man is necessarily better than a small man. Or a big mistake better than a little mistake, for that matter. It all depends on the school.

PHONY ASSUMPTION #5: That a teacher with ten years' experience is better than a teacher with only one and therefore should be paid more.   Nope. One of my profession's oldest chestnuts is that a teacher may simply have had one year's experience over again ten times.

PHONY ASSUMPTION #6: That an athlete is usually a dummy.   This is an insufferable manifestation of smug superiority emanating from some of our self-styled intellectuals. In all the high schools where I ever worked, the athletes had a higher collective grade point average than did the nonathletes.

PHONY ASSUMPTION #7: That memorizing things in school is hopelessly stultifying.   The multiplication tables may be a little square, I suppose, but children must learn to memorize them anyway. And they must memorize key dates, names, and events in history, the letters of the alphabet, the continents of old earth, and the planets of the solar system, especially these days. And ability to call trippingly to the tongue certain passages of great poetry and prose can certainly brighten up an otherwise humdrum and even dreary mortal safari through this vale of tears. Memorization in school is a must. Today we don't ask pupils to do enough of it.

PHONY ASSUMPTION #8: That school dress and personal appearance codes are outrageous, tyrannical, and even unconstitutional.   The theory here is that school is a place which society subsidizes expensively so that every kid can turn on, blow his mind, and do his own thing. Sorry. It isn't. And society doesn't. School is a place where teachers try to establish a climate conducive to organized, systematic, and disciplined learning. Anything which interferes with a scholarly atmosphere is inimical to good education, and should be tossed out on its exhibitionistic ear. Hence school dress codes. And personal appearance standards. And disciplinary rules. And a lot of other things.

PHONY ASSUMPTION #9: That school policy should be set by the students and/or faculty.   This concept is patently and outrageously undemocratic. Any public, tax-supported institution must be run by those who pay the taxes, not by those who benefit from them. This means that public schools and colleges have to have their policies set by representatives responsible to all the people, not by stray groups of students and instructors responsible to nobody on God's earth except themselves alone. The latter should be heard, true enough, if only because they are the ones most directly and immediately affected by the policies adopted. But welcoming their participation in the policy-making process doesn't mean abandoning the whole shebang to them, lock, stock, and barrel. In any democratic society, you simply cannot turn the institutions over to the inmates.

PHONY ASSUMPTION #10: That report cards are meaningless status symbols, catering to an unhealthy parental craving to experience vicarious success at the expense of their children.   Tommyrot. Report cards are precisely what their name implies; they inform parents how their children are doing in school. Like any other school tool—including books, maps, or tests—report cards are subject to abuse at the hands of a stupid teacher or to misinterpretation by an hysterical parent. But the fact that a valuable tool is capable of being misused is no reason to revile the tool itself, nor to relegate it to the junk pile.

PHONY ASSUMPTION #11: That modern technology and the welfare state are producing better education than the schools did a generation ago.   Enters now from the wings one Prof. Sir Cyril Burt, who in 1970 completed a study showing that English school children in 1914 scored higher in every category of scholastic achievement than did their counterparts of 1965. And on the same tests, too.

Here's the way the generation gap shaped up:

	1914	1965
Reading	101.4	96.7
Spelling	102.8	94.6
Arithmetic	103.2	95.5

Oh, I know. The argument has always been: "But back in those days, the less able didn't stay in school very long. So the ones who took the tests were a select group compared to the school children of today. It's a rigged comparison."

Sorry. It won't wash, as the English say.

The youngsters tested in 1914 were just ten years old; so were the ones tested in 1965. And while I'm sure a lot of teenagers weren't going to school in pre-World War I Britain, I'm equally sure they were enrolled when they were ten. I'm almost as sure, incidentally, that American test figures would show similar results, if we had them.

How now, fellow educators? After a half-century of new ideas, new techniques, new psychologies of learning, why should the horse-and-buggy kids of Grandma's day show up so well, and our own progressive, permissive swingers show up so sorrily?

It's even worse than the cold statistics show. Hear Sir Cyril further: "A comparison of essays written by average school children in 1914 and fifty years later reveals yet more obvious signs of decline."

Bear in mind that the England of those dim, dead days before the guns of August ushered in our current century of wars and wickedness was a land of startling extremes: stately homes and ghastly slums, magnificence and squalor, the very rich and the abysmally poor. Where does this leave the educational environmentalists, who swear so confidently and so copiously that culturally deprived children cannot learn as much or as well as their less disadvantaged peers? Surely the welfare state which Britain has become since 1945 has less abject poverty than did the Britain of a half-century ago. Surely, too, the English youngsters of 1914 had less food, less medical care, less of everything than do their grandchildren. Yet they could read, spell, and cipher today's crop of well-fed scholars right off the map.

How to explain it?

In part, it's a failure of will and nerve. School in those days was a hair-raisingly competitive proposition. It was survival of the fittest, root hog or die. No one expected to enjoy himself in class. It was more like going to the dentist; you knew it was going to hurt, but you also knew the alternative was a whole lot worse. So you went and you endured and you gritted your teeth. And you learned.

Today, school is expected to be amusing and sparkling and fitted accommodatingly to the "felt needs" of each individual. It counsels and it psycho-analyzes and it entertains its pupils, but even as it does all these delightful things it educates them ever less effectively in the use of the intellectual tools which it was originally created to burnish and to hone and to hand down from one generation to the next.

There's a little more to it than mere slackened application, though. Somewhere along the long line since 1914, between the blaze of wars and the dry rot of depressions, we lost sight of the real nature of education. It's not fun and games. It's not intended to entertain or to divert. It's far too important to be watered down and gussied up and made palatable for a generation which prefers a placebo to a physic, even as all generations would have chosen to their disaster had their elders been stupid enough to give them a choice.

We and our English cousins have shortchanged the children during the past fifty years. I wonder. What will the same tests show in the year 2000?

PHONY ASSUMPTION #12: That tomorrow's school problems can be solved by more permissiveness.   As one who has spent his life simultaneously loving education and criticizing it, I'm more than a little miffed at the recent Carnegie Corporation study report which portrays American public schools as a cross between Sing Sing and a General Motors assembly line. Aside from the execrable grammar involved in the phrase, I don't object one whit to telling it like it is. I do object more than somewhat to the indiscriminate use of pejorative adjectives such as "oppressive," "grim," and "joyless" to describe our educational system as a whole, thus telling it like it certainly is not.

According to the report's author, Charles Silberman, the schools are regimented, the curriculum is banal, the teachers are slaves, and the pupils are being "educated for docility." That last crack sent my eyebrows clear up to my receding hairline. Our youngsters today are many things; docile they aren't.

However, let's go on. Mr. Silberman recommends a radical restructuring of the classroom along more "informal" lines so that the student will be free to use his own interests as a starting point for his education. Above all, he must avoid any kind of "domination" by the teacher.

Sound familiar? It should. The disciples of John Dewey were spreading whole layers of this kind of guff all over the country back in the thirties, like so much malignant margarine. The entire fabric of "life adjustment" education is shot through with this bland, infuriating assumption that the child knows more than the adult, the pupil more than the teacher.

There's more. In the elementary schools, it seems, much of what is taught "isn't worth knowing as a child, let alone as an adult, and little will be remembered." Like the ability to read, Mr. Silberman? The multiplication tables, perhaps? The United States Constitution? Punctuation and sentence structure? How to spell?

Quite a few adults manage to remember these things, and even to regard them as pretty important.

What does Mr. Silberman recommend in place of this nation-wide educational disaster area his report limns so luridly?

Well, for one thing, he wants to abolish lesson plans. Each child should be allowed to go at his own pace, select his own subject matter, and structure the curriculum in terms of his own personal "interests." "The child," he states, "is the principal agent in his own education and mental development." So let him organize his own education.

Good Grief! This is the sort of permissive pap I was being fed back in 1939, when I was first training to be a teacher. It was swallowed hook, line and sinker by enough schools and teachers to produce a generation composed of entirely too many quasi illiterates. We broke with this "do as you please" philosophy after we looked up during the late fifties and found Sputnik I beeping merrily all over our American skyspace. Now Mr. Silberman wants to resurrect it and breathe new life into its ancient flab.

Children have interests appropriate to their stages of development: bubble gum and dolls at one stage, dune buggies and Tom Jones records at another. But we teachers are paid to prepare them for life in the extraordinarily complicated world of the twenty-first century, and units in gum-chewing, doll-dressing, and jalopy-driving are not precisely what the parents of those children had in mind when they paid us their hard-earned tax dollars to share our knowledge with their offspring.

School in the days beyond tomorrow should be interesting, granted. It should also be important. And the things it teaches should be those which adults have found to be indispensable, not things which they found enjoyable at the age of ten and then discarded at the age of twelve.

The trouble with gearing a curriculum to the interests of children is precisely that: they *are* children. But education is for life.

Having disposed of the phony assumptions which have kept my profession bottled up in port so long for all the world like a semantic minefield, I've now cleared my decks for action and am ready to advance my predictions along the whole line of battle. Each is supported by its own auxiliary vessels of argument and reinforced by its independent squadron of supporting developments summoned fresh from the teeming shipyards of current educational happenings. Let us then consider the armada well launched into the mysterious future and the combat fairly joined.

PREDICTION A: The oversupply of teachers will get worse and will have perfectly splendid spin-offs.   In 1940, I was one of 220 eager beavers who qualified for high school teaching credentials at UCLA. About 20 of us got jobs. I had haunted the university's placement office for months. Finally the director took pity on me and offered me a job nobody else wanted.

"Where is it?" I asked gratefully.

"Trona, California," he replied.

"Where in blazes is that?"

"Search me. Let's look on the map."

I quickly discovered that when I said "blazes" I was righter than I knew. Trona turned out to be thirty miles from Death Valley as the crow flies, except that no crow in his right mind would have flown over that cauldron without an atmospheric reentry heat shield. The thermometer got stuck above 110 degrees for weeks on end, once in a while bubbling up to a balmy and salubrious 120. A huge chemical plant spewed odorous potash fumes all over the lunarlike landscape where nothing grew except a certain kind of salt tree imported from the Great Australian Desert.

The job itself left something to be desired, though certainly not in the way of variety. I was expected to teach seven periods per day, each period in a different field of preparation. After school I coached football and track for a couple of hours to keep myself from the clutching hands of sloth. Even with the teacher surplus now building up, a wet-behind-the-ears graduate of one of today's mod and swinging teachers' colleges, confronted with an offer like that, would send for the little men with the white coats and the butterfly nets.

I took it, and was darned glad to get it. It paid me the magnificent sum of $1,750 a year. I've never regretted it. In many ways, it was the best job I ever had.

Now, after more than three decades, the pendulum has swung back to 1940. What's causing the current glut in the teacher market? Two things.

First, the American birthrate started swooning and collapsing all over the charts back in 1964. Right now it's the lowest ever. Demographic projections indicate that the slump in number of warm bodies has hit the elementary schools during the early seventies, will drain the high schools by the end of the decade, and will hit the colleges and universities like a blockbuster around 1980.

Second, there was a big push in 1967-1968 and since toward "public service" career preparation—things like VISTA, the Peace Corps, ecology, welfare work, and of course teaching. This has switched tens of thousands of college graduates from careers in business and science to careers of do-goodism, vocations which don't produce fallouts of wars, napalm-brewing, and air pollution. *Result:* a lot more people than usual artificially propelled into teaching, and a resultant buyers' market in education of colossal proportions.

There's no indication that this state of affairs is going to change much in the foreseeable future. And there are a lot of implications emerging from this unexpected phenomenon, all of them good.

One is that we're not going to need many new schools for a while.

Another is the beckoning invitation to lower class sizes, with all which this implies in the way of increased attention to the needs of individual pupils.

Still a third is the opportunity, unique since Depression days, to exercise more selectivity in the hiring of new teachers. An administrator who adds to his faculty headaches from now on by employing either lethargic bores or wild-eyed, obscenity-spouting activists will deserve exactly what he gets.

PREDICTION B: There will be better education in the big cities without forced busing.   Mandated busing is one of the real wild hares of our time. Our descendants are going to think we were out of our minds when they study this aberration in their history classes. Mind you, there is no question about the need to equalize educational opportunities, especially for Blacks. But busing fails to take one stark, inescapable fact of life into consideration: in huge, sprawling areas of de facto segregation such as New York, Chicago, and Los Angeles, busing cannot possibly work. When a ghetto extends for miles and miles in all directions, there simply is no logistically or financially conceivable way to transport or to redistribute the millions of Black and White youngsters who would have to be shipped all over the map to attain any kind of ethnic balance in the schools.

The future's solution to this problem?

1. Compensatory education will be provided wherever and whenever we find children who need it. And if this means spending more money on better equipment and smaller class sizes for Black children, that's the way it's going to be.
2. Every state in the union during the next twenty years will adopt a policy which requires the best school buildings and supplies to be placed in the slums and ghettoes.
3. Slum school teachers will be paid more—a lot more—to stay and teach in slum schools. Too often, the finest, most inspirational instructors dodge assignment to the schools where the need for their services is greatest. You can't blame them. They don't like to be mugged and robbed and placed in sordid surroundings any better than the rest of us. But it is absolutely vital that our best teachers, not our worst, be placed in these schools. And the only way to get them to stay put is to make it worth their while.

What happens to racial integration of the schools, you ask? It will occur when whole cities and neighborhoods are integrated naturally, and not before. As far as real education is concerned, racial balance is happily irrelevant, no matter what Coleman and others have said. A school with decent facilities, reasonable class sizes, good materials, and excellent teachers is a school where children will learn. And I don't care if those children are all Negroes, Caucasians, Eskimos, or Berbers.

PREDICTION C: The frequency of teacher strikes will decline to zero.   In every state, teacher strikes are unprofessional and immoral; unprofessional because teaching is a self-proclaimed learned profession, and members of learned professions don't strike; immoral because leaving classrooms unsupervised and pupils uninstructed for prolonged periods of time hurts children who cannot defend themselves.

In most states, teacher strikes are illegal as well. This serves to point up the recent bankruptcy of the educational establishment as contained in a statement by Robert Chapin, general counsel for the National Education Association: "We don't view a strike as a planned strategy. Usually it's something teachers are forced to do. Sometimes you can make progress by testing what you think are unjust laws."

A fascinating philosophy, Mr. Chapin. Suppose I get the idea that the existing homicide laws are "unjust." Should I "test" them by murdering someone? Like an NEA general counsel, for instance?

Any school child above the age of ten knows that if he considers a law to be unjust, his proper recourse is to work to get it changed, not to go out and break it. I'm not even going to comment on the idiocy of the statement about teachers (or anyone else) being "forced" to strike. If our successors during the eighties and the nineties aren't smart enough to figure this one out, there probably won't be any society around to support schools for teachers to picket.

But it won't be illegality or immorality or unprofessionalism that will blow the whistle on teacher strikes. It will be the fact that such strikes are counterproductive. Allow me to quote from an article in a major national publication, published in February of 1971:

"Teacher strikes are backfiring, no longer serve their intended purpose, say private reports being sent from AFL-CIO headquarters to teachers' unions. Officials at the American Federation of Teachers tell local groups that strikes 'have done more harm than good.'"

And that's why, by the time the year 2000 has rolled around, teacher strikes will be as extinct as the dodo and the passenger pigeon. A final quote on this topic, this one from East St. Louis teacher union boss Donald Miller, just after his strikers trooped back into their classrooms after a twelve-week walkout:

"The new contract certainly is no great improvement over the one we had last year. However, at least we're hired back, and I think that's a victory in itself."

Oh brother! Using reasoning like this, Napoleon actually won at Waterloo. After all, he did get out of the battle alive, and received a free sea voyage to St. Helena into the bargain.

PREDICTION D: Mandated statewide use of standardized tests will be universal.   During the 1960s, California adopted regulations requiring the annual testing of all public school children in certain grades. The tests were in reading, mathematics, and English usage. The first year the tests were given, the city of Los Angeles ended up low man on a twenty-city totem poll in regard to how well its children knew how to read.

The test results didn't exactly come as a surprise to those of us who had been begging Los Angeles to junk its obviously inadequate reading techniques and start teaching phonics to its first graders as soon as they arrived in school. Neither were we surprised by the initial reaction to the horrendous test scores. Everybody denounced the tests. This is precisely comparable to the hospital patient with a high fever who denounces the doctor's thermometer.

Fortunately, Reaction No. 2 was more interesting. Feeling the heat from the newspaper headlines, Los Angeles promptly invested in several thousand so-called "phonics kits" and distributed them to all its elementary teachers, along with no-nonsense orders that they had to be used. *Result:* The next year, the test scores went up, and the next year they went up even higher.

The important thing, however, is that mandated standardized testing in the fundamentals did three things:

1. It raised the curtain and showed how bad things were.
2. It generated irresistible demand for reform.
3. It pointed the way to make results better in the future.

For years beyond counting, the leaders of my profession have been dosing the laity with anesthetic bromides like these:

"Teaching good citizenship is more important than teaching mere subject matter."

and

"Competence in reading as in other subjects will spring naturally from the felt needs of the child, and when the proper maturation level of the individual has been reached."

and

"A teacher's effectiveness can never be measured by objective testing in the so-called fundamentals."

Poppycock.
Every one of the above platitudes is demonstrably false.
First, subject matter—especially reading—is far and away the most important thing the schools exist to teach. Good citizenship springs from familiarity with our nation's history, from knowledge of its government, from at least a nodding acquaintance with great literature, and from a lively interest in current hap-

penings. None of these wellsprings of good citizenship, you will notice, can be tapped by the nonreader.

Second, competence in reading does *not* spring spontaneously from the felt needs of the child. It springs from an efficient, inspirational teacher and from interesting, challenging books, both dedicated to the proposition that learning the letters of the alphabet, the sounds of those letters, and how to combine them into syllables is the best possible way to teach anyone how to read.

Third, bosh to the comfortable theory that good teaching is so ethereal and intangible a commodity that it can't be measured objectively. Right now, and probably on into the next century, an effective elementary teacher will be one who sees that the children in her class learn to read easily and fluently before she ships them on to the next grade. In other words, if she's effective, her kids will learn to read.

Standardized testing has its weaknesses. But the future will use it the way California used it—to measure its progress in curricular areas which lend themselves to measurement. And what's wrong with that?

PREDICTION E: More and better vocational education is in the cards, and for a lot more children than are getting it now.   Never in any nation's history has there been such a hue and cry after vocational education as the one in which we have been engaged—with indifferent results—since the middle sixties. The Youth Corps and the Job Corps have been nosing into every likely copse and thicket, quivering with eagerness at even the slightest hint of short-cut methodology stirring within and pointing rigidly whenever a bashful new technique whirred unexpectedly from cover.

The beaters and gunbearers of the Economic Opportunities Act were flushing the countryside in all directions, seeking not only the elusive quarry of trainable and willing unemployees, but also the game bags labeled "job rehabilitation" in which to bear the spoils of the chase triumphantly back to the nearest vocational training center.

The whole power of Uncle Sam was unleashed during a period of full employment to get into the hands of unskilled labor the tools and the skills needed to transform it into skilled labor. Now the unemployment rate has risen and the bloom is off the boom. Yet the problem underlying vocational education is still essentially the same.

We are still being told that the aircraft industry is crying for all sorts of strange and esoteric mechanical abilities, and that the schools are going to have to install in the future everything from micromillimetric measuring devices to nuclear reactors in order to train the highly specialized technicians needed to service both the Air Age of today and the Space Age of tomorrow. The same claims are being made for an increasing segment of both light and heavy industry.

There's no doubt that this is basically true. In the decades ahead, and regardless of how the historical ball bounces, we're going to need more and better trained experts in many industrial fields, and it's perfectly true that this will mean more complex and expensive vocational courses in the schools. But important as this is, it isn't the real problem.

For every exotic job opportunity involving advance knowledge of slide rules and electronic transistors there are now, and will continue to be at least through the mid-eighties, twenty job opportunities which will involve nothing of the sort.

Want to know the kind of qualifications these jobs require? Here they are:

1. Ability to read without lip-moving and without a glazing of the eyeballs whenever a word of more than two syllables comes along.
2. Proficiency in making simple change out of a cash drawer, which in turn requires certain minimum essentials in adding and subtracting.
3. Moderately acceptable vocal speech patterns—that is, the ability to conduct a conversation with a customer, with relatively few gross grammatical errors, and with absolutely no reliance upon such ineffable verbal crutches as "Blast off, weirdo!" and 'De cat ha just split."
4. Willingness to shut up, take orders, and work hard.
5. Cheerfulness, helpfulness, and a civil tongue in one's head.

I submit that all five of these qualifications will be in uncommonly short supply during the years ahead, even with a major emphasis on supplying them. I submit further that the schools are in excellent posture to supply all five. And I'm willing to bet that in the vast majority of jobs available tomorrow and twenty years from tomorrow the applicant who has mastered all five is not only going to get hired; he's going to stay hired.

The proprietor of a combination garage and gas station cornered me the other day after a meeting, backed me into a corner, and prodded me on the chest with a meaty and slightly discolored forefinger.

"I hire a lot of kids just out of high school," he began, breathing heavily. "And I have to fire a lot of them pretty quick. Not because they don't know how to operate the equipment. Heck, I can teach them that in a day or two."

"Oh, no," he went on. "It's because they don't know how to work. They lean on a broom or a grease gun for ten minutes, and they want a coffee break. Leave 'em unsupervised for five minutes, and they're over in the corner rapping about last Saturday's rumble or next Friday's rock festival. Dock 'em when they come in late, and they think you're one of the bad guys in the black hats."

He eyed me despairingly.

"Why don't you school fellows forget about how to operate the lathe and how to set the band saw rigging and all that until you've taught these kids the right *attitudes*? If they've got that, we can give 'em the rest, right on the job."

I told him I'd do my best to spread the word. As he walked away, he looked back over his shoulder.

"And while you're at it, try to talk 'em into shaving, getting a haircut, and throwing away the sandals. I've got no objection to some character going around looking like Peter the Hermit but I'm hanged if he's going to work in my place."

This is what the vocational education instructor of the future is going to have to teach first: attitudes.

PREDICTION F: Ethnic studies will be as important in the curriculum as etruscan tomb-carving, and no more so.   The most futile "cause" of the Sixties has turned out to be the ethnic studies hassle. Remember five years ago when all the bedlam and brute force were used to compel colleges to institute classes in black history, brown culture, and the like? Well, here's what happened in the biggest state of the union, and in the biggest city of that state.

Los Angeles Valley College, under pressure from militants whose abundant hair fairly bristled with outraged indignation, launched an elaborate program of ethnically oriented courses in 1968–1969. The rioters and cop-cursers, who had done their best to turn California campuses into bloody battlefields, won their fight. Their demands were met in full.

So what happened? Valley College gave an ethnic party, but nobody came. Half the bitterly fought-for classes didn't even open a year later. *Reason:* hardly anyone wanted to take them, apparently. The Mexican-American courses attracted exactly four eager students. Black studies enrollments told the same deflating story, particularly in regard to Afro-American literature, a class in which only three students registered.

The same surprise on a somewhat less spectacular scale occurred at Los Angeles' California State College, which had a sizable enrollment of 21,000, of which 2,310 were Negroes and Mexican-Americans. All of Cal State's ethnic courses lumped together drew 500 students, about 2.5 percent of the total student body.

Let me stress here that there's nothing at all wrong with establishing college courses in the culture and history of our racial minority groups. But there's a lot wrong with letting immature kids unilaterally change the entire curriculum of an institution of higher learning, with all the time, money, and energy which this requires. For results, you need look no farther than Los Angeles.

Hopefully, our grandchildren in A.D. 2000 will have learned from our sad and somewhat sappy experience.

PREDICTION G: Merit pay for teachers and modification of tenure laws are coming up around the bend of the time stream.   Long before the year 2000 comes along, if we are still refusing in this country to pay good teachers more money than we pay poor teachers, then public education will be permanently becalmed in a Sargasso Sea of insipidity. And unless we drastically reorganize the state laws governing lifelong, ironclad tenure for teachers to permit firing the senile, the stupid, and the subversive, public education is going to be a dead duck. We are the only profession which refuses steadfastly to police its own ranks and to weed out its loafers, its incompetents, and its loose nuts. Because the future cannot coexist with this nonsense, the nonsense will cease to exist.

Merit pay and tenure revision are in the wings getting ready to come onstage into the spotlight because they have to be; there is no alternative.

PREDICTION H: Better textbooks are already on the way.   This is an easy prophecy to venture. Today's elementary readers are demonstrably better than were their predecessors of ten years back. Remember Dick and Jane and Tom and Susan and Spot and all the driveling milksops of the early sixties? The new readers are better; our grandchildren's will be still better. Excerpts from the great children's classics—hero tales from American history, stories from Greek and Roman mythology—these are the ingredients which save children's reading from being stale and which make it savory.

Aside from the brain-numbing effect upon the youngsters of the old primers, consider what years of having to deal with the paltry vocabularies and the dry-rot repetitiveness may do to the unfortunate teacher. There is a story, perhaps but not necessarily apocryphal, of the first grade teacher who had saved up enough of her small salary to buy a gleaming new compact car. The first night she had it, she parked it in front of her apartment, and a large truck inadvertently squashed it like a beetle. Wakened by the crash of metal and the tinkling of broken glass, poor Miss Guggenslocker turned on the porch light, stood there helplessly wringing her hands, and in words conditioned by a decade of first grade readers sobbed: "Oh! Oh! Oh! Look! Look! Look! Damn! Damn! Damn!"

Science texts are so much better than the ones I had when I was a boy that I can hardly wait to see what the next few years will bring. There is still vast room for improvement, however, in the history and other social science texts, many of which show an almost creepy resemblance in both content and style to a UNESCO fund-raising appeal or to an ACLU brief.

PREDICTION I: Both a longer school year and school day seem in the cards.   It's pretty safe to assume that there will be a longer school year before long. Three months off each summer no longer makes sense. But there is even greater justification for a longer school day, if only because the humanities are gradually being shoved out of big-city high schools and junior high schools by the shortening of the school day which occurred for financial reasons during the past ten years.

Unless there is a seven- or eight-period day in secondary schools, such valuable subjects as art, music, and home economics are going to continue to be muscled aside by "must courses" such as math, science, English, and history. I just can't believe that America in the final quarter of the twentieth century is going to let this happen, especially when we are being bombarded from all sides by forecasts of shorter work weeks and increasing leisure time. Unless education can somehow take up the slack that seems to be accumulating, we're going to see all this extra time occupied in watching television daytime serials and nighttime wrestling, and this I postively refuse to contemplate.

PREDICTION J: More student participation in school administration will be occurring.   This is particularly true in the area of teacher evaluation, where thoughtful and constructive student rating of instructors is both practicable and appropriate.

The trend, however, is apparent in school policy making as well. In California in 1968, students began serving on local school boards and even on the state board of education. Alabama recently added student representatives to every one of its college and university governing boards. Stimulated by the recent constitutional amendment giving eighteen-year-olds the right to vote, this trend will continue and probably accelerate.

PREDICTION K: More part-time students and off-campus courses.   Both higher and secondary education are starting to branch out. Prospects are for more correspondence courses, televised home "extension" classes, and college off-shoots out in Podunk, so that adults especially can benefit from lifelong learning. Nothing in all education's cloudy crystal ball shines more brightly than this almost certain development.

PREDICTION L: School and teacher accountability will be demanded.   Before the end of this century—hopefully before the end of this decade—we will challenge successfully the arrogant assumption that educators should not be held responsible for the product they turn out. The best way I know to establish the principle of accountability is to rate teachers at least in part on how much subject matter and how many effective skills they have been able to impart to their pupils as shown on the standardized tests advocated under Prediction D.

At this juncture, I can hear the dismal wails and piteous ululations emanating from the educational establishment, sobbing that such regimented goings-on will dehumanize the instructional process, to say nothing of ignoring such valuable intangibles as good citizenship, artistic appreciation, and —inevitably—relevance.

No matter. Such evaluation will certainly show how well Teacher is doing in the fields being evaluated. Right now, I'll settle for that.

PREDICTION M: There will be a change in the selection and training of school administrators.   For some time we've been operating on the theory that a good teacher will automatically make a good principal or superintendent. As Gershwin said about something else altogether. "It ain't necessarily so."

Long before the next decade has run its course, we will be recruiting school superintendents and business managers from the business world rather than from the academic community, and we will be giving them prolonged on-the-job intern training. It's about time.

These, then, allowing for a reasonable margin of error, are what will be happening in education during the years ahead. There are also a few things which will *not* be happening.

For example, American children will not become mere wards of an all-powerful state, with the schools taking over the traditional functions of the home. That trend has been running now since World War II; it's about due to reverse itself.

Teachers are not going to be replaced by machines. It's certainly true that these electronic gadgets light up, whir, click, and buzz enticingly, none of which the human teacher can do without considerable difficulty. It's also true that one of the ultimate realities in education is the interplay of the personality of the teacher with that of the pupil, and a machine, no matter how impressive its memory banks, has no more personality than a tin can. A machine can certainly help a teacher test, drill, and present material. But it cannot—nor will it ever—really teach.

Finally, schools and classrooms will not be museum pieces in the year 2000. They'll still be around and recognizable, if only because children need to be with each other during an important part of their lives. More, they need the motivation to learn and to study which cannot be provided in the average home and which only a teacher-classroom milieu can supply.

As I said at the beginning, education has always moved more like a glacier than like a prairie fire. In the long haul, this is probably a good thing; most of us would not like prairie-fire education very much even if there were some way it could be made available. Actually education is a bridge on which perhaps we may be able to meet our successors halfway.

But more than anything else, education is a great mirror, reflecting always the strengths and the weaknesses, the follies and the frailties which add up to the nation which supports and populates the schools, and which first called them into being on this continent. Those of us whose life work calls upon us to look deeply and regularly into that gleaming surface find it fascinating, almost hypnotic. A crowded, swarming, colorful caravan unrolls before us every day—as old Omar said, "A moving row of magic shadow-shapes that come and go." America, drawing now toward the end of the thunderous, cataclysmic twentieth century, passes in review, in all its baffling profusion, its tumult and its shouting, in the persons of its children.

Unlike the more conventional looking glass, however, the mirror which is education takes unto itself two additional and somewhat unorthodox dimensions.

First, it reflects not only the faces of people and the appearance of things, but also the semblance of ideas themselves. They troop like armed battalions across the shining surface, and even as they pass they war with one another.

Is it to be education as the pursuit of truth for truth's own sake, or is it to be the easy, comfortable adjustment of the child to his environment? Shall it be schooling to impart the accumulated and well-weighed wisdom of the ages to the citizens of the future, or schooling to impose unilaterally and tyrannically upon a malleable and captive daily audience a particular socioeconomic or political dogma? Are we to have instruction or indoctrination? pedagogy or demagoguery?

And even as we try to winnow from among the struggling, grappling mirror images a true depiction of the future, the great glass shifts and changes into its second strange dimension: the depiction in its glowing, enigmatic depths of what Wells called the Shape of Things to Come, seen darkly perhaps and teeming with uncertainties, but nonetheless and in the long run certainly.

Like the children of Hamlin town so long ago, following an inscrutable Piper into an unimaginable world, a strange, enchanted land of mixed beauty and balefulness, our younglings have set their feet upon a path which leads to a universe where a million—that number which has loomed so large to us—will be a very small number indeed, whether in terms of dollars, or of miles, or of human beings; a society where hard, monotonous physical labor will be as quaint and forgotten as are slavery and witch burning; a mind-boggling commonwealth not of nations alone, nor even of continents, but of whole planets, flung in ordered profusion across the spangled immensity of the night sky.

Mothers' and fathers' breaths have always caught, and their brows have furrowed, as the little ones went off so wide-eyed to school on that first day of all September days. In the Seventies, the Eighties, the Nineties, the breath-catching and the brow-furrowing will be doubly warranted. For upon the schools and upon the teachers, upon the books and the lessons and the tapes and the films, above all upon the educational way of thinking about life embodied in the schools' philosophy, today as in no other day, hang all the keys to the future and the survival of our children's America as a land of freedom and a bastion of democracy in a world which becomes a little less free, a little less democratic with each passing year.

A mirror faithfully gives back the shadow, not the substance. By itself, it is helpless to remedy old evils, to redress the ills of days gone by, to straighten the passageway which stretches ahead, with all its promise and peril. Used properly and with due regard for its built-in limitations, the mirror tells its user the simple truth. It enables him to tally the good against the evil. It arms him against surprise. It warns him against approaching danger. It is incapable of flattery. It counsels wisely and well.

Even so is education, now and in the days ahead. We who wield it and who love it can use it as we choose. We can employ it for the great purposes of life and learning, as the mirror in the laboratory picks up the light waves which confirm some towering experiment, or we can utilize it for causes as vain and as foolish as the aimless focusing of the sun dance on some garden wall.

Education is not magic. It works with what is given to it. In the years ahead, it will be as it was in the days of Plato and of Aristotle— as it will be in the time of our remote descendants.

Yesterday, today, or tomorrow, the faces which look out hopefully or fearfully from its gleaming, passionless surface are always our own.

■ Examine Dr. Rafferty's first three "phony assumptions." In what ways do his descriptions fit your own educational experience? In what ways do you agree or disagree with him that the assumptions described are "phony"?

■ Rafferty attacks *Crisis in the Classroom* by Charles Silberman ("...the recent Carnegie Corporation study report...") for its use of words such as "oppressive," "grim," and "joyless" in describing the American public-education system. If you are not familiar with *Crisis in the Classroom*, obtain a copy and read Silberman's accounts of the schools that prompted him to use the above descriptions. Afterwards, explain why you agree with either Rafferty or Silberman. What three words would you select to describe your own experience as a secondary-school student?

■ Consider Rafferty's predictions. Which of them are reaching fulfillment at this time? If you are not familiar with George Leonard's *Education and Ecstasy* (New York: Delacorte Press, 1968), it would be informative for you to read it and compare Leonard's utopian projections for the turn of the century with those made in Rafferty's article.

■ Because Rafferty represents a significant attitude toward public education, it is important to know his philosophy as well as his reasoning. Obtain either of his popular books, *Suffer, Little Children* (Old Greenwich, Conn.: Devin-Adair Co., Inc., 1962) or *What They Are Doing to Your Children* (New York: New American Library, 1963), and arrange a group discussion on the positions Rafferty presents.

"Most people, least of all educators, do not understand what education really is."

Consider Montagu's observations in light of the excerpts from the "Seventh Annual Gallup Poll of Public Attitudes Toward Education" (Section One).

We're Botching the Business of Education

Ashley Montagu

Education is the essence of the American opportunity—and it is being muffed.

In the Age of Space we continue to muddle along with horse and buggy ideas which are of as much use to the victims of them as an abacus is to a computer systems analyst.

Complaints about educators and education are as old as education itself. In 1531 Sir Thomas Elyot, in his magnificent book "The Gouverneur," resumed the criticism of educators most appositely, when he wrote, "Lorde god, how many good and clene wittes of children be now a dayes perished by ignorant school maisters."

In our own time, students, revolted by the irrelevance of so much that passes for education, have rebelled against the system and demanded that what they are taught have some relevance to the world in which they are living and to the world that is coming into being.

Ashley Montagu, "We're Botching the Business of Education," *The Washington Star,* 24 October 1971. Reprinted by permission of the author.

Ashley Montagu is Professor and Head of the Department of Anthropology at Rutgers University. He has also been a member of the departments of anthropology at Columbia University, Harvard University, and the University of California, Santa Barbara. The author of articles for journals and magazines, he has also written numerous books, including: *Man's Most Dangerous Myth: The Fallacy of Race; The Natural Superiority of Women; The American Way of Life;* and *The Direction of Human Development.*

It is significant that the revolt started on the Berkeley campus of the University of California. On that campus it had long been the boast of the university that there were 27,500 students. The emphasis was placed on the quantity of the students rather than on their quality.

Professors celebrated the fact that they had 1,600 students in their classes, and that they hardly knew the names of more than one or two of them, and that on the street they would not recognize more than a few of them. The relation between teacher and student was strictly anonymous, and professors often remarked what a good place a university would be to work in if only there weren't any students!

INFORMATION BIN

The student was regarded as an information bin who, at certain ritual occasions, would be required to regurgitate onto blank sheets of paper the information he had acquired. Those having the highest regurgitative capacities being the most highly rewarded with the appropriate grades.

Eventually the student would graduate with a degree, perhaps go on to higher degrees—in the process dying both intellectually and spiritually by degrees.

Many students resented this mechanized, inhuman processing, the remoteness and apparent indifference of the teacher toward them, the anonymity of what should have been a creative relationship between teacher and student. And so students began to protest, there were campus disturbances, culminating in the unerasable tragedy of Kent State, and the despair of far too many students.

Some have dropped out, others have copped out, while still others have decided that the system can be beaten, and will therefore stay and hope to change it from within.

Already students have succeeded in producing more changes within the educational system than has been achieved by any other agency within the last hundred years or more.

Such students, and those who are to follow them, need all the help they can get. What they most need is an answer to the question—a very simple question—What is education for?

It is my view that no less than the continuation of the human species depends upon the manner in which that question is answered.

Let us quickly come to the point. Most people, least of all educators, do not understand what education really is. The confusion is well-nigh universal which leads most people to identify instruction with education.

Instruction is what goes on in our schools today. Education is practically, and has for a long time been, nonexistent.

Instruction—to spell it out—is training in "the three R's," in techniques and skills, mainly for the purposes of making a living.

Instruction lays emphasis upon the rote-remembering of facts, upon practice and repetition, its goal is knowledge for use, and it treats every child, every student, as if his aptitudes, capacities, abilities, motivations, and interest, were identical with those of everyone else in the classroom. Hence every child, every student, must learn exactly the same things in exactly the same way.

"Education for everyone," desirable as that is, has been interpreted to mean "instruction alike for all alike," instead of "Education for each," each according to his own uniquenesses, interests, and aptitudes.

By education is to be understood the nourishment of the student's potentialities for growth and development as one who is able to work, to love, and to play. Those are the three chords of might, the criteria of mental health. That, in my view, as a student of the origin and evolution of humanity, should be the purpose and the goal of all education: the development of a human being who lives as if to live and love were one.

WHOLE OF NATURE

For it seems to me that unless we learn to live not only with our fellow human beings everywhere, but also with the whole of nature, in such a cooperative manner, man will in the not too distant future destroy himself.

We have lost the sense of belonging to the environment, and behave as if the environment belonged to us. Similarly, we have lost the sense of belonging to a community of man, and have become increasingly alienated, disengaged, from our fellowman.

We have developed strange and destructive enmities, xenophobias. Knowledge has increased at a spectacular rate, and understanding decreased as rapidly, with the result that not having any genuine understanding of what knowledge is for, we continually misuse it to the detriment of the environment and man's place in it. And all this is largely due to the fact that most of us have not understood what knowledge is for, to the failure to understand the difference between instruction and education.

Instruction is important, but first it must always be adjusted to the aptitudes, abilities, and goals of the individual child, and second, all instruction must be regarded as secondary to the prime purpose of all education, the ability to love, to work, and to play.

Instruction in the service of education, and not education in the service of instruction. The school must become an experience in the learning of the art, that is the practice, and the science, that is, the theory upon which that art is based, of human relations, *not* an institution for training in the three 'Rs.' And the first qualification required of every teacher shall be the ability to love, for the care of the student begins with caring for the student, and the only way one ever learns to become a loving human being is by being loved.

To students this answer to the question, "What is education for?" makes the best of all sense. It is one, in any event, that they have already worked out for themselves.

Now we need communities and school boards, and superintendents, and principals, and teachers to go with the students. The trouble with most students is that they don't have a sufficient number of educators who have caught up with them.

The students belong in the Space Age, most educators belong in the days of the horse and buggy. Educators have a lot of catching up to do. They have a great deal of revaluing of entrenched and outmoded values to do. Will they?

Teachers and the community must fully appreciate that the educator is really the most important member of the community, for in addition to the parents, it is he who has the making of the growing and developing human being in his power.

Very few if any communities anywhere in the world yet recognize this fact, for everywhere the educator is among the most modestly paid members of the community. The most important members of the teaching profession, those in the elementary and secondary school, are among the lowest paid.

In fact, we encourage the teacher to take a vow of perpetual poverty, and in this way encourage the efficiently second-rate and mediocre in positions that should be the privilege of the most highly developed members of the community of man. And they should be rewarded for what they are worth: The makers of humanity, the acknowledged legislators of the world, the highest and most important of all callings.

So much for instruction, education, and the teacher. What now of methods?

There are methods courses given in colleges that prepare teachers. These courses belong in the Stone Age of Education and are a disgrace to those who give them and an affliction to the students who are wearisomely forced to sit through them. What these courses deal with are the most banal and for the most part utterly useless "methods" of improving teaching. These are not the methods that, in the age of the computer, should be taken seriously by anyone.

COMPUTER AS TUTOR

The computer renders "education" as we know it today and have known it in the past, obsolete.

The computer will make possible an education tailored to the individual's needs, and assist each student to realize his own uniqueness, to become an active participant in the process of educating and creating himself, so that he in turn may become the educator and creator of others.

Teachers will be liberated from the Sisyphus-labor of drilling repetition, and grading, and will be able to devote themselves to being human.

It has been shown that during the actual time that the teacher is in the classroom with her students in elementary school, during only about 15 percent of that time is the teacher engaged in teaching. The computer can do a great deal better than that, for it can serve as an individual tutor always at the service of the student.

It is quite possible to replace the teacher altogether by a computer, but I think this undesirable. Teaching, as I have said, begins with caring for the student. While it is not impossible to communicate caring through a computer, it is not quite the same thing as having a warm, loving, human being in the classroom.

Once the computer is adopted as a learning aid it will undoubtedly remain for centuries the greatest advance in educational methodology since the invention of the alphabet. For what the computer will achieve, among other things, is the important and long overdue advance of placing the learning process under the individual control of the learner.

INDIVIDUAL ATTENTION

In the classroom each student will have his own console with TV screen, at which he can receive the individual attention of the computer, no matter where he may stand in relation to every other student in the class and no matter what the subject he may be concentrating on at the moment.

The computer makes it possible for each student to receive individual attention consonant with his particular needs.

Since the computer can remember the problems and weaknesses as well as the strengths of the student in prior performances, no advance will be made until the computer is satisfied that the student has mastered every step in learning the subject.

At the college and university levels the computer as an aid to teaching and learning will become a tool of major importance, not alone in the expansion in the understanding of techniques, skills, and human relations, but in the application of these to active participation in the problems of society, at every level, social, ideological, political, technological, scientific, and so on. In this manner community, university, students and teachers will be brought together in one large integrated community, instead of being separated as they for the most part still are, into "Town" and "Gown," "Faculty" and "Students."

In the Age of the Computer the working together for the common good of all these elements will be the new style, and the old style, prevailing today, will be looked back upon as belonging to the Stone Age of education.

For what the new style of education in the Computer Age will be emphasizing will be what the word "education" originally meant, namely, "to care, to nourish, and to cause to grow," from the Latin *educare*.

It is a good thing to Anglicize the pronunciation of that word, for what it means is essentially the development of the ability to care for others. And since that is what education should, fundamentally and for the most part, be all about, the emphasis on the caring is the missing principle that the new education will restore to humanity, and make more readily achievable through the computer.

Thus, for the first time in man's history, will an effective means, the computer, be joined to a visionary dream: The achievement of a genuine civilization of humanity, in which the race between education and catastrophe that H. G. Wells said is civilization will have been won—by education.

■ Ashley Montagu is a well-known popularizer of social-anthropological material. What are his key objections to the traditional concept of education, and what alternative viewpoint does he propose?

■ Montagu calls for a return to a feeling of community to counter what he considers to be a growing alienation among the young, an alienation enhanced by the low status of teachers. On the basis of your own experience and observations, in what ways does his charge appear to be accurate or inaccurate?

■ If you have had any experience with computers in instruction, do you feel Montagu is assessing the potential of this technology accurately?

*"...the primary function of schools is the
development of basic skills and the training
of minds."*

Consider Smith's article in relation to the
National Commission's "Recommendations
for Improving Secondary Education" and
excerpts from the "Seventh Annual Gallup
Poll of Public Attitudes Toward Education" (both in Section One).

The Reforms Most Needed in Education

Mortimer Smith

The leading article in the *Bulletin* for January dealt with the topic "Are the
Schools Worth Saving?" The revolutionaries, of course, answer "no" to this
question, maintaining that the assumptions on which public education is
founded, and the basic structure and many of the procedures of school organization, are invalid. On the other hand, the reformers (as we pointed out in the
earlier article) accept certain propositions governing the management of schools
and believe that within an organizational structure incorporating these propositions, it is possible to improve the quality of elementary and secondary education.
We listed the following propositions as being acceptable to the reformers: a
public system of education is not only a convenience but a necessity; schooling
has to be formalized, with required attendance, sequential courses and schedules;
the teacher and the taught are not equal partners in the educational process; given
the economics of the school situation, large-group instruction is a necessity;
ability grouping in one form or another is desirable.

Mortimer Smith, "The Reforms Most Needed in Education," *Council for Basic Education Bulletin*, **13**, no. 7 (March 1969). Reprinted by permission.

Mortimer Smith is a social historian, biographer, and writer on education. One of the
founders of the Council for Basic Education, he was editor of the *CEE Bulletin* until 1974.
Author of numerous articles in magazines and anthologies, he is also author of *A Consumer's Guide to Educational Innovations; A Citizen's Manual for Public Schools; The
Diminished Mind;* and *And Madly Teach.*

If one accepts the conclusion that our schools as presently designed are salvageable, the logical next step is to ask what reforms are needed, or to put it another way, what can we do within the framework of the present system that will result in strong schools rather than mediocre or poor ones? But there is a prior matter to be settled: before any reforms are possible there has to be a clearing of the philosophical air; that is, we have to come to some firm conclusions as to why we have schools. It is surprising that after a dozen years of vigorous public debate about education there is still so little agreement about aims and purposes. Thousands of educators still accept the view recently advanced by Donald C. Weaver of the School of Education at Western Michigan University. Writing in the January issue of *The Community School And Its Administration,* he states that the traditional view of the school as 'an intellectual skill center'' is no longer acceptable. He calls for the creation of an institution that will serve as "a laboratory for the management of human behavior," a school where "no program is considered inappropriate so long as it serves an educational need of persons within the jurisdiction of the school." We have already moved considerably in the direction of this all-inclusive view of purpose. How to drive a car and what to think about sex are but two of the many non-academic subjects now almost universally accepted as appropriate parts of the school program.

A sounder view of the function of the school has been expressed by psychologist Kenneth B. Clark: "I am old-fashioned in believing that schools have a specific educational function, that principals and teachers are not social workers and psychologists, and that part of our problem is that this specific function of the schools has become confused and ambiguous by a lot of things called progressive education or social concern. My belief is that schools tend to take on peripheral functions and can't do them well precisely because they do not perform their primary function well." (*The Center Magazine,* published by the Center for the Study of Democratic Institutions, November, 1968.)

CBE is on Clark's side of the debate about function and purpose. There has never been any doubt on our part that the primary function of schools is the development of basic skills and the training of minds. Bearing this idea of the function of schools in mind, let us return to the question of what reforms are now desirable. Here are some of the things for which there is an imperative need: 1. Improved reading instruction. 2. Better teacher education. 3. Clearer and better measures of educational achievement. 4. More critical evaluation, in practice, of innovations. 5. Higher aspirations for children of the ghetto.

Reading, of course, is the essential first skill and the child who has an inadequate grasp of it is doomed to academic failure all along the line. It is hardly necessary to point to the failure of most of our schools in teaching this skill; indeed, published (and unpublished) test scores show that the failure amounts to a scandal. CBE believes that the root of the trouble is the faulty whole-word method in beginning reading that has predominated in American schools for so many years. Until fairly recently, organized phonics, or what it is becoming fashionable to call decoding, has been frowned on by almost all the reading specialists. Those who wanted to improve reading had to buck a monopoly and had to try to persuade schoolmen to stop being intimidated by the "experts" and to try new approaches. Now there is reason for cautious optimism about reading improvement. In recent years a half dozen different phonics-based reading systems have come into successful use. Our very rough estimate is that 15 per cent of American school children are now learning to read by these systems. Enough comparative studies of the old and new systems have been made to indicate the overwhelming superiority of the latter. The reform of reading instruction is a slow process, but one indication that it is coming is that many leading publishers are now moving in the direction of a phonics, or code-emphasis, approach.

In the second area where reform is most needed, teacher education, there has been some progress in recent years. There have been some changes in certification practices and some honest attempts to make a broad liberal education the basis of the teacher's preparation. Some of the changes have certainly been superficial, like changing the name of Bear Hollow State Teachers College to Bear Hollow State University. The complaint made a few years ago by Conant and Koerner that teacher education is a monopoly of the educationists is still valid. They, rather than the academicians, remain in charge. The mechanisms available to them—their schools and departments of education, their national educational and accrediting associations, and for the most part, their certification requirements—still flourish and still dominate the field. We must be grateful for the undoubted advances that have been made. But until the old establishment is willing to make some fundamental changes we will continue to feed into the schools each year a crop of undereducated teachers.

A third area where reform is needed is in measuring achievement. As we have often pointed out in these pages, there is an amazing lack of over-all information about what students learn. The paucity of information has its roots in the reluctance of educators to release data about achievement to the public, and their morbid fear of comparison, that is, of measuring one school system against another. A layman who is interested in knowing how state or town A's schools compare with state or town B's, must for the most part go by hunch and impression. The picture is not all dark, however. California and New York now have uniform programs of state-wide achievement testing at the elementary level and some of the results have become available to the public. This month the first phase of a national assessment program will get under way. The Committee on Assessing the Progress of Education (CAPE) will start to collect, by random sampling, information about educational attainments, abilities, and skills of students aged 17, to be followed in the fall by students aged 9 and 13. The results will not enable one to make judgments about particular school districts but will give some national picture of educational attainment. Such an assessment is long overdue. Perhaps it will prepare the way for evaluation procedures that will improve our ability to judge the competency of individual schools and school systems.

We come now to the need for better and more critical evaluation of various educational innovations in practice. Since Sputnik, American public education has turned to experimentation and has shown willingness, at least in some directions, to abandon old methods for new ones that seem to hold more promise. The discovery method, foreign language laboratories, individually prescribed instruction, nongraded schools, the new math and the new English, programmed instruction, and team teaching are some of the innovations that have found favor with schoolmen. In some circles there has been a tendency to accept these innovations as necessities or as infallible devices; and there has also been a tendency to rely on them rather than on better teaching to improve the over-all educational program. Along with an admirable willingness to try new things school people have sometimes seemed to think that all change is good or of equal value. Some of the innovations mentioned above have undoubtedly been effective, but we submit that most of them have not been subjected to rigorous critical evaluation. As the pressures increase for schoolmen to "innovate," there is a pressing need for critical studies to determine the effectiveness of the great number of innovations already in operation.

The final reform of which we would speak has to do with ghetto education. One of the most urgent tasks of public education at the moment—in view of the consequences of failure, one is tempted to say *the* most urgent task—is to improve the quality of education in big-city schools. This involves a change of attitude on the part of many adults and the adopting of higher aspirations for children of the ghetto. Many educators and teachers have developed a sort of determinism about ghetto education, although the rationale may not always be the same. This determinism may be based on differing notions of the nature of the slum child, especially the Negro slum child. Some teachers, including many Negro teachers, believe he is an undisciplined savage, too dumb to learn. Others are inclined to rhapsodize about his naturalness and spontaneity and to point out that such an unspoiled child of nature may suffer a trauma by having "middle class" education or mores imposed on him. (It is teachers of this sort who are apt to tell us that we mustn't corrupt slum dialects by insisting on standard English.)

Those holding these opposing views of the nature of the slum child seem, however, to agree on one thing: millions of American young people in our cities are innately "different," non-verbal and non-bookish children who will find irrelevant the kind of preparation in reading and writing that has always been one of the main tasks of the schools. Educators and teachers may be divided over the question of whether the slum child is imp of Satan or child of God, but many of them are united in thinking he is uneducable.

Effective ghetto education is further hamstrung by the sociological view that the schools cannot do much for the child until the community and the home change. If you accept the conclusion of the well-known Coleman report that "schools bring little influence to bear on a child's achievement that is independent of his background and general social context," then it may be futile to spend much time trying to improve the school's instructional program. You might better be employed in changing the child's home and social environment, or at least in trying to make the school a branch of the welfare department.

Ironically, many slum parents realize better than do their children's mentors the importance of learning the basic skills. In our judgment, the most important of the reforms outlined in this article is the upgrading of ghetto education. A first step toward that reform would be the assumption on the part of all those working in ghetto schools that the children in their charge are capable of learning.

There is nothing fundamentally awry with the structure and organization of American schools. Very often there is a great deal wrong with the aims and programs of schools. We believe the schools are salvageable, and in this article have named some of the reforms which, if effectively carried out, can turn poor or mediocre schools into good schools. To sum up, we need to improve reading; upgrade teacher education; provide clear measures of educational achievement; engage in critical evaluation of current innovations; and above all, change ghetto schools from ineffective custodial institutions into effective educational institutions. There is no miracle pill around that will make the schools what they ought to be. Only such a program of reform, calling for dedication and hard work, will do the job.

■ Mortimer Smith is a well-known critic of educational practices. What groups would find his criticism most welcome? Who would be his opponents? Compare Smith's views with those of Toffler in "The Psychology of the Future," earlier in this section. What major points of disagreement between the two writers can you identify?

■ One of the points of view expressed during recent debate over educational change has been that of Ivan Illich, who proposes that society abandon its schools. If you are not familiar with Illich's position, obtain a copy of his book *Deschooling Society* (New York: Harper & Row, 1972) and present a summary of his "radical" ideas to your fellow students. What is your reaction to Illich's arguments?

■ It may be said that Smith's comments in this article are also "radical." The kind of education he calls for differs markedly from what occurs in many classrooms. Discuss in what sense Smith may be considered a "radical."

■ What arguments can you develop for aligning yourself with Smith or Illich, or with an in-between position?

"...education is not a neutral subject, nor is it an isolated subject. It is a deeply political issue in which we guarantee a future for someone and, frequently, in guaranteeing a future for someone, we deal somebody else out."

Relate Bruner's ideas to those of Colin Greer in "Romanticism, Rheumatism, and Public Education" (Section Three).

The Process of Education Revisited

Jerome S. Bruner

Ten years have passed since *The Process of Education* was published—a decade of enormous change in the perspective and emphasis of educational reform. I am torn between beginning my account as an archaeologist reconstructing that period by its products, or beginning with a message of revolutionary import. I shall moderate both impulses, begin with a bit of archaeology, and show how my excavations lead me to a certain revolutionary zeal.

Let me reconstruct the period in which *The Process of Education* came into being. Nineteen fifty-nine was a time of great concern over the intellectual aimlessness of our schools. Great strides had been made in many fields of knowledge and these advances were not being reflected in what was taught in our schools. A huge gap had grown between what might be called the head and the tail of the

Jerome S. Bruner, "The Process of Education Revisited," *Phi Delta Kappan* **53**, no. 1 (September 1971), pp. 18–21. Reprinted by permission.

Jerome Bruner is Watts Professor of Experimental Psychology, Oxford, England. He was, for many years, professor of psychology at Harvard University where he was also founder and director of the Center for Cognitive Studies. Among his books are *Beyond the Information Given; On Knowing: Essays for the Left Hand; The Process of Education; Toward a Theory of Instruction.* His provocative work *The Process of Education* was written following the famous Woods Hole, Massachusetts conference on educational methods. Its basic concept is that the elements of science and the humanities can be grasped by children much earlier than has been traditionally assumed.

academic procession. There was great fear, particularly, that we were not producing enough scientists and engineers.

It was the period shortly after Sputnik I. The great problem faced by some of my colleagues in Cambridge at the time was that modern physics and mathematics were not represented in the curriculum, yet many of the decisions that society had to make were premised on being able to understand modern science. Something had to be done to assure that the ordinary decision maker within the society would have a sound basis for decision. The task was to get started on the teaching of science and, later, other subjects. They were innocent days. But beware such judgments rendered in retrospect. At worst, the early period suffered an excess of rationalism.

The prevailing notion was that if you understood the structure of knowledge, that understanding would then permit you to go ahead on your own; you did not need to encounter everything in nature in order to know nature, but by understanding some deep principles you could extrapolate to the particulars as needed. Knowing was a canny strategy whereby you could know a great deal about a lot of things while keeping very little in mind.

This view essentially opened the possibility that those who understood a field well—the practitioners of the field—could work with teachers to produce new curricula. For the first time in the modern age, the acme of scholarship, even in our great research institutes and universities, was to convert knowledge into pedagogy, to turn it back to aid the learning of the young. It was a brave idea and a noble one, for all its pitfalls. It is an idea that still bears close scrutiny, and we shall give it some later.

It was this point of view that emerged from the famous Woods Hole conference on improving education in science (the impetus and inspiration for *The Process of Education*). No curriculum project in the first five years after that was worth its salt unless it could sport a Nobel laureate or two on its letterhead!

The rational structuralism of Woods Hole had its internal counterpoise in intuitionism—the espousal of good guessing, of courage to make leaps, to go a long way on a little. It was mind at its best, being active, extrapolative, innovative, going from something firmly held to areas which were not so firmly known in order to have a basis for test. Of course, everybody knew that good teachers always have encouraged such use of mind. But perhaps good teachers were being driven underground by the prevailing literalism. . . .

At Woods Hole and after there was also a great emphasis on active learning, poking into things yourself, an emphasis on active discovery rather than upon the passive consumption of knowledge. It too derived from the idea that making things one's own was an activity that would get things structured in one's own way rather than as in the book. Some enthusiasts ran away with the idea of the "discovery method," that one should even discover the names of the constellations! It is a modest idea, but with profound consequences, some of which were not understood at the time—and we shall come back to it.

During the early sixties, in various projects, it was discovered again and again how difficult it was to get to the limit of children's competence when the teaching was good....No wonder then that we concluded that any subject could be taught in some honest form to any child at any stage in his development. This did not necessarily mean that it could be taught in its final form, but it did mean that basically there was a courteous translation that could reduce ideas to a form that young students could grasp. *Not* to provide such translation was discourteous to them. The pursuit of this ideal was probably the most important outcome of the great period of curriculum building in the sixties.

With all of this there went a spirit and attitude toward students. The learner was not one kind of person, the scientist or historian another kind. The schoolboy learning physics did so as a physicist rather than as a consumer of some facts wrapped in what came to be called at Woods Hole a "middle language." A middle language talks *about* the subject rather than talking the subject.

I recall a dark day on Cape Cod, the day after the conference ended. It was raining. We, the steering committee, thought surely the whole enterprise had been wrongly conceived. We would end, we feared, by turning the educational Establishment against us and science. Then *The Process of Education* was published. It was acclaimed. I want to tell you about acclaim. Acclaim is very hard to cope with if you have business in mind. For once something is acclaimed it can be ignored in a noble way. The acclaim from which we suffered was that each reader-teacher picked the part he liked best and proclaimed it was exactly what *he* was doing! But the period of being acclaimed into impotence passed as new curricula began to appear.

Producing curriculum turned out to be not quite as we academics had thought. Something a bit strained would happen when one caused to work together a most gifted and experienced teacher and an equally gifted and experienced scientist, historian, or scholar. There was much to be learned on both sides and the process was slow and decisions had to be made about the level at which one wanted to pitch the effort—the college-bound, the "average," the slum kid?

There were aspects of the undertaking that we had not counted on—mostly after the production. One was the problem of bureaucracy in education, the subject of an entire yearbook recently published by the ASCD—the issue of adoption, of distribution of materials, and so forth. A second was an even deeper problem: the training of teachers to use curricula. Both of these remain unresolved—the first constrained by fiscal difficulties, the second by the genuinely puzzling questions of teacher recruitment, training, and supervision. I cannot pretend to competence in this area....

So much for the archaeology. What I should like to do now is shift to other matters more concerned with present and future.

The movement of which *The Process of Education* was a part was based on a formula of faith: that learning was what students wanted to do, that they wanted to achieve an expertise in some particular subject matter. Their motivation was taken for granted. It also accepted the tacit assumption that everybody who came to these curricula in the schools already had been the beneficiary of the middle-class hidden curricula that taught them analytic skills and launched them in the traditionally intellectual use of mind.

Failure to question these assumptions has, of course, caused much grief to all of us. Let me quote from the preface of a book I have just written, *The Relevance of Education:*[1]

> This book is built around essays written between 1964 and 1970, years of deep and tumultuous change. They were disturbing years. They had an impact in their own right, amplified by my increasingly strong involvement during the period with very young human beings. These were my "subjects" in experiments and observations. The contrast between the exterior or social turbulence and the human helplessness I was studying kept imposing itself.
>
> The period of these essays is the period of the elaboration of youth culture, with its concomitant revolt against "establishment" schooling. It extends from Berkeley to Columbia, through the Harvard bust and the Sorbonne riots, to the Prague spring and summer, and the beginnings of the long and cruel winter that followed. In our own universities we have gone from the salad days of "new colleges" to the present "hard line" of so many faculties. The young began the period in political activism; then there was the sharp fire of a new extremism; now, in...early...1971, it is a new disengagement.
>
> Through the turmoil and idealism of these years has run a theme of "naturalness," of "spontaneity," of the immediacy of learning through direct encounter. A distrust of traditional ways has brought into question whether schools as such might not be part of the problem—rather than a solution to the problem of education. American educational reform in the early sixties was concerned principally with the reconstruction of curriculum. The ideal was clarity and self-direction of intellect in the use of modern knowledge.
>
> There were brave efforts and successful ones in mathematics and physics, in chemistry and biology, and even in the behavioral sciences. The faltering of the humanists at this time was puzzling, though it later became clearer. A revision of the humanities involved too many explosive issues, we were to discover.
>
> In the second half of the decade, the period of these essays, deeper doubts began to develop. Did revision of curriculum suffice, or was a more fundamental restructuring of the entire educational system in order? Plainly, the origins of the doubt go deep and far back into the changing culture and technology of our times. But our ruinous and cruel war in Vietnam led many who would have remained complacent to question our practices and priorities. How could a society be so enormously wealthy, yet so enormously and callously destructive, while professing idealism? How wage a war in the name of a generous way of life, while our own way of life included urban ghettos, a culture of poverty, racism, and worse?
>
> We looked afresh at the appalling effects of poverty and racism on the lives of children, and the extent to which schools had become instruments of the evil forces in our society. Eloquent books like Jonathan Kozol's *Death at an Early Age* began to appear.
>
> It was the black community that first sought "free schools," freedom schools. They were to help black identity, to give a sense of control back to the

---

[1]Anita Gil (ed.). New York: W. W. Norton, 1971.

community. Just as the civil rights movement provided models for social protest at large, so, too, the drive for free schools for the children of the black poor produced a counterpart response in the intellectual middleclass community. The revolt against the system very quickly came to include the educational Establishment. Generous-minded men like Ivan Illich and Paul Goodman, inveighing against the deadening bureaucratic hold of teachers and educational administrators, voiced a new romanticism: salvation by spontaneity; "dis-establish" the established schools. It was a view that, as we know, took immediate root in the "in" youth culture.

But if romanticism was solace for some, despair was the order for others. By the spring of 1970, when Elizabeth Hall, one of the editors of *Psychology Today,* asked me what I thought about American education at the moment, all I could answer was that it had passed into a state of utter crisis. It had failed to respond to changing social needs, lagging behind rather than leading. My work on early education and social class, for example, had convinced me that the educational system was, in effect, our way of maintaining a class system—a group at the bottom. It crippled the capacity of children in the lowest socioeconomic quarter of the population, and particularly those who were black, to participate at full power in the society, and it did so early and effectively.

It is not suprising then that this little volume, arranged roughly in chronological order, should begin with an essay that bears the title, "The Perfectibility of Intellect," vintage 1965, and end with one called "Poverty and Childhood," a product of 1970.

And so a half decade passed. By 1970 the concern was no longer to change schools from within by curriculum, but to refit them altogether to the needs of society, to change them as institutions. It is no longer reform but revolution that has come to challenge us. And it is not so plain what is the role of the academic in such an enterprise.

What would one do now? What would be the pattern at a Woods Hole conference in 1971? It would not be in Woods Hole, in that once rural, coastal setting. More likely, we would gather in the heart of a great city. The task would center around the dispossession of the children of the poor and the alienation of the middle-class child. In some crucial respect, the medium would surely be the message: the school, not the curriculum, or the society and not even the school. And in my view, through my perspective, the issues would have to do with how one gives back initiative and a sense of potency, how one activates to tempt one to want to learn again. When that is accomplished, then curriculum becomes an issue again—curriculum not as a subject but as an approach to learning and using knowledge.

The rest of what I have to say concerns these issues—of activating a learner, of giving him his full sense of intent and initiative.

Consider first getting people to want to learn something, how to make the learning enterprise sustained and compelling. In a recent article in the *Saturday Review,* I proposed that it is possible to conceive of a Monday-Wednesday-Friday curriculum covering the standard topics, and a Tuesday-Thursday and indeed Saturday way of doing things in which immediate and compelling concerns are given the central place—activism? Let them on Tuesdays and Thursdays prepare "briefs" in behalf of their views, make a case for things they care about. Let them prepare plans of action, whether they be on issues in the school, on the local scene, or whatever. What is important is to learn to bring all one's resources to bear on something that matters to you now. These are the times for the migratory questions that wander on long after their answers are forgotten, just because they are great questions. And there must be more time for the expressive elements—the encounters, the hates, the loves, the feelings. All this need not be antic nor need it all be in the manner of presenting one's case. I have seen experiments using improvisational theater, drama, film, and the like to teach and to question history, projects in which one learns to construe events through different sets of eyes. To what an extraordinary extent do films and plays of the contemporary scene matter in this! Ionesco or Pirandello are not so much concerned with absurdity but with how not to be caught with the obvious. This is not something to be prescribed. But it can surely be explored how it is we are perplexed by the texture of the society in which we live.

An extraordinary, moving book called *Children of Barbiana* is about a contemporary Tuscan hill town in Italy. The children there had failed so many times in so many ways in school that they had given up generation after generation—consigned to unskilled labor. A priest came to the parish. He started a school in which nobody was to fail, a school in which it was expected that everybody had to pass. It was everyone's responsibility to see that everybody in the class mastered the lesson before anybody could go on to the next lesson.

A community is a powerful force for effective learning. Students, when encouraged, are tremendously helpful to each other. They are like a cell, a revolutionary cell. It is the cell in which mutual learning and instruction can occur, a unit within a classroom with its own sense of compassion and responsibility for its members.

These were matters we did not do enough with at Woods Hole. We did not think about mutuality because we were stuck on the idea of curriculum—in spite of the fact that our laboratories and our very curriculum projects were set up rather like communes!

Inevitably, somebody will ask, "Well, how are you going to grade them?" You might also ask, "How in the world are you going to grade all of these distinguished colleagues who write collaborative articles among themselves and their graduate students?

There is a group of high school girls in Concord, Massachusetts, who are tutoring in the local elementary school. Those who are acquainted with cross-age tutoring will know, as I discovered, the extent to which those who help are helped, that being a teacher makes one a better learner. But should it be such a surprise? Is this not what is meant by passing on the culture?

What we say of the peer group and the near-peer group holds for the different age levels within the society. For in some deep way, what is needed is the reestablishment of a "learning community" beyond formal school, which as now constituted is far too isolating. It is not just by removing the barriers between elementary and high school students or by establishing a lifetime relationship to one's college where one can return for sustenance and become part of a broader learning community again. M.I.T. pronounced a few years ago that an engineer's education is obsolete after five years, so he must be brought back to bring him up to date. Let him come back, yes, but let the price of admission be that he discharge his obligation then to those who are just beginning—teacher, tutor, guide, what?

Finally, I would like to explore, in the interest of relevance, whether we might not recapture something of the old notion of vocation, of ways of life, or to use the expression of so many undergraduates today, of "life-styles." I am impressed with contemporary concern for life-styles. I have just finished a term as master of Currier House, a Radcliffe-Harvard house, and I assure you of the genuineness of this concern. But I am appalled that it is rarely translated into what one *does* with a life-style, the kind of vocation and livelihood in which we can express it. Could it be that in our stratified and fragmented society, our students simply do not know about local grocers and their styles, local doctors and theirs, local taxi drivers and theirs, local political activists and theirs? And don't forget the styles of local bookies, aspiring actresses, or illegitimate mothers. No, I really believe that our young have become so isolated that they do *not* know the roles available in the society and the variety of styles in which they are played. I would urge that we find some way of connecting the diversity of the society to the phenomenon of school, to keep the latter from becoming so isolated and the former so suspicious.

Let me add one last thing not directly connected with *The Process of Education*, but a problem of the first order today. One cannot ignore it in talking of education. We shall kill ourselves, as a society and as human beings, unless we address our efforts to redressing the deep, deep wounds that we inflict on the poor, the outcast, those who somehow do not fit within our caste system—be they black or dispossessed in any way. If there is one thing that has come out of our work with the very young, it is the extent to which "being out," not having a chance as an adult, or as a parent, very quickly reflects itself in loss of hope in the child. As early as the second or third year a child begins to reflect this loss of hope.

When any group is robbed of its legitimate aspiration, it will aspire desperately and by means that outrage the broader society, though they are efforts to sustain or regain dignity. Inequity cannot be altered by education alone, another lession we have learned in the past decade. The impact of poverty is usually transmitted through the school as well. It cannot be counteracted by words unless there are also jobs and opportunities available to express society's confidence in what is possible after school.

There must be ways in which we can think honestly of reformulation of the institutions into which our schools fit, as one integral part. Surely it requires that we redirect our resources, re-order our priorities, redefine our national effort, and come to terms with the fact that we have a deep and brutal racism in us—in all of us. We must learn how to cope with that. The young know it; they despise our failure to talk about it and our other difficulties. History may well side with them.

In the end, we must finally appreciate that education is not a neutral subject, nor is it an isolated subject. It is a deeply political issue in which we guarantee a future for someone and, frequently, in guaranteeing a future for someone, we deal somebody else out. If I had my choice now, in terms of a curriculum project for the seventies, it would be to find a means whereby we could bring society back to its sense of values and priorities in life. *I believe I would be quite satisfied to declare, if not a moratorium, then something of a de-emphasis on matters that have to do with the structure of history, the structure of physics, the nature of mathematical consistency, and deal with it rather in the context of the problems that face us.* We might better concern ourselves with how those problems can be solved, not just by practical action, but by putting knowledge, wherever we find it and in whatever form we find it, to work in these massive tasks. *We might put vocation and intention back into the process of education, much more firmly than we had it there before.*

A decade later, we realize that *The Process of Education* was the beginning of a revolution, and one cannot yet know how far it will go. Reform of curriculum is not enough. Reform of the school is probably not enough. The issue is one of man's capacity for creating a culture, society, and technology that not only feed him but keep him caring and belonging.

■   The writings of Jerome Bruner have had a profound effect on education, not because he was pointedly critical, but because he formulated an idea of how curriculum could be organized that struck a responsive chord in both academics and educators. Yet in this essay Bruner complains that he was misunderstood. What was the basis for the misunderstanding and what were its consequences?

■   What does Bruner feel is basically wrong with the educational process that utilized his ideas? Does Bruner maintain hope that reform of education is possible? What would be the most important reform he would advocate now?

Five percent in a national survey believe "There are no problems...[with] which the public schools in this community must deal...."

Examine the attitudes expressed in this poll against the ideas of Phyllis Myers in "Alternative Schools: Creative Rebellion Against the Public System" (Section Two).

Seventh Annual Gallup Poll of Public Attitudes Toward Education

George F. Gallup

...The Gallup education polls are now an established source of reliable information concerning trends in opinion about significant school questions. For school officials, the polls can be valuable in two important ways. They alert decision makers to overall public reaction to a variety of school programs and policies. And they serve as a national benchmark against which local attitudes can be measured....

The present survey has sought to discover the views of American citizens toward their public schools. It is the seventh annual survey in the series launched in 1969. This year the survey was funded by the Ford Foundation. Previous surveys were sponsored by CFK Ltd....

MAJOR PROBLEMS CONFRONTING THE PUBLIC SCHOOLS IN 1975

Respondents have been asked each year in the seven surveys in this series to cite the most important problems of the public schools in their own communities.

George F. Gallup, "Seventh Annual Gallup Poll of Public Attitudes Toward Education," *Phi Delta Kappan* 57, no. 4 (December 1975). Reprinted by permission.

George Gallup began his famous poll taking in 1933, focusing at first on social and political issues. Dr. Gallup has served as head of the journalism department at Drake University (Des Moines, Iowa) and as a professor of advertising and journalism at Northwestern University. He is founder of the American Institute of Public Opinion and the Audience Research Institute, as well as the author of *Public Opinion in a Democracy, A Guide to Public Opinion Polls,* and *The Sophisticated Poll Watchers Guide.*

In six of these seven surveys, including the present one, the problem most frequently mentioned is "lack of discipline." The percentage of those interviewed who cite discipline has not differed significantly from the first survey: Approximately one person in four names discipline as the most important problem.

The major problems which the public names this year, 1975, are substantially the same as those mentioned in the 1974 survey, with one exception. This year, for the first time, the number of respondents mentioning "crime" (vandalism, stealing, etc.) is great enough to place this problem among the top 10. Actually, in number of mentions, it ranks in eighth place. And this year, for the first time, "drinking" (use of alcohol) is mentioned by enough respondents to establish a new category, although it is not one of the top 10.

Comparing this year's findings with those of 1969, the first survey, brings to light a significant drop in the number who say that "lack of proper facilities" is a major problem in their local schools.

Below, in order of mentions, is the list of the top 10 problems of the public schools, as viewed by the public, in the year 1975:

1. Lack of discipline
2. Integration/segregation/busing
3. Lack of proper financial support
4. Difficulty of getting "good" teachers
5. Size of school/classes
6. Use of drugs
7. Poor curriculum
8. Crime/vandalism/stealing
9. Lack of proper facilities
10. Pupils' lack of interest

RATING OF THE PUBLIC SCHOOLS

In the 1974 survey, an effort was made to establish a rating of the public schools that would provide a base for future comparisons. A five-point scale was used, one which the schools themselves have employed historically. This question was asked:

Students are often given the grades A, B, C, D, and FAIL to denote the quality of their work. Suppose the *public* schools themselves, in this community, were graded in the same way. What grade would you give the public schools here—A, B, C, D, or FAIL?

During the year, a significant drop has been registered in the number of persons giving the schools a grade of A. The change is from 18% last year to 13% this year.

The lowest ratings of the public schools come, understandably, from parents whose children are now attending independent/parochial schools. In this group, only 5% give the public schools an A rating; 34% give them a rating of either D or FAIL.

The public's rating of the schools may be influenced by the general loss of confidence in and respect for all American institutions. Education and the church, it should be pointed out, still have much higher confidence ratings than Congress, the Supreme Court, organized labor, or big business. A Gallup Poll released in July, 1975 shows that the public gives a high confidence rating of 67% to the schools as opposed to a 40% confidence rating for Congress, a 38% confidence rating for organized labor, and a 34% rating for big business.

Apart from this, it should be pointed out, the media have given wide publicity this year to the increasing crime and vandalism in the schools throughout the nation and to the declining test scores as reported by national college entrance examinations.

Ratings given to the public schools in 1974 and those given in 1975 indicate these changes during this period:

	National Totals	
Ratings Given the	**1974**	**1975**
Public Schools	%	%
A rating	18	13
B rating	30	30
C rating	21	28
D rating	6	9
FAIL	5	7
Don't know/no answer	20	13

ATTITUDES TOWARD STUDENT RIGHTS

Although the Supreme Court has upheld rights of students in recent rulings, the weight of opinion in the nation is that students have too many rights and privileges. Those who say students, generally speaking, have "too many" rights and privileges comprise 45%; those who say "not enough" or who say these rights and privileges are about right total 37%.

When the same question was asked in the 1972 survey, 41% said that students had "too many" rights. This compares with the 45% in the present study. More important, parents of children in the schools are increasingly of the opinion that students have too many rights. The percentage of parents with children in the public schools who say "too many" has increased from 40% to 47%; those with children in parochial/private schools, from 40% to 56%.

The question:

Generally speaking, do the local public school students in this community have too many rights and privileges, or not enough?

	National Totals %	No Children In Schools %	Public School Parents %	Parochial School Parents %
Too many	45	43	47	56
Just right	27	22	35	22
Not enough	10	10	11	9
No opinion	18	25	7	13

TRAINING PROGRAMS PLANNED BY THE PUBLIC SCHOOLS

In most of the seven annual surveys in this series, questions have been asked about training programs for students who are not interested in the usual curricular subjects and who stay on in school only because they are required to by law.

The public has favored by large majorities all the proposals for dealing with these young people—all except the plan to let them quit school and go it alone without supervision.

While the public has recognized the problem presented by students who are wholly uninterested in academic work, still no program has emerged or been put into effect on a national scale.

The public schools, if they follow the public's wishes, have an opportunity to work out a special program that will combine educational and vocational training. The public favors giving the schools this responsibility by an overwhelming vote of 86%.

Most European nations have wrestled with this same problem and have devised programs that are successful. And, as a matter of fact, so have some public school systems in the United States.

Many of these programs call for a combination of technical training and on-the-job experience, with attention given to communication and mathematical skills that are deemed essential.

If experiments with this kind of program are devised and tested, almost certainly a way will be found to deal with students in the 15- to 18-year age group who are uninterested in academic subjects and who all too often become troublemakers in school.

The question:

It has been suggested that the public schools be given the responsibility to set up special job training programs for young people, age 15 to 18, who are out of work and out of school. Would you favor or oppose such a plan?

	National Totals %	No Children In Schools %	Public School Parents %	Parochial School Parents %
Favor giving schools this responsibility	86	87	85	84
Oppose	11	9	12	15
Don't know/ no answer	3	4	3	1

THE NONGRADED SCHOOL

The nongraded school concept has wide appeal. In fact, all major groups of the public favor the idea by margins of more than two to one. The high percentage favoring nongraded schools indicates that the public is ready to accept innovations in a period when many persons are inclined to blame new methods and new viewpoints in the educational world for an apparent decline in student performance.

When the same question was asked of the general public in 1972, a slightly higher favorable figure was obtained. In that year, the national totals showed 71% favoring the nongraded school concept as opposed to 64% in the present survey. In the earlier study, 22% were opposed, which compares with 28% today.

The question:

Should a student be able to progress through the school system at his own speed and without regard to the usual grade levels? This would mean that he might study seventh-grade math, but only fifth-grade English. Would you favor or oppose such a plan in the local schools?

	National Totals %	No Children In Schools %	Public School Parents %	Parochial School Parents %
Favor	64	62	66	73
Oppose	28	28	28	25
No opinion	8	10	6	2

AWARENESS AND ATTITUDES WITH RESPECT TO OPEN EDUCATION

The open concept of education, which came originally from England and which has been adopted in many schools throughout the United States in recent years, is still relatively unknown to a majority of Americans and even to parents whose children now attend the public schools.

Slightly more than one-fourth (27%) of all individuals questioned in the survey said that they knew what is meant by the "open" education concept or idea.

And when asked to describe, in their own words, what an "open" school is, most of these proved their familiarity with the concept. Only a negligible few said that it meant "schools open to all."

In the case of parents with children in private or parochial schools, a higher proportion (33%) claimed familiarity with the "open" school concept and, significantly, a higher proportion of this group approved of open education.

These questions were asked:

Do you happen to know what is meant by the "open" school concept or idea?

If yes:

In your own words, how would you describe an "open" school?

How do you feel about "open" schools? Do you approve or disapprove of them?

	Awareness of Open Education			
	National Totals %	No Children In Schools %	Public School Parents %	Parochial School Parents %
Said they knew what is meant by open schools	27	24	30	33
Didn't know	60	63	56	54
Weren't sure	13	13	14	13
	Attitudes Toward Open Education*			
Approve of open schools	13	12	14	18
Disapprove	10	8	12	11
Don't know/ no answer	4	4	4	4
	27	24	30	33

ALTERNATIVE PUBLIC SCHOOLS

In some U.S. cities, parents of schoolchildren are being given the choice of sending their children to a special public school that has strict discipline, including a dress code, and that puts emphasis on the three Rs. If you lived in one of these cities and had children of school age, would you send them to such a school or not?

---

*Percentages of those who said they knew what is meant by open education.

	Yes %	No %	Don't Know/ No Answer %
National totals	57	33	10
Sex			
Men	54	35	11
Women	60	31	9
Race			
White	57	33	10
Nonwhite	57	29	14
Age			
18 to 29 years	43	51	6
30 to 49 years	59	31	10
50 years and over	65	21	14
Education			
Elementary grades	58	25	17
High school	58	34	8
College	54	37	9
Community size			
1 million and over	61	28	11
500,000 to 999,999	55	40	5
50,000 to 499,999	58	34	8
2,500 to 49,999	53	37	10
Under 2,500	57	30	13
Region			
East	55	33	12
Midwest	57	36	7
South	60	28	12
West	56	35	9

■ Opinion polls frequently exert an important influence on public policy, on television programming, and on political decisions. Reviewing the data regarding Gallup polls of opinion on education, what conclusions do you reach concerning the influence of public opinion on the program of the schools?

■ *The Gallup Polls of Attitudes Toward Education, 1969-1973,* a paperback publication, is available from Phi Delta Kappa, International Headquarters Building, Eighth and Union, Bloomington, Indiana 47401. A complete account of the 1974 poll is also available; the entire 1975 poll is printed in the December 1975 issue of *Phi Delta Kappan* magazine. Examining the polls across a period of time reveals a wide range of vantage points from which to examine major issues in public education.

■ Consider the figures listed under "Rating of the Public Schools"; what explanations can you offer for the range of grades from A to Fail? What events or experiences do you think caused a shift in ratings from 1974 to 1975?

"The seemingly enlighted educators who had pressed. . .changes toward flexibility and enrichment had focused their energies entirely on making the process of learning in school more lively and rewarding. But they had not perceived that larger social forces were calling into question the relevance of education."

Read and compare ideas expressed by Gross with those of Neil Postman and Charles Weingartner in "A History of the Hollering" (Section One) and with Lawrence Cremin in "The Free School Movement—a Perspective" (Section Three).

From Innovations to Alternatives: A Decade of Change in Education

Ronald Gross

For the past 10 years, first at the Ford Foundation, later with the Academy for Educational Development, I've been acting as a kind of Typhoid Mary of education, picking up new ideas and practices wherever I found them, then spreading them around to the susceptible.

This experience has given me a chance both to examine the state of American education and to make my own judgments about the new ideas and programs. Some of the things I've learned are small and simple. From Herb Kohl in Berkeley, for instance, I learned how teachers can start off in moving toward a freer classroom by devoting only 10 minutes a day to new ideas. Nothing frightening in that—despite Kohl's insistence that his revolutionary strategy comes straight out of Che Guevera!

Ronald Gross, "From Innovations to Alternatives: A Decade of Change in Education," *Phi Delta Kappan* **13**, no. 1 (September 1971). Reprinted by permission of the author.

Ronald Gross is the co-editor of *High School* (with Paul Osterman), and *Radical School Reform: The Revolution in the Schools.* He is also author of *The Teacher and the Taught: Education in Theory and Practice from Plato to Conant.* Mr. Gross has also published two unusual collections of poems: *Pop Poems* and *A Handful of Concrete* (with Beatrice Gross). The author of numerous magazine articles, Mr. Gross was associated with the Ford Foundation's educational program and has been a consultant for the United States Office of Education and the United States National Commission for UNESCO.

From John Holt I found out how students sabotage their own education, learning to please the teacher by "psyching out" the tests. And from Neil Postman I discovered that students and teachers can use "judo" rather than violent confrontation to get their schools to change.

The movement for change in recent American education has moved through three phases: first, "innovation"; second, "radical reform"; and the phase just emerging, "alternatives" to traditional concepts of schooling.

When I first entered the field of education in the mid-fifties, it was in the midst of a flurry of what came to be called "innovations." I'm thinking of the various new curricula exemplified by the new math—ideas like team teaching and programmed instruction, the use of technologies such as television and the language laboratory, the first serious experiments with nongrading.

These innovations were sparked by a fresh concern with educational quality, both personally and nationally. Every parent was concerned about whether his child was getting a good enough education; the "sheepskin psychosis" was hitting high gear. And for the nation as a whole, that superb visual aid called Sputnik had made many citizens look down from the skies and into the classrooms—with dismay at the supposed educational causes of our technological failure. So a corps of master plasterers was recruited to patch up the intellectually disreputable facade of American education.

These "innovative" programs were undertaken in well-established schools with fairly conventional philosophies. They were not based on new ideas about the role of education, or the nature of the child, or the place of culture in a democratic society. They focused on practical methods of achieving the traditional end of schooling—the mastery of basic skills and subject matter.

These innovative approaches changed the climate of American public education in the late fifties and early sixties. What they achieved has been important, but what they failed to achieve, unfortunately, has been even more important.

A DEEPER MALAISE

For even as these innovations relieved the rigid programs and teaching practices in many schools, a deeper malaise was developing, unnoticed, in American education. The seemingly enlightened educators who had pressed these changes toward flexibility and enrichment had focused their energies entirely on making the process of learning in school more lively and rewarding. But they had not perceived that larger social forces were calling into question the relevance of education.

In the urban ghetto schools, starvation budgets, the impact of the slum environment, teacher indifference and sometimes unconscious racism had reduced the schools to mere disciplinary or custodial institutions. And in the suburbs, the shadow of college preparation and social conformity had blighted the process of growing up—less brutally but with comparable efficiency.

By the mid-sixties black parents in the ghettos and white students on the campuses and in the suburban high schools began to revolt against the educational system. The riots of the big-city slums and the demonstrations on the campuses of the multiversities made it shockingly clear that the educational and social system had reached a point where it could no longer continue without basic, radical changes in its structure, control, and operation.

As a result, over the past five years a new breed of radical theorists and teachers has emerged in American education.

True learning and healthy growth are sabotaged in most American schools today, these critics argue, because of an authoritarian atmosphere in which the emphasis is on the teacher teaching rather than on the student learning. The whole process of schooling is frozen into a rigid lockstep through the grades, chopped up mechanically into blocks of time and different subjects, dominated by a curriculum fixed in advance and imposed from above. There is no real regard for the students as individual people, with real concerns of their own and inherent drives to know, understand, and create.

For John Holt, "To a very great degree, school is a place where children learn to be stupid." Paul Goodman "would not give a penny to the present administrators, and would largely dismantle the present school machinery." Jonathan Kozol demonstrates that the schools of one of our major cities destroy the minds and hearts of black children. George Leonard, Peter Marin, and Edgar Friedenberg see schools stifling the finest and most passionate impulses of young people. The high school students who formed the Montgomery County (Maryland) Student Alliance testified that "From what we know to be true as full-time students it is quite safe to say that the public schools have critically negative and absolutely destructive effects on human beings and their curiosity, natural desire to learn, confidence, individuality, creativity, freedom of thought, and self-respect."

These charges, which were considered beyond the pale of "responsible criticism," have been officially substantiated by such recent reports as Charles Silberman's *Crisis in the Classroom* and the *Schools for the Seventies* publications project of the NEA's Center for the Study of Instruction.

THE RADICALS' PLATFORM

On what principles would the radical reformers reconstitute education? Here the diversity of such an individualistic group of writers makes it difficult to generalize, but among the propositions most frequently found in these writings, and embodied in radical programs, are:

1. Students, not teachers, must be at the center of education.
2. Teaching and learning should start and stay with the students' real concerns, rather than with artificial disciplines, bureaucratic requirements, or adults' rigid ideas about what children need to learn.

3. The paraphernalia of standard classroom practice should be abolished: mechanical order, silence, tests, grades, lesson plans, hierarchical supervision and administration, homework, and compulsory attendance.
4. Most existing textbooks should be thrown out.
5. Schools should be much smaller and much more responsive to diverse educational needs of parents and children.
6. Certification requirements for teachers should be abolished.
7. All compulsory testing and grading, including intelligence testing and entrance examinations, should be abolished.
8. In all educational institutions supported by tax money or enjoying tax-exempt status, entrance examinations should be abolished.
9. Legal requirements which impede the formation of new schools by independent groups of parents—such as health and safety requirements—should be abolished.
10. The schools' monopoly on education should be broken. The best way to finance education might be to give every consumer a voucher for him to spend on his education as he chooses, instead of increasing allocations to the school authorities.

Based on some of these new principles, positive, fresh starts have developed throughout the country. Silberman, in his book, focuses on one such trend at the elementary level: the adoption here of the so-called British infant school approach. He also cites impulses toward reform at the high school level, in such schools as Murray Road in Newton, Massachusetts, Parkway in Philadelphia, and John Adams in Portland. In my books, *High School* and *Radical School Reform,* I provide case studies written by participants or close observers of all of these schools. I report on many other promising experiments throughout the nation: Herb Kohl's Other Ways School in Berkeley; Harlem Prep in New York City; George Dennison's First Street School; the CAM Academy in Chicago; Shule ya Uhura, a freedom school in Washington, D.C.; a middle-class free school in suburban Montgomery County, Maryland; the super-free public school called Fernwood in rural Oregon; and others.

THE NEW ULTRA-RADICALS

In the last years, a new viewpoint has emerged in this continuing debate over American education. More radical than radical school reform, this viewpoint asserts that reforming schools is impossible.

One practicing teacher who came to this conclusion is James Herndon, who teaches in a suburban junior high school outside of San Francisco. Some years back when Herndon wrote the best book about ghetto teaching, *The Way It Spozed To Be,* he was fired. For the past 10 years, he has been trying his damndest to humanize his school. He and his *simpatico* colleagues began by pushing the idea of freedom as far as it would go. They made classes voluntary, had the kids decide what would go on when they came, gave no grades. But the students didn't turn on; the teachers realized that the children couldn't tell them what and how to teach. "We were both waiting around. Together, we amounted to zero."

Then suddenly, out of this zero, out of reaching bottom, it all came together: a school-within-the-school in which they concentrated on teaching reading, found their own answer, and succeeded handsomely. They simply recreated the convivial, "inefficient," noncompetitive atmosphere in which kids learned to read before schools made it such a big deal. The story of their success shows stunningly what can be achieved when teachers seriously re-examine what they are doing and why—as Charles Silberman has urged so eloquently.

But the experiment was murdered. The successful reading approach they demonstrated was rejected by the school bureaucracy, which preferred to follow mindlessly the latest state education department ukase. "Public education is a game you can't whip," said the principal when he delivered the *coup de grace.*

Herndon's conclusions are dark. He believes the U.S. public school blights the whole learning process, that it is hopelessly hung up on ramming children into bureaucratic categories, dividing them destructively at every level into winners and losers.

He rests his hopes, therefore, not on the possibility of changing education, but on just getting it off people's backs. "There is no law any more that people must go to church or pay attention to the church," Herndon writes, "and so many people don't, while others do. That is the best you can expect, and good enough. . . . The public school is the closest thing we have in America to a national established church, Getting-an-Education the closest thing to God, and it should be possible to treat it and deal with it as the church has been treated and dealt with."

At the center of this line of thought is Ivan Illich, that extraordinary mastermind who works out of the Center for Intercultural Documentation in Cuernavaca, Mexico. Illich seems to be having the same kind of impact on social criticism in this country that Marshall McLuhan had, operating out of Toronto in the late fifties. Illich argues that the reason our schools seem to be doing everything wrong these days is that schools *are* basically wrong, *per se.* He believes that schools and all the other service institutions by which we have sought to maintain and enhance our lives actually oppress and degrade us. Schooling, in Illich's view, has little to do with learning. Each of us has learned most of the useful, lovely, or engaging things he knows from his life rather than from his teachers. Learning comes about through association with people and books and things and institutions, through trying to grow up.

Illich demands the "dis-establishment" of schooling: the repeal of compulsory education laws, provision of constitutional guarantees against discrimination on the basis of possession of a high school or college diploma or advanced degree, rollback of public support of public schools, and an "edu-credit" card which each individual may use to receive his equal share of public education resources (broader than the voucher plan, because Illich would not confine its use to schools).

MY OWN VIEW

I do not see deschooling coming to America the way the deschoolers would like. Rather, I envisage a various, halting, impulsive, sometimes troubled groping toward more diverse options, finer possibilities. My hope is that through the gradual erosion of those constraints of place, time, age, and mode of learning which now define schooling, it will gradually become impossible to tell where school begins and life stops—a more feasible goal which would reinstate, under more benign conditions, the pre-industrial unity of learning and living.

Already there are "schools without walls," free universities, human potential growth centers, the *Whole Earth Catalog,* and a myriad of other initiatives, inside and outside the formal education system, for enabling what I call "free learning" to commence. Many educators seem reconciled to the fact that the present generation of 10- to 20-year-olds is just about the last one that will voluntarily trudge through the lockstep from kindergarten to college. Something has got to be done—or many, many things.

I have seen too many good classrooms in the past 10 years to agree that the schools are going to shrivel up and die, or should. Many, many children are spending many, many happy and fruitful hours in our schools at every level. Particularly heartening is the emergence of a new spirit among some groups of teachers, joining together through what Joseph Featherstone calls "a common conviction of what it means to do a good job." Once teachers and students together begin to take themselves seriously, to ask what they are really doing in school, why they are doing it, and what they could and should do, I think we will see some extraordinary changes.

But at the same time I would like to see a real flowering of other options, other avenues to growing up, other milieu in which youngsters and grownups could learn from each other. Institutions that have a monopoly, like schooling, grow impervious to reform. The church was oppressive and rigid when it had a monopoly and could force people to heed its dicta. Now it is more enterprising in defining its authentic role in the modern world.

Alternatives can do the same for education. Schools themselves will benefit from the creation of many options and alternatives to the present monolithic system. But the chief benefit will be for our children, who will have the chance to grow up in a society of autonomous men rather than coercive institutions.

■   Some critics of education would like to see the entire system of schooling changed radically. What evidence can you offer to place Gross in such a group of critics?

- What does Gross see as the way to eliminate current dissatisfaction with education? Do you find Gross's case convincing? Why or why not?

- Examine the ten propositions of the radical's platform for education. What items would you add or subtract from the list? Explain your decision(s).

- If you are not familiar with the writers and books mentioned in this article, you may find it informative to obtain one or more of them and to report on their theses to your classmates.

*"The school curriculum was substantially
the same in 1957 as it was in 1917. There
were, of course, some silly courses that had
not existed ten or fifteen years earlier, but
the school curriculum in its modern version
began to form in the 1880's, became more
or less established in the 1920's, and remains intact, alas, in most schools to this
day."*

See Ashley Montagu's "We're Botching the
Business of Education" for a point of reference (Section One).

A History of the Hollering

Neil Postman and Charles Weingartner

John Dewey was just beginning to get comfortable in his grave when the
Russians, of all people, reached down and stuck a spear into his heart. It was
1957. Dewey had died five years earlier, secure in the knowledge that he was
America's preeminent education philosopher. And then the Russians launched
Sputnik I. As Walter Cronkite might say, this meant that we were behind in the
race for space. A lot of Americans went into a grim panic. In those days, you may
remember, whenever things went badly for us, the custom was to assume that one
of our own had sold us out. On this occasion, Dewey was fingered.

The indictment went something like this: John Dewey was the father, and
maybe the mother, of the Progressive Education movement. Progressive education was a kind of gooey, precious, romantic philosophy which stressed permissiveness and life adjustment. There was no place in it for rigorous thinking, disci-

"A History of the Hollering," in Neil Postman and Charles Weingartner, *The School
Book.* Copyright © 1973 by Neil Postman and Charles Weingartner. Reprinted with permission of Delacorte Press.

Neil Postman and Charles Weingartner have been successful collaborators on numerous
publications: *Teaching as a Subversive Activity; The Soft Revolution: A Student Hand-
book for Turning Schools Around; The School Book,* and textbooks in language study.
Dr. Postman is professor of English education at New York University and is also on the
faculty of Harlem Preparatory School. He is a former elementary and secondary-school
teacher. Dr. Weingartner was a professor of education at Queens College (New York) and
is now professor of English education at the University of South Florida (Tampa).

pline, or social responsibility. Moreover, progressive education was championed by know-nothing education professors and had taken over as the dominant philosophy of American schools. As a result, our country had been burdened with at least two generations of self-indulgent ignoramuses—specifically, kids who had no stomach or preparation for building rockets and other important things. And that's why we were losing to the Russians. *Life* magazine and the *New York Times* stressed these points pretty hard, but they were moderate in comparison with Admiral Hyman Rickover, who, for a time, devoted most of his energies to attacking the schools and their Dewey-istic learnings. Rickover, the father (and maybe the mother) of the atomic submarine, was among other things, under the impression that a child's school day was mostly absorbed by "frill" subjects such as basket weaving and free-form dancing. He ferociously denounced the waste of it all, urging that we return to what he called the basics. He was joined by many others who accused the schools of quackery and of not understanding the perilous position we occupied as leader of the free world.

A good history of those times does not exist, and we are not prepared to give one. But it is necessary for us to make these points: (1) The reaction immediately following the launching of *Sputnik I* represents the first phase of what might be called contemporary school criticism; (2) most of the complaints during that period were made by politicians, military men, and college professors, not by teachers, students, or parents; and (3) most of the criticisms were prodigiously misinformed. For example, it was *not* true that the philosophy of American schools was dominated by Dewey's "progressive" ideas. It probably *was* true that professors of education rated Dewey the foremost theoretician in their field, but this did not mean much in the day-to-day functioning of most schools. In other words, there did not exist then, nor does there now, a great confluence between theory and practice.

Neither was it true that students were spending an inordinate amount of time on "frill" subjects. The school curriculum was substantially the same in 1957 as it was in 1917. There were, of course, some silly courses that had not existed ten or fifteen years earlier, but the school curriculum in its modern version began to form in the 1880s, became more or less established in the 1920s, and remains intact, alas, in most schools to this day.

Finally, Dewey was badly misinterpreted by critics who had obviously not read him "personally." To the extent that teachers were being permissive, they were probably more influenced by their conceptions of Freud than of Dewey. If Dewey stands for anything, he stands for rigorous thinking, self-discipline, and social responsibility. (So does Freud—but that's another matter.) It is virtually impossible to read Dewey without coming to this conclusion, unless of course, the reader is in a curiously mangled state of mind.

But for all the misinformed ill will of post-*Sputnik* school criticism, there was at least one positive aspect to it. For the second time in this century (the "progressives" had done it first), the question was raised, What are schools for?

Of course, for many critics, the question was rhetorical. Their purpose in raising it was to give a preformed answer: schools were an instrument of national foreign policy, a weapon in the cold war. It followed from this that the best thing schools could do was to produce inspired scientists and competent technicians, and fast. Thus, the first and shortest-lived phase of modern school criticism—let us call it Panic Phase 1—amounted to an attack on such "frill" courses as existed and a call for an increase in science and math programs. But the question, What is school for?, hovered about, and in a short time, a new group of critics was to grab hold of it and give it a very different set of answers.

But that did not come until the second phase of school criticism had ended. The second phase began roughly in 1960 and was concerned, as Jerome Bruner has put it, principally with the reconstruction of curriculum. What happened was that the professionals moved in. Not the "know-nothing educationists," who were still reeling from the blows aimed at them in Phase 1, but the "real" professionals: professors of mathematics and science. And then, a bit later, professors of history and English. As the professionals saw it, if the schools were to produce good scientists and engineers, then it was up to our best scientists and mathematicians to turn out the programs that would do the job most efficiently. What they did, in effect, was to bypass the question, What is school for?, and go straight to the question, What is a subject for? In a now famous conference held at Woods Hole, Massachusetts, in 1959, the professionals—led by Jerrold Zacharias of MIT and Jerome Bruner of Harvard—mapped out their strategy. Some curious things followed. For one, as the scientists began to ask themselves, "What is physics for?" or, "What is chemistry for?" they found themselves turning back to John Dewey. As Bruner put it, "The ideal was clarity and self-direction of intellect in the use of modern knowledge"—an elegant way of saying that the scientists rejected the notion that a student's head needed to be filled with someone else's answers to someone else's questions—that is, a lot of facts. Instead, they embraced the idea that the purpose of studying a subject was to learn *how to think*, which is not only the title of one of Dewey's most famous books, but also a lifelong concern of his.

In *The Process of Education* (1960), a report on the Woods Hole Conference, Bruner introduced the phrase "the structure of a discipline." By that term he meant to convey that each subject has a unique way of asking questions and finding answers, and that this "structure" is what students ought to learn. Moreover, he recommended that the best way to learn it is by doing it. Which, of course, is what John Dewey had been saying for roughly forty years. Thus, in the early 1960s the phrase "inductive method" became popular, as the scientists tried to invent problems that would engage students in a process of inquiry, presumably to help them become self-directing, creative thinkers. At this point, Dewey started to rest comfortably again in his grave.

It came to pass, of course, that professors of history and English wanted to get into the act (there were lots of government grants available), and within two or three years—certainly by 1965—we had not only the New Math and the New Science, but the New English and New Social Studies as well. Moreover, since the scientists and other university scholars learned fairly quickly that there is more to schooling than they had at first supposed, there developed a rapprochement between the scholars (who knew about subjects) and the educationists, including workaday teachers (who knew about students). Organizations like the National Council of Teachers of English and the National Council of Teachers of Social Studies invited the active and influential participation of prominent university specialists, who advised elementary and secondary school teachers on content. The teachers contributed their knowledge of children and the realities of school life. Together, they would solve the problem of the schools by teaching students to learn how to learn.

For a while, somewhere around 1964 or 1965, it seemed as if they could. One thing was sure: the United States was back in the lead in the race for space. No thanks to the schools of course, but at least the schools had gotten back on the right track and were protected from the charge of quackery through their alliance with our best scholars. Everything looked rosy, except for a few minor details. One of them was the problem of the ghetto school. Everyone knew that in such schools, reading scores were low and dropout rates high, but amid the prevailing optimism, the belief was strong that these problems could be overcome by the application of proper techniques. The New Curricula could fix most of what was wrong, and if they couldn't, we would just work harder to fix the new curricula. At some point, we would know enough about language learning, reading difficulties, and the rest so that ghetto schools could benefit as much as any from the "revolutionary new approaches," as they were called.

Up to this point, the public had not had much to say, and the students nothing at all. True, laymen had been aroused to a state of concern by the early critics, but only for a short time before the professionals moved in. When that happened, everyone kept still in deference to the great American religion called Expertise. There is an analogy to be drawn on this point between the school problem and the space problem. In the early 1960s, the technicians at Cape Kennedy, née Canaveral, were working on the problem of how to get to the moon by 1970. Since no one was asking whether or not we *should* go to the moon, and since laymen had no qualifications to discuss how to get there, silence was the only option. Similarly, in the early 60s, since no one was asking what a school is for, and since laymen believed they had no qualifications for discussing the reconstruction of curriculum, a comparable silence followed. But not for awfully long. The experts, as usual, had asked the wrong question, and this fact could not go unnoticed forever. Paul Goodman noticed it. And so did Edgar Friedenberg. And Jules Henry.

Goodman and Friedenberg were sociologists, Henry an anthropologist, and what they noticed, first of all, was that the dropout rates were going up among all social classes; that "psychic" dropout rates were astronomical; that in spite of the enthusiasm of many teachers and professional organizations for the new curricula, students were becoming increasingly alienated from learning and from almost anything else related to school. They also began to notice the ways in which school, as a social institution, functioned to support other institutions, some of which did not need or want people to be self-directing and creative. They explored the gap between the official rhetoric about the purposes of school (e.g., to widen the horizons of students) and the *real* purposes of school, and they found it enormous. In short, they discovered that the problem of the schools had not been seriously confronted. Rickover had only touched the subject. Zacharias and Bruner had avoided it altogether. The problem had to do with the question of what school is for in the first place, and had little to do with how to make instruction more efficient. As a matter of fact, from the point of view of Goodman, Friedenberg, and Henry, the schools were astonishingly efficient. According to them, schools trained the young remarkably well to be obedient, passive, and mechanical, and to accept alienation as a way of life.

Two things must be noted at this point. First, the insights of Goodman and the others were not really discoveries. Social scientists rarely discover anything new, in the sense that biologists do. For the most part, social scientists *re*discover. They call attention to things people once knew but have forgotten. There was nothing new in showing how schools serve the needs of corporations, government, advertisers, even demogogues, but the reminders were nonetheless astonishing and reopened philosophical (why) rather than technical (how) questions. Second, Goodman, Friedenberg, and Henry were slightly ahead of their time. Their publications came between 1956 and the early 1960s, when very few people were thinking seriously about the schools. Their work was, so to speak, only the gathering clouds. The first drops of rain came in 1964, in the form of John Holt's *How Children Fail* and Bel Kaufman's *Up the Down Staircase*. The books caught on almost immediately, to a large extent because they were written by teachers who could speak in concrete terms about what schools did to children. These were no abstract sociological analyses. Instead, they were an almost daily record of how fear of failure and obedience to rigid conventions destroyed the curiosity and natural love of learning of real children.

Soon after, the trickle became a deluge. From everywhere, and seemingly simultaneously, there appeared dozens of books, each one stronger than the other in its denunciation of a school system devoted not to the welfare of children, but to the service of a war-loving state and a dehumanizing economy. It was as if the question Admiral Rickover asked in the late 1950s was finally getting an answer. What are schools for? Well, not to help build atomic subs, baby. So answered the new wave of school critics, who, significantly, seemed to come from all walks of life. There were, of course, the practicing teachers, such as Jonathan Kozol, Herbert Kohl, and James Herndon. There were also journalists and writers, among them George Leonard, Nat Hentoff, and George Dennison. And psychologists, men like Carl Rogers, William Glasser, and Jerome Bruner (who by now understood the error of his earlier ways). And sociologists David Rogers, Frank Riessman, and Marilyn Gittell. And parents, such as Ellen Lurie. And students, such as Donald Reeves. And even a couple of know-nothing education professors, Postman and Weingartner. Education magazines began to sprout all over the place, as did education conferences and antischool organizations. Inevitably, some people—feeling that the public schools were beyond reform, let alone redemption—began to start their own schools, thus beginning what is known as the Free School movement.

Between 1965 and 1970, there was more ferment over the schools than anyone had seen since the heyday of progressive education. And just to excite matters a little more, people in the ghettos became aroused, then militant. Although few school critics were black or Hispanic, the messages they were sending were not lost among the poor and disenfranchised.

What were those messages? The new indictment went something like this: Somehow, during the last thirty years, control of the American school had passed out of the hands of the people and into the hands of the bureaucrats. Perhaps the people didn't care enough, occupied as they were with an affluence achieved by the vice of a war economy. More likely, their indifference was the result of a pervasive cultural trend toward moving people farther and farther away from control over their own institutions. In any event, it was clear that school was not devoted to the interests of individual children, to helping them become autonomous, creative, inquiring people who have the will and intelligence to determine their own destiny. In fact, the new critics argued, the school functions to defeat such goals. Instead, it now functions as a service agency to the dominant bureaucracies of our society. Almost all the conventions of school—grading, grouping, labeling, record keeping, bell ringing, testing, etc.—are designed to make students accept the decisions of others, accept fear, accept alienation. Moreover, the argument went, it is no accident that children in the ghettos fail repeatedly. The conventions of school are so arranged as to guarantee that result. Our present economy still demands a large source of cheap labor, and the school is deeply implicated in a kind of conspiracy to keep the poor, poor. As for the curricula, even the newest of them, they are at best irrelevant, at worst, obsolete—all in all, a source of distraction that prevents students from thinking about the true nature of their situation.

So ran the indictment. The defendants, who in this case consisted mostly of beleaguered teachers and administrators, replied by denouncing the critics as romantic and, in some instances, paranoid. The trouble with such criticism, the defense argued, is that it comes from people who are not familiar with what really goes on in school, and who expect the schools to implement utopian schemes. To which the critics replied that they were only too familiar with the realities of school (which in some cases was not true) and that there was hardly anything utopian in their proposals (which in most cases *was* true). In fact, it should be stressed that in spite of the idealized images of school evoked by the "romantics," most of their complaints were against the conventions of the schooling process, not its basic structure. For example, the critics did not, for the most part, question whether or not the schools should exist, or even whether or not students should be compelled to attend them. What they wanted was an overhaul of the procedures governing the relationship among students, teachers, and administrators. They took for granted that schools *could* function humanely; they were angry about the fact that they didn't.... Assuming, then, within this limitation, that our narrative of the recent history of school criticism is accurate, what does it all mean?

Well, in the first place, school critics, like other critics, tend to overestimate the influence of their ideas. The fact is that many schools in the country have not been touched by any of this....

■   The authors of this selection won a large audience both inside and outside the field of education for their book, *Teaching as a Subversive Activity.* Their writings since have been received favorably in many areas, not only because of their lively literary style, but because of their direct and forceful critical appraisals. Postman and Weingartner claim that despite the criticisms leveled against the schools, public education remains relatively unchanged. In what ways do you agree or disagree with their position?

■   Can you cite examples of the ways schools as you have experienced them have seemed to respond to criticisms?

"The content of traditional high school curricula should be revised to eliminate busywork components designed merely to occupy the time of adolescents who are in school only because the law requires it."

Examine the position taken by Phyllis Meyers in "Alternative Schools: Creative Rebellion Against the Public System" and by Frederick Bock and Wanda Gomula in "A Conservative Community Forms an Alternative High School" (both in Section Two).

Recommendations for Improving Secondary Education

The National Commission on the Reform of Secondary Education

The reform of secondary education cannot be accomplished by educators working alone. It requires the ingenuity and assistance of many people in the community served by a particular school. The recommendations of the Commission must be considered in this framework.

RECOMMENDATION NO. 1: Defining Secondary School Expectations. Every secondary school and its subordinate departments must formulate a statement of goals and develop performance criteria for students. Goals and objectives should be published in information bulletins for students and parents and be posted in a conspicuous place within the school building.

From *The Reform of Secondary Education: A Report to the Public and the Profession* by the National Commission on the Reform of Secondary Education (New York: McGraw-Hill, 1973). Reprinted by permission.

The National Commission on the Reform of Secondary Education was sponsored by the Kettering Foundation. It included representatives from the teaching profession, teacher-training institutions, and high-school student councils, as well as from such educational organizations as the American Association of School Administrators, National Congress of Parents and Teachers, National Association of Secondary School Principals, National Catholic Educational Association, and the North Central Association of Colleges and Secondary Schools. B. Frank Brown of the Institute for Development of Educational Activities was chairman.

RECOMMENDATION NO. 2: Community Participation in Determining Secondary School Expectations. Schools will not be able to achieve their purposes without increased help from the people in the communities they serve. Communities must participate in the formulation of goals and in continuing efforts to refine and adapt the statements of goals and objectives. The communities as a whole, not solely the subsection called schools, must achieve the goals.

RECOMMENDATION NO. 3: The Basis for Curricular Revision. The high schools should no longer be required to perform purely custodial functions. Attempts to keep in school adolescents who do not wish to be there damage the environment for learning. The content of traditional high school curricula should be revised to eliminate busywork components designed merely to occupy the time of adolescents who are in school only because the law requires it. Revitalization of the curriculum will require attention to the earlier maturation of adolescents. Intelligent evaluation of curricular revision must grow from valid measurements of the degree to which students are achieving the stated goals and objectives of their school.

RECOMMENDATION NO. 4: Teacher Training. Teacher training institutions should revise their programs so that prospective teachers are exposed to the variety of teaching and learning options in secondary education. New teachers should be able to work in several instructional modes.

Extensive in-service programs should be instituted to retrain teachers presently employed to equip them with a greater variety of approaches and skills. This need will become increasingly acute as the decline in birth rate encumbers the schools with aging teaching staffs.

RECOMMENDATION NO. 5: Bias in Textbooks. State legislatures must ensure that procedures are established so that textbooks and materials used in the schools do not present inaccurate accounts of the contributions of various ethnic groups or inaccurate portrayals of the role of women.

RECOMMENDATION NO. 6: Bias in Counseling. Counselors should ensure that all students, regardless of sex or ethnic background, are afforded equal latitude and equally positive guidance in making educational choices.

RECOMMENDATION NO. 7: Affirmative Action. Every high school should establish an affirmative action committee composed of students, former students, faculty, and community representatives. The purpose of this committee is to examine and report to the administration on instances of inequality and discrimination involving students or groups of students at the school.

RECOMMENDATION NO. 8: Expanding Career Opportunities. Secondary schools must realign their curricula to provide students with a range of experiences and activities broad enough to permit them to take full advantage of career opportunities in their communities. To meet this objective, basic components of the school program will have to be offered in the late afternoon or in the evening for some students.

RECOMMENDATION NO. 9: Career Education.   Career education advisory councils including representatives of labor, business, community, students, and former students should be established to assist in planning and implementing career education programs in comprehensive high schools.

Career awareness programs should be initiated as an integral part of the curriculum to assure an appreciation of the dignity of work.

Opportunities for exploration in a variety of career clusters should be available to students in grades 8 through 10.

In grades 11 and 12, students should have opportunities to acquire hard skills in a career area of their choice. This training should involve experience in the world outside school and should equip the student with job-entry skills.

RECOMMENDATION NO. 10: Job Placement.   Suitable job placement must be an integral part of the career education program for students planning to enter the labor force upon leaving school. Secondary schools should establish an employment office staffed by career counselors and clerical assistants. The office should work in close cooperation with the state employment services. Agencies certifying counselors for secondary schools should require such counselors to show experience in job placement as a condition for granting initial certification.

RECOMMENDATION NO. 11: Global Education.   The education of the nation's adolescents must be superior to that of their parents. Part of this superiority must be an enhanced sense of the globe as the human environment, and instruction to this end must reflect not only the ancient characteristics of the world, but emerging knowledge of biological and social unity. All secondary school students should receive a basic global education.

New instructional material for global education must be prepared if this recommendation is to be effective. State departments of education should require teacher training institutions to design programs which prepare teachers to present such programs.

RECOMMENDATION NO. 12: Alternative Paths to High School Completion.   A wide variety of paths leading to completion of requirements for graduation from high school should be made available to all students. Individual students must be encouraged to assume major responsibility for the determination of their educational goals, the development of the learning activities needed to achieve those goals, and the appraisal of their progress.

RECOMMENDATION NO. 13: Local Board Responsibilities for Funding Alternatives. Whenever a student chooses an acceptable alternative to the comprehensive high school, local school boards should fund his education at the level of current expenditure computed for other students.

RECOMMENDATION NO. 14: Credit for Experience. Secondary schools should establish extensive programs to award academic credit for accomplishment outside the building, and for learning that occurs on the job, whether the job be undertaken for pay, for love, or for its own sake. Community involvement will, of course, be required in such a program and should be as encompassing as possible.

RECOMMENDATION NO. 15: Secondary Level Examination Program. The College Level Examination Board should expand its College Level Examination Program to include a comparable Secondary Level Examination Program. The tests should be routinely administered quarterly or monthly to help adolescents to obtain credit for work done outside the classroom.

RECOMMENDATION NO. 16: Broadcast Television. Major funding sources, including both foundations and the National Institute of Education, should initiate and support extensive research into the influence of television on students' attitudes, perceptions, and life styles. The purpose of this research should be to suggest changes in school curricula and instructional approach.

The broadcasting industry should establish media fellowships designed to afford secondary school teachers and instructional leaders the opportunity to study the use of broadcast commercial television for educational purposes.

RECOMMENDATION NO. 17: Classroom Use of Broadcast Material. Copyright laws and union contracts should be written to make sure that classroom use of broadcast materials copied off the air is not unnecessarily restricted. Television programs should never be asked to carry instructional burdens alone. Books and pamphlets must be specially and carefully prepared to accompany all instruction via television. Both the instructional television program and the printed materials should be available in public libraries as well as in schools.

RECOMMENDATION NO. 18: Cable Television. When cable franchises are awarded, the local school system should have exclusive use of three channels during the daytime, with possible use of more as needed. At least one—and preferably all three—of these cable channels should continue to be available for nighttime viewing by school students or for purposes of adult education.

RECOMMENDATION NO. 19: Flexibility of Alternative Programs. Differing time sequences—hourly, daily, weekly, yearly—must be made available so that educational programs can be adapted to the needs of individual students.

Schools are already moving away from the Carnegie Unit and are beginning to grant credit on the basis of competence, demonstrated experience, and a host of other assessments. It is recommended that this practice be expanded and that the Carnegie Unit become merely one of the alternative ways of granting credit.

RECOMMENDATION NO. 20: Rank in Class.   Articulation between secondary schools and post-secondary schools must be improved, with each level seeking to support the educational efforts of the other. Personnel representing both levels must cooperatively develop alternatives to grade-point average and rank in class for assessing the scope and quality of the education received by students at the secondary level. High schools should stop calculating student rank in class for any purpose.

RECOMMENDATION NO. 21: Planning for School Security.   All secondary school systems should develop security plans to safeguard students, faculty, equipment, and facilities. Specific procedures must be developed for faculty members to follow in case of disruption.

RECOMMENDATION NO. 22: Records of Violence.   State legislation should be enacted to require principals to file a detailed report on all serious assaults within schools. The information contained should form a data base from which security personnel could identify potential trouble areas and move to alleviate future problems.

RECOMMENDATION NO. 23: Code of Student Rights and Obligations.   Every secondary school should develop and adopt a code of student rights and obligations. This code should be published and distributed to every student. It should include all school rules, regulations, and procedures for suspension and expulsion with explanations of how students can defend themselves through established process.

RECOMMENDATION NO. 24: School Newspapers.   A school newspaper is a house organ which is operated, financed, and therefore controlled by the school system, which may be legally liable for its contents. In cases where students and school administrators become deadlocked over censorship, a student-faculty-community committee should decide the issue. Some schools may find it necessary to withdraw financial support, allowing students complete freedom of expression in what would then be entirely their own publication, with a corresponding liability for what is printed.

RECOMMENDATION NO. 25: Right of Privacy.   A student's school records must contain only factual information necessary to the educative process. The entire file must be available at all times for review by students and their parents but must not be accessible to "persons not in interest." Records should be forwarded to another school system, university, or prospective employer only at the written request of the student, his parents, or the receiving school.

That part of a student's records which pertain to his mental health should contain only entries made under the direction of the student's physician and must be kept separately from his academic records. The complete record or any of its contents should be released only to the student, his parents, or to his physician at the student's or parent's request.

RECOMMENDATION NO. 26: Corporal Punishment.   Several states have outlawed corporal punishment with no resulting loss in control or authority. Corporal punishment should be abolished by statute in all states. In the modern world, corporal punishment is necessarily "cruel and unusual."

RECOMMENDATION NO. 27: Student Activities.   Scholarship should not be a requisite for participation in sports, band, singing, cheerleading, or other student activities important to the social development of adolescents. Neither the local school nor state activities associations should establish scholarship standards. Any student in good standing in a school should have the right to participate in any of the school's activities with the exception of honor societies specifically established to reward scholarship.

RECOMMENDATION NO. 28: Compulsory Attendance.   If the high school is not to be a custodial institution, the state must not force adolescents to attend. Earlier maturity—physical, sexual, and intellectual—requires an option of earlier departure from the restraints of formal schooling.

The formal school-leaving age should be dropped to age fourteen. Other programs should accomodate those who wish to leave school, and employment laws should be rewritten to assure on-the-job training in full-time service and work.

RECOMMENDATION NO. 29: Free K-14 Public Education.   The Congress of the United States in conjunction with state legislatures should enact legislation that will entitle each citizen to fourteen years of tuition-free education beyond kindergarten, only eight of which would be compulsory. The remaining six years should be available for use by anyone at any stage of his life. Congressional involvement is essential to assure equal access in an age of interstate mobility.

RECOMMENDATION NO. 30: Youth Organizations.   The National Association of Secondary School Principals, a professional organization for school administrators, currently operates two of the largest organizations affecting public high school youth: the National Student Council Association and the National Honor Society. The principals' group should dissociate itself from these organizations and help them become independent national youth organizations.

RECOMMENDATION NO. 31: Sexism.   School administrators and school boards, at both the state and local levels, must set forth commitments to eliminate all vestiges of sexism in the schools.

Areas of immediate concern are equal employment and treatment of the sexes in instructional and administrative positions, equal opportunities for female students to participate in all curricula areas, including career education, and the elimination of all courses required of only one sex.

Individual teachers should make sure they are not focusing their teaching toward either sex.

All female students who become pregnant should be permitted to remain in school for the full term of pregnancy if they wish to do so and their physician considers it feasible. They should be permitted to return to school following childbirth as soon as released by their physician. There must be no denial of the right to participate in activities because of pregnancy or motherhood, whether the girl is wed or unwed.

RECOMMENDATION NO. 32: Females in Competitive Team Sports.   School boards and administrators at the local level must provide opportunities for female students to participate in programs of competitive team sports that are comparable to the opportunities for males. The programs must be adequately funded through regular school budgets.

Outstanding female athletes must not be excluded from competition as members of male teams in noncontact sports. The fact that a school offers the same team sport for girls should not foreclose this option.

State activities associations should be required by statute to eliminate from their constitutions and bylaws all constraints to full participation in competitive team sports by females.

If state activities associations are to continue to have jurisdiction over female sports, they should be required by state statute to have equal sex representation on all boards supervising boys' and girls' athletics.

■   Recommendation five suggests the monitoring of textbooks for inaccuracies regarding ethnic groups and women. Examine at least two of your current texts (or other learning materials) for such inaccuracies. Remember that inaccuracies may be "sins of omission" as well as "sins of commission." Organize a panel discussion that will allow the members of your class to more fully recognize how textbooks in a variety of subject areas treat ethnic groups and women.

■   What evidence can you cite to determine whether the thirty-two recommendations of this report are radical, conservative, or "something else"?

■ Recommendation nineteen indicates that some secondary schools are moving away from the Carnegie Unit. What is the Carnegie Unit and how does it function in the academic careers of most American students? The Commission's recommendations suggest that students be allowed to receive credit for experience and as the result of other assessments. For what experience and in what other ways might you have been granted credit at the secondary-school level?

■ Recommendation twenty-six speaks of corporal punishment as "necessarily 'cruel and unusual'." Examine recent efforts to reestablish corporal punishment in various parts of the country. What reasons are offered for these efforts? Historically, how is the Commission's recommendation a "modern" one?

■ In what ways are recommendations eight, nine, and ten, concerning expanding career opportunities," "career education," and "job placement," innovative? Consider those recommendations in light of the comments made by Mortimer Smith in "The Reforms Most Needed in Education," earlier in this section.

Annotated Bibliography

ALLEN, DWIGHT W., and JEFFREY C. HECHT, eds. *Controversies in Education*. Philadelphia: Saunders, 1974.

A sprightly and controversial collection of original pieces, most of them short, which highlights many of the issues regarding school reform that are of interest to educators. Represented are Illich, Mortimer Smith, Asimov, and Lieberman, among others. (549 pp.)

BRUNER, JEROME S. *The Process of Education*. Cambridge, Mass.: Harvard University Press, 1962.

Probably the most influential book in education of the past two decades. The analysis of curricular and instructional problems presented in this slim volume has had a major impact upon curriculum planning in all areas. (97 pp.)

COLEMAN, JAMES S. "The Children Have Outgrown the Schools." *Psychology Today* 5, no. 9 (February 1972), pp. 72–75.

Coleman describes". . . a revolution in the concept and practice of educational institutions in modern society. . . . The role of the school must undergo. . . transformation if the school is to continue to aid society in its critical socializing function."

EURICH, ALVIN C., ed. *High School 1980: The Shape of the Future in American Secondary Education*. New York: Pitman, 1970.

Over twenty educational sages have their chance to predict how, why, and in what direction the secondary school may change by 1980. Are they overly optimistic about the possibilities of changes? (304 pp.)

FRIERE, PAULO. *Pedagogy of the Oppressed*. New York: Herder and Herder, 1971.

A radical leader in Brazil until expelled because of his work with the impoverished peasants, Friere developed a theory of education for such individuals and extended it to the whole of education. This small volume has been widely read and quoted by those who feel that the "official" school systems are oppressive and designed primarily to protect and retain the status quo. (186 pp.)

GENTRY, ATRON *et al. Urban Education: The Hope Factor*. Philadelphia: Saunders, 1972.

A series of special essays devoted to an analysis of the problems of urban schools and discussion of some innovative experiments designed to meet the special needs of such schools. Particularly valuable for hard data and perceptive writing, though the overall impact is one of rather muted hope that urban schools can in fact be changed basically. (130 pp.)

GOODELL, CAROL. *The Changing Classroom.* New York: Ballantine, 1973.

Shows the contemporary classroom in concrete detail and thus provides helpful data for evaluating the current criticism of these classrooms. Useful in providing a contrast between the ideal and the actual. (339 pp.)

GUTHRIE, JAMES W., and EDWARD WYNNE, eds. *New Models for American Education.* Englewood Cliffs, N. J.: Prentice-Hall, 1971.

A number of leading American educators discuss the need for new models for American education and describe some that hold promise for the future. Included are new incentives for change, a systems approach, community control, the achievement of racial integration, new approaches to school finance, and the role of the family and out-of-school sources in learning. (258 pp.)

HERNDON, JAMES. "Jail." *How to Survive in Your Native Land.* New York: Simon and Schuster, 1971, pp. 97–98.

"All you can tell is, they'd rather come to your class than go to jail," expresses Herndon's point that as long as school is compulsory, teachers can never know whether kids are really happy or really learning.

KATZ, MICHAEL. "The Present Movement in Educational Reform." *Harvard Educational Review* **41**, no. 3 (August 1971), pp. 355–359.

From an historical perspective, the author suggests the current educational reform movement is near a close. The movement's demise rests on its inability to face and resolve various unexamined conflicts among leading reform proposals, such as compensatory education, integration, community control, radical pedagogical reform, and teachers professionalism. The author offers proposals for rehabilitation of the reform movement, including the "radical" notion that schools concentrate on teaching skills and avoid teaching attitudes.

KATZ, MICHAL B., ed. *School Reform: Past and Present.* Boston: Little, Brown, 1971.

Provides some significant and hard-to-find statements on reform from historical sources. A valuable background for assessing current reform movements. An unusual source book, particularly for the historically minded. (303 pp.)

KOZOL, JONATHAN. *Death at an Early Age.* Boston: Houghton-Mifflin, 1967.

Winner of the National Book Award, this is a "classic" from the early days of the free-school or alternative-school movement. The author describes his experience teaching in the slum schools of Boston with such anger and vividness that the urgent need for reform becomes obvious. (242 pp.)

MILHOLLAN, FRANK, and BILL E. FORISHA. *From Skinner to Rogers: Contrasting Approaches to Education.* Lincoln, Neb: Professional Educators Publications, 1972.

Presents a clear summary of the theoretical positions of Skinner and Rogers and shows what the implications of these theories are for classroom and student learning. (128 pp.)

O'NEILL, WILLIAM F., ed. *Selected Educational Heresies.* Glenview, Ill.: Scott, Foresman, 1969.

> Well-selected essays and commentary on the state of education, with prescriptions for change. Particularly interesting for the wide range of commentators, some of whom are seldom included in educational readers: Susan Sontag, Paul Tillich, Norbet Wiener. (372 pp.)

RAINES, MAX R., and GUNDER A. MYRAN. "Community Services: Goals for 1980." *Junior College Journal* **42** (April 1972), pp. 12–16.

> One of the most innovative areas of American education is the junior college. This article suggests various ways in which these two-year colleges must adapt to the needs of future students.

THOMAS, DONALD R. *The Schools Next Time: Explorations in Educational Sociology.* New York: McGraw-Hill, 1973.

> From the viewpoint of the educational sociologist, the author presents succinct commentary on the current dilemmas of education, and analyzes various prescriptions for change. The last chapter, "Does Reform Have a Future?" is particularly thought-provoking. (225 pp.)

TYACK, DAVID B. "Needed: The Reform of a Reform." In *New Dimensions in School Board Leadership*, ed. William E. Dickinson. Evanston, Ill.: National School Boards Association, 1969, pp. 29–51.

> A noted educational historian provides an overview of school reform, with focus on the crucial role of school boards; he discusses the problems of centralization versus decentralization in this light.

WASSERMAN, MIRIAM. "School Mythology and the Education of Oppression." *This Magazine is About Schools* **5**, no. 3, (Summer 1971), pp. 23–36.

> A four-way review of Silberman's *Crisis in the Classroom,* Althusser's "*Idéologie et Appareils Idéologiques d'État*", and Friere's *Cultural Action for Freedom* as well as *Pedagaogy of the Oppressed,* this article questions several premises of the works reviewed. "What constitutes the crisis of the schools is that students, no longer accepting their oppressiveness as morally and intellectually legitimate, are turning off, cutting out, and fighting back. And, in the face of drugs, truancy, and rebellion, the schools are less and less able to perform their socially necessary functions."

WATSON, GOODWIN, ed. *Change in School Systems.* Washington, D. C.: National Education Association, 1967.

> This collection of essays is particularly useful for theoretical statements regarding the processes of change in institutions, with special reference to the peculiar nature of the school system. (115 pp.)

vs.

"I'm not learning anything, I'm developing cognitive skills." [1]
Reproduced by permission of PUNCH

Harold: "...They send the [Bennington] girls out for part of the year. To take jobs...a third of the school year...."

Louise: "A third of the school year."

Harold: "Yes." (Louise breaks into laughter...) "What's funny?"

Louise: "I was thinking of some of the girls I used to know—in high school—who had to go right into jobs at Woolworth's—or Hank's Diner—and never knew they were getting a third of a Bennington education....Oh God, I hate all those schools so much!"[5]

In most alternative schools, teachers don't lecture, they discuss. Teachers and students frequently are on a first-name basis. Students don't sit at desks in rows, they sit on the floor or on lounges or at tables. Lessons aren't always held during the normal school day.[2]

It's time for the school system to stop experimenting with our kids.[6]

INNOVATIVE. Anything different in the content or technique of education, the assumption being that anything different is better (if you are a liberal) or dangerous (if you are a conservative).[3]

Schools never reform themselves.[4]

The only meaningful change will come from within the system.[7]

SOURCES FOR VERSUS

1. © *Punch*, London.

2. Donald Johnston, "Made-to-Order High Schools," *The New York Times*, 31 August 1975.

3. Richard Armour, *A Diabolical Dictionary of Education* (New York: The World Publishing Company, 1969).

4. Robert Gordis, quoted in *The American Character: A Conversation* (Santa Barbara, California: The Fund for the Republic, Inc., 1962).

5. Oliver Hailey, *Father's Day* (New York: Dramatists Play Service, Inc., 1971).

6. Parent of a student, quoted in *The Washington Post*, 14 November 1974.

7. Commencement speaker at the graduation exercises of a large suburban high school which had just come to the end of a year marked by student protest.

SECTION TWO
Starting New or Piecing Together

Section One attempted to provoke questions and stimulate thinking about "the need to create something different." Section Two provides some immediate follow-up by focusing on efforts that have been made to develop alternatives within and outside formal educational settings.

Richard Armour's facetious definition of "innovative" on the *Versus* page for this section underscores the extremely varied connotations of the word. Before you read this section, it may be informative for you to write your own definition of "innovative" as it relates to schooling. Check the dictionary for the definition that appears there. After you have completed this section, reexamine your definition in relation to the articles read, the dictionary definition, *and* Mr. Armour's statement.

As you read the articles by Joel Denker ("Boredom, Utopia, and 'Unprofessional Conduct' "), Evans Clinchy ("Murray Road: Beyond Innovation"), Thorwald Esbensen ("Family-Designed Learning: Accountability as Customer Satisfaction"), and Jane S. Shaw ("The New Conservative Alternative"), imagine yourself as a teacher in the circumstances described. Are you equipped with the academic content and educational methodology to function effectively in any/all of these environments? If any of the articles describes a situation you would enjoy, what goals must you set in order to be able to strive toward similar employment?

One of the critical generalizations made about alternative-schooling designs of the last fifteen years is that they do not last. After a year or two, the programs outside the school system disappear entirely, while the ones within are absorbed and modified into older (or still newer) programs, or are eliminated altogether. It could prove revealing to contact the sources referred to in these articles to determine how many of the schools described are still in operation and to what degree they function as described here. You may also wish to contact the Center for Options in Public Education, School of Education, Indiana University, Bloomington, Indiana 47401. Information about conservative alternatives is available from the Council for Basic Education, 725 Fifteenth Street, N.W., Washington, D.C. 20005.

To generally familiarize yourself with this section, consider the article titles listed and read, at the top of the first page of each article, the excerpts quoted. What conclusions do you reach about the range of experiences described? In what ways do you see, already, a relation or extension of ideas and issues raised in Section One? Do you know of schools not described here that have made efforts to find alternative ways of functioning? A possible assignment would be to write an article that could be included in this section. In what tentative ways could you argue that any/all of the situations described here will produce a Galatea or a monster?

As in the other sections of the book, an annotated bibliography follows the articles. The books and articles listed should prove helpful in further pursuing the in-depth issues and concerns explored in this section.

Some questions to bear in mind:

- How does one resolve the issues of ethics and integrity when confronted with a teaching situation repulsive to one's own values?
- To what degree can the schools permit students to make their own decisions about curriculum and organization of study?
- How much right does society (as represented in the immediate community) have to require the schools to engage in certain teaching/learning activities?
- What other alternative forms of education exist—or might exist—beyond those described in this section?

After reading the section articles, you might wish to return to the *Versus* page and debate the issue presented in items four and seven. On what side of the argument would you place yourself and what evidence can you offer to support your position?

"The seeds of rebellion against the public school monopoly are sprouting in city after city, nourished by more than a decade of documentation and passionate debate over the multiple failures of the public education system."

Consider Myers' remarks in light of the Ford Foundation's "Matters of Choice" (Section Two) and of Mortimer Smith's "Is Common Sense Breaking Through?" (Section Three).

Alternative Schools: Creative Rebellion Against the Public System

Phyllis Myers

Back in the early 1800s, when universal public education was not a subject of scorn but rather a glint in radical eyes, one of the knottiest issues before the fledgling nation had to do with diversity. Would its youth be better served by a single system under public auspices or should it continue, with public support, the kind of education the well-to-do were already getting—in small, independent institutions spawned by different, then usually religious, groups?

The heated debate was finally stilled, as we know, for more than a century, with the establishment of "common schools," free, compulsory, and open to all. It was a victory for democracy, equality, and freedom—or so it looked at the time—erasing distinctions of class, ethnicity, and religion and helping mold the incoming immigrant into an American.

Phyllis Myers wrote widely in the field of urban education as a member of the Urban Coalition. She was a senior staff member of the Rockefeller Task Force on Land Use and is now a senior associate of the Conservation Foundation. She has written numerous articles on state land-use legislation for the Foundation and a book, published by the Foundation, on neighborhood conservation.

Now it looks as if that debate might blow up all over again. The seeds of rebellion against the public school "monopoly" are sprouting in city after city, nourished by more than a decade of documentation and passionate debate over the multiple failures of the public education system.

It is a highly creative rebellion, in which parents and professionals alike are breaking away from the common school and putting together, with spit and string, their own schools. They try to charge little or no tuition, and some of them are beginning to talk about public support.

The rebellion (or, perhaps better, movement) goes by many names: alternative schools, parallel systems, educational options. It takes many forms: community schools, free schools, new schools, open schools, learning centers, street academies, community schools. They all begin with the thesis that most schools are mind-binding institutions which go against the nature of children. Thus the preset curriculum, teacher domination, and competition are readily discarded. There is far less worry over content than process—encouragement of curiosity, creativity, and inquiry.

But, as the proliferation of names suggests, behind the generalized impetus for change is a mind-boggling potpourri of pragmatic, romantic, and anarchistic hopes, ranging from innovation in the classroom to a radical restructuring of all society, from control by the community to control by a new set of professionals, from providing an escape valve for some children to institutionalizing escape valves within the system, from reforming public schools to giving up on them.

This confusion is welcomed by the New Schools Exchange Newsletter, a kind of "in" clearinghouse in Santa Barbara, Calif., aimed at the growing number of "people involved in alternatives in education." Recently, the Exchange asked its readers, rather as a put-on, to write in what they thought free schools were. Among the entries the Exchange delightedly printed:

"A free school is a nonpublic, nonelite, nondenominational school."

"A free school is a place where kids of all ages and sizes jump out of the bus and burst in the door yelling 'Hooray!' "

"I think of a free school as a learner-directed, loving, community-controlled, inventive, spontaneous place where all people live and learn together."

"A free school is a good place to make love. . . ."

"A free school is not a school. . . it is an attitude of an individual or group to pursue that which interests them."

To the sons and daughters of the middle class, who use the word *free* most often, the word has to do with working out a new relation to authority and compulsion—teachers, rules, parents, work, war.

But *free* can and does mean other things. In the community schools coming out of the desperation in the ghettos, it early on meant a school open to all on a first-come, first-served basis, like a public school, but free of the public school bureaucracy and having to do with "our freedom as black people."

Counting broadly from "progressive and liberative" through the most radical schools, the Exchange estimates there are 1,600 "new schools," involving

60,000 students, 10,000 staff, and 80,000 parents. Glowingly, the Exchange projects that by 1975 there will be 25,000 free schools, constituting "a major alternative to the public system" and draining away 1.4 million "responsive kids," 150,000 "innovative teachers," and 2 million parents.

San Francisco and Boston are the hottest outposts of innovation, and New York, Philadelphia, Milwaukee, Minneapolis, and Berkeley are not far behind. Conferences on "alternatives" abound, on California hillsides and in staid District of Columbia ballrooms.

It is the stuff of which Ph.D.'s are created and magazines are sold. But even as the media take up the pitch, all but proclaiming the dawn of a new day in education, there is an uneasiness—which visibly mounts the closer one gets to people who are out there on the line—that their efforts are being blown up far too fast. With memories of what happened to so many other "solutions," they fear another cult is washing over us, soon to ebb away.

Their questioning tends to follow several recurring themes: the applicability of the innovative models to the nation's top-priority educational dilemma, the inner-city school; doubts whether enough resources, either dollars or people, are available for expanding the number of experimental schools; and a damned-if-you-succeed-and-damned-if-you-don't fear that sudden popularity might result in change that is more form than substance, particularly as the "system" adopts its own versions of nonsystem models.

Is the aim to permit parents and students to choose among independent schools, paying with a government chit, or is the aim change in the system? The latter raises the whole question of how to bring about change in a system. Is it by the creation of compellingly successful models outside of the system; by "planting" innovative new staff in the system to spark change by example; by taking over an entire public school, or how? All of these strategems are being tried. All have succeeded by some measures and failed by others. And in what time frame should "success" be gauged?

"I can't believe that rapid change would be good change," warns Edward Yeomans of the National Association of Independent Schools. A courtly New Englander, he was one of the group of early admirers of British primary school reforms whose success in seeding similar approaches here can be measured by the marked Anglophilia of the reform movement. "Things have moved far ahead of what I could have hoped three or four years ago. But there are obvious risks. People tend to be faddists and want instant results. We can be killed with kindness as well as opposition."

Yeomans clearly hankers for the orderly, sensible way the British have gone about reforming their system, with professional leadership and initiative, with slow expansion—so far over a 15-year period—as results have warranted.

He is also very worried that the free school movement is being wrongly linked to British reforms. "Free schools and the Leicestershire model are not the same thing," warns Yeomans, referring to the best known British center of change, which became a generic term for awhile for the new educational approach. Yeomans prefers the term "integrated day," since it describes the multiplicity of activities and choices that replace the set sequential pattern of study in traditional classrooms.

The crucial difference, says Yeomans, between free schools and the integrated-day schools is that, while both represent rebellion against traditional schools, the first has aspects of a "utopian dream," while the second "is confined conceptually to a classroom." The latter has to do with "deep respect for sustained achievement, for orderly relationships, for shared experiences...and for rising expectations." Behind the buzz of activity and the apparent chaos of the integrated-day school, its advocates insist, is a definite structure of learning experiences—no less a structure because children "bump into experiences" instead of being lectured at. Harvey Haber, editor of the Exchange Newsletter, puts is succinctly: "Leicestershire is about schools, and ultimately we're against all institutions."

Between Haber and Yeomans are a lot of people who are unwilling to pin labels on what they're doing, or prescribe for others. They are too caught up in the hard work of moving beyond the words of the theorists to the question of What do you do today? "The biggest myth," says one young headmaster of a new school, "is that there's an 'it' around, ready to be implemented. I don't know what the optimal role of the teacher is, nor does anyone else."

Some of the deepest questioning of both the Leicestershire and free school models is coming out of the black community alternative schools. "The free school comes out of white society reform," says Kenneth Haskins. Haskins was one of the first principals of a community-controlled school, the Morgan Community School in Washington, D.C., which like most community schools has many of the trimmings of the open-structure schools: ungraded classes, interest centers, individualization of activities, informality in the classroom, and so on.

"Right now, the model we use is not as important as who makes decisions. It is true that when black people take over schools and start thinking about what they want, they end up talking about respect, more freedom, no suspensions. They want the kids treated as individuals, the slow kids not kept down. But we don't need the Leicestershire model to tell us what to do about these," says Haskings, who adds wryly that when he was at Morgan, people from Leicestershire came to visit *him* at Morgan because they had heard of his success with black, poor children.

"The British system, with its colonial derivatives, is no model for us in racial terms," agrees Yeomans. "Our data will soon be far ahead of theirs on this." He is nonetheless convinced that universal qualities underlying the learning of all children take precedence over the differences between black and white, city and suburb, poor and rich—although these must be taken into account. The British reforms, which emerged out of its teaching profession, are also no model in terms of accountability to a community, a unique concept here that puts special strains on reforms. "The black parents don't like the rigidities of the public schools," says Yeomans, "but neither do they necessarily want the freedom they perceive in the British approach." They are nervous about reading and math, and having put so much into getting their community schools going, want to make very sure their children are going to "make it." Surprisingly, their concern is not always understood or even welcomed by the white reformers involved in these schools, and a we-they split along community-professional lines is not infrequent as community schools veer toward more structure and direction.

The nervousness over skills is shared by many white parents. For so long, when schools looked like schools, there was little questioning of institutional failure. With the security of familiarity gone, parents need reassurance that something called education is going on.

Most people staffing experimental schools are too turned off by testing to use it, even in their own defense. Not New York City College Professor Lillian Weber, whose conversion of P.S. 84—one-third black, one-third white, one-third Spanish—into an exciting "open corridor" school has been widely reported. She is shrewd enough to buttress reports on the unique aims and accomplishments of the school with data about success in conventional terms as well: "99 percent of the children in an open-corridor class were reading by the time they left first grade. This has never happened before. . . . "

Mostly, the people involved in such schools prefer to rest on the visible evidence—so striking to anyone who visits these schools—of the remarkable openness, curiosity, and interaction among the pupils, so much in contrast to the apathetic, glazed-over look that is the earmark of many public school classrooms. It looks like the essence of real learning, but it's hard to capture in the pages of evaluative reports.

And it could be lost in scaling up too fast. "We are at the stage of little schools," says Yeomans. "We still have to prove ourselves. Then we can stand the pressures of system-wide implementation."

It is not at all clear whence the leadership will come to spur and finance these little schools, assess their accomplishment, and steer good models into wider use. In England, reforms came out of the profession and were supported by the system. But Professor Weber and her work at P.S. 84 are exceptions in the United States, where the teacher training colleges and the profession are, at best, in the rear guard of any march towards change.

One of the main needs of the new schools seems to be money. Although schools crop up in stores, abandoned factories, and religious schools whose clientele has vanished, and staffs often live on subsistence wages, funds are still needed. Bake sales go just so far, and the exhaustion of staffs is sometimes laid as much to scrounging for money as to long hours of teaching and planning. Many schools go under the first year.

The Ford Foundation has put about $2.5 million so far into alternatives: in New York City, the Children's Community School, Harlem Prep, the Street Academies, and the East Harlem Block Schools; in Boston, the Federation of Community Schools. Some of its support is going to new options within the system: in Philadelphia, the Parkway School Without Walls, and in Berkeley, the Other Ways integrated day program. Other foundations have pitched in too, as well as some corporations, opening up the possibilities of pyramiding small grants. In New York City, for example, the New York Urban Coalition was able to package local business, foundation, and school system support for a group of innovative minischools aimed at "problem students" and employing "street workers" as a link between students, their neighborhoods, and the schools.

But the big money is in Washington and, not surprisingly, the federal government's attitude has been ambivalent. The development of alternatives is "very scary to the establishment," says Martin Engel, an HEW official with an intensive interest in the free school movement. "The Office of Education likes to talk about innovation, but its funds are tied to the system."

Last year the Office of Economic Opportunity, which has taken up some of the slack, was ready to go with a "major priority" $10-million program on "alternatives"—to encourage fledgling free schools and assess their effectiveness, particularly with low-income children. This was shot down, as one staffer sees it, because "The Administration wanted to work closely with established systems."

The federal government's showcase effort in experimental schools is just under way in the Office of Education. With a $12-million appropriation for its first year, director Robert Binzwanger wants to "stop tinkering with reforms and put all the pieces together." Grant recipients must meet some tough standards—programs must deal with a kindergarten-through-12th-grade continuum, work with a student enrollment of 2,000 to 5,000, focus primarily on low-income children, and be supportable after federal developmental money stops. Such criteria, says Dr. Binzwanger, assure meaningful impact. They also seem to mean that money will go to systems, and not outside them, to already promising efforts rather than to riskier, experimental ventures.

The federal government's most radical venture into alternatives—limited to planning and feasibility money—was OEO's support of the educational voucher idea, a concept that would institutionalize the old idea of diversity within the system by permitting parents and students to shop with public funds among a variety of schools.

Prospects for such rerouting of the educational pipeline have dimmed. Support is easing off even among advocates of alternative schools who seem to doubt that the system could really bring itself to support the kinds of schools they have in mind. More likely, they think, vouchers will prop up parochial schools and white academies—particularly if no money is around to seed new schools.

Meanwhile, the fact is that most of the new schools have a tough time making it into the second year. There are many who think this is more of a people problem than a money problem. One of the outstanding impressions of these new schools is how hardworking, dedicated, and drawn with exhaustion the staff is—in contrast to the relaxed, happy children. They may be black or they may be white, they may have degrees or they may be dropouts, their commitment may stem from professional excitement or community-based dreams. Whatever, can such commitment be sustained or—even more important—induced?

Increasingly, as schools go on into their second or third year, they are looking for people with teaching experience and even maturity—in addition to flexibility, commitment, love of children, and so on. "The key is talent," says an official of the Ford Foundation, which is sponsoring workshops and training centers this summer on the open-structure approach, as are the National Association of Independent Schools, a number of universities, and other groups. Cross-Atlantic visits of teachers—bringing British ones here, sending ours there to bring home the gospel—are increasingly common. Such a training process is obviously gradual, as many believe it must be if a creditable, viable reform movement is to take hold here. Otherwise, says the Ford spokesman, "We're going to founder and everyone will say it's because it hasn't worked when it hasn't been tried."

The fate of the "alternatives movement" depends in large part also on the response of the public school system itself. To the extent it resists, then the outside-the-system alternatives could well burgeon the way the Exchange predicts. To the extent that successful models have an impact on public schools, that new kinds of teachers and teaching find a place with the system, these changes will absorb much of the energies previously involved in fighting it. The prospect is exciting and may spell "success." The danger—and it is a big one—is that when the system makes something its own, the something loses the ingredients that made it special. Already there are fancy learning centers where the teacher gives out set assignments and "schools without walls" run by principals who have worked within the system for 20 years.

The reverse prospect is equally discouraging—that many excited people will "do their thing" with small numbers of young people, as by far the larger number go through the system untouched by change. It is this possibility that makes Haskins worry that the alternatives movement might be "diversionary. People fool themselves that they are really changing things when they're not," he says.

Writing in the Evergreen Review, Ford Foundation officer Joshua Smith has likened the alternatives movement to the opening of Pandora's box, which according to different versions of the myth, either let loose a swarm of evil or a shower of blessings. Not knowing where it will all end up many, like Charles Lawrence, black lawyer turned principal of the Highland Park Free School in Boston, are just going ahead. "The alternative schools movement," say Lawrence, "could save public education. If not, well, it is saving some children from the public schools right now."

■ Debate this point: "The teacher training colleges and the profession are, at best, in the rear guard of any march towards change" in education.

■ Reflect on your years in elementary and secondary school and attempt to determine those former classmates who might have been "saved" by attending alternative schools. What characteristics did those classmates possess that lead you to believe they would have performed differently in an alternative setting?

"For myself, the ideal is to become a co-learner."

Look at Denker's experience in relation to ideas expressed by Jane S. Shaw in "The New Conservative Alternative" (Section Two) and by Mortimer Smith in "The Reforms Most Needed in Education" (Section One).

Boredom, Utopia, and
"Unprofessional Conduct"

Joel Denker

Public high schools in suburbia are exploding; in the last two years boycotts, sit-ins, and other acts of rebellion have shattered these outwardly placid communities. But these are only the more visible signs of the disaffection which white middle-class kids feel. Many activist students burn themselves out trying to transform their schools. Others are too pessimistic about the possibility of bringing about any substantive change to even try. It is to these students that the idea of starting their own school, outside the system, has the greatest appeal. All over the country, small groups of students are beginning to band together in order to form free schools. They are doing this with the aid of discontented teachers, parents, and other friendly souls, but it is their own boldness, more than anything else, that supplies the real energy for these projects. Dropping out of school means not only overcoming the resistance of one's parents but also confronting the many regulations which the state has set up to hedge in the freedom of the young—the com-

Joel Denker, "Boredom, Utopia, and 'Unprofessional Conduct'," this article first appeared in *High School,* eds. Ronald Gross and Paul Osterman (New York: Random House, 1971). Reprinted by permission of the author.

Joel Denker is completing his doctorate at the Harvard School of Education. In addition to the experiences described in this article, he has been a teacher in the American Studies Department, State College of Old Westbury, Long Island (New York), and in programs at University College, Rutgers College, Staten Island (New York) Community College, and has been president of New Educational Project, Inc., Washington, D.C. He was also a volunteer teacher at the Kurasini International Education Centre, Dar es Salaam, Tanzania. He is co-author of *No Particular Place to Go: The Making of a Free High School.*

pulsory attendance, labor, antiloitering, and other laws. Already a newsletter, *The New Schools Exchange*, has been started to serve as a clearinghouse of information for people who want to start schools, teachers who want to teach in them, kids who want to drop out. That many more kids are dropping out of school than ever before is important in itself. That they are dropping out in order to develop counter-communities that may in time further destroy the legitimacy of public schools in the eyes of parents and their children is even more significant.

I helped to create a free high school in Washington, D.C., and have been active in it for the past two years. In 1967-68, I was a teacher in a high school in suburban Maryland. I had just returned from a year of teaching in a refugee school in southern Africa. All my past teaching experience had been with black students in educational projects in the ghetto and in the South. Like many other activists my age, I felt that the black community was where the action was. When my graduate school placed me in a predominantly white high school, Montgomery Blair High School in Silver Spring, Maryland, I was very upset. I thought that the kids would be soft and complacent, that they would experience none of the anguish that is the common condition of black Americans.

After a few months of "cultural shock," I really began to enjoy my work. Not the classroom teaching but the relationships I was beginning to develop with the kids I was meeting in the building. Many were virtually suffocating from their routinized existence at Blair. Reciting Shakespeare or learning English vocabulary made little sense to them when they were experiencing acute personal tensions. A drug experience, a romance, a desire to free oneself from parental restrictions, an interest in the Poor People's Campaign—none of these concerns was a legitimate part of the curriculum. And they had little time during the school day to talk to their classmates about the things that were tearing up their guts. Attention had to be focused on the teacher, if they were to be ready for the next question. I would frequently meet kids who skipped their classes to walk out to the grove or wander the corridors just to seek out some social contact.

That fall, a number of students asked me to serve as a sponsor for an organization they wanted to start, to be called the Student Organizing Committee. They wanted it to be a discussion group that would deal with things that were banished from the school curriculum—the draft, race, rock music, experimental education, for example. But the school administration did not like the fact that the kids would be organizing independently of the official channels. The principal said that there was already a "critical issues" forum sponsored by the Student Council. He was also bothered by the role he expected me to play in the group. I was not going to mediate between the students and the school administration. Nor was I willing to be a moderate force in the group, to be there to introduce a note of caution whenever the kids got too self-reliant. And many of the faculty did not like the close, personal ties that were developing between me and the kids. They wanted to maintain their distance from the kids; their style was one of cool reserve. Later in the year, the principal told me that some members of the faculty had criticized me for "unprofessional conduct" because they had seen me sitting on the floor talking with students.

Our first conflict with the administration developed when one of the organizers of SOC placed a copy of Jerry Farber's article "Student As Nigger" on some of the school's bulletin boards. Beneath the article was an announcement that SOC (still not an official organization) would sponsor a discussion of that article at the end of the school day. Much to my surprise, the poster said that I would be leading the discussion. The fellow who had put it up had forgotten to tell me this. The administration panicked. They claimed that the article would inflame racial tensions at the school. We gave in too quickly on this issue. We didn't hold the discussion and we took down the posters.

For much of September and October we had what seemed an endless round of discussions with the administration about the formation of SOC. The principal wanted to know whether we intended the group simply to be a discussion rather than an action organization. He was disturbed by the name we had given to our group and wanted us to change it. We stood fast. When we responded that it was impossible to separate critical thought and discussion from action, he was baffled. He was also concerned lest we present only one side of an issue. He maintained that the school's function was to make a balanced presentation of all social problems. I was learning how the rhetoric of "objectivity" could be used to conceal real biases and self-interest. For example, the Montgomery County school system, like most public systems, prohibited the circulation of leaflets and the posting of announcements without prior permission. They rarely gave permission to anyone who wanted to distribute controversial material—on the draft, on the war, on student rights. We were later to encounter tremendous resistance from the principal when we asked that the annual "military service" assembly (at which representatives from all the services spoke to the senior class) include a discussion of alternatives to the draft.

Both the school administration and its allies in the student council placed a number of procedural roadblocks in our way. We had to prepare a constitution and we were told on a number of occasions that we had made grievous errors in submitting it. They told us, for example, that we had given them an insufficient number of copies. One of our friends on the newspaper unearthed the fact that another student group, The Model Rocketry Club, had quickly been approved by the student government and recognized by the administration.

We finally were approved as an official school organization after much parliamentary and procedural hassling. We quickly organized a series of programs that enabled us to build a solid base of support among the students. Our first program brought the Nighthawk, a black disk jockey from the District, to Blair to expound on soul music. The gym was filled to capacity. Discussions on the "psychological hangups of teachers" (led by a local psychiatrist), on Buddhism, on the American right followed.

But kids in the group wanted to do more than talk. Some of them wanted to organize protests against the county regulations on leafleting and against the forthcoming military service assembly. Yet it would be misleading to describe SOC as an effective vehicle for political action. We talked much more than we acted. We never were able to attract enough student support to carry out a successful action and most of our plans fizzled. I suspect that we never quite believed that our actions would make the slightest dent in the way the administration ran the school. We had learned a lot from our experience organizing SOC about the resistance the administration would put up to even the most minor change in the status quo. Much of our energy was sapped in simply trying to survive from day to day in the school. A good number of the kids got stoned on grass just to get through the day. I myself returned home feeling physically exhausted from my struggles trying to cope with that absurd universe. We expended so much nervous energy simply trying to stay on our feet that we had little left over for practical organization.

The talking we did together and the close personal ties that began to develop between us were profoundly important. For more than anything else, SOC was a community. We were free to get to know each other without regulation from a classroom timetable. Kids who had once felt awfully alone, who had personalized their problems, met others who were in the same situation. The enthusiasm that many of the SOC kids expressed came from having acquired a new identity, an identity rooted in their involvement in a cohesive group. Free from many of the standardized roles and superficial forms of communication we had previously been locked into, we began to analyze the educational system that had been repressing us. We tried to figure out why schools were organized in the way they were. We tried to envision what learning would be like in a really free environment.

One night in February two students from Blair, a civil rights lawyer, Bill Higgs, and I were having dinner together at the home of another one of the kids, Norman Solomon. We were discussing the perennial topic of conversation, life at Blair, when Bill in a perfectly straightforward way asked us: "Why don't you guys start your own school?" Bill had a way of making the most outlandish experiments seem easy. At the suggestion of this idea, all of us became very excited. It was a perfectly outrageous idea that answered all our most immediate needs; that we hadn't thought of it ourselves was a measure of how constricted our vision had been. Blair was our universe; nothing else seemed quite real.

For the next several days and for several weeks thereafter, we talked in a visionary way about the idea and began to tell a number of our friends about it. We had to keep convincing each other that the idea could become real, that it just wouldn't stay in the fantasy stage. The compelling thing about creating our own school was that it would be something we would control and own. All our efforts to change conditions at the school had been going nowhere. We were becoming increasingly frustrated and had no answers for those who asked us what alternative we had for the present system. Here was an opportunity to begin living what we had been preaching, rather than waiting for utopia someday to come.

The kids at Blair who became involved in the project and I had one thing in common. We were all bored. No common ideology, no common view of what our school's purpose should be, bound us together. The atmosphere at Blair, we said to ourselves, was choking us to death; we wanted out. It was the atmosphere, more than any specific acts of repression directed against us, which made us leave; we were rebelling against a total environment.

Many people in the radical movement constantly talk about whether it is better to stay within the established institutions or to leave them and create alternative structures. But this issue didn't bother us at all at the time that we started organizing the school. It was an abstract consideration compared to the acutely personal impulses we then felt. We acted out of personal necessity; we had no other options. Neither the kids nor myself could survive another year in a public high school. One of the kids most active in the project has told me since that if the school hadn't come along he would have hit the road for California. It was only in the course of our day-to-day work in the school that we began to get a glimpse of the direction we might go in, the goals we might set for ourselves.

One movement organizer in the Washington area accused us of being utopian, as if this were a cardinal sin. She felt, and I think her point of view is shared by some segments of the left, that it was a cop-out for teachers and students to leave public schools. If students stayed locked in the jaws of Leviathan they would be radicalized, which was to be desired; teachers should also remain in the school to give political direction to the struggles their students would then undertake. This view makes suffering into a virtue and ignores the profoundly liberating effect of leaving the school system.

The center for organizing the school was Blair. I was teaching there and the kids most committed to the idea were students at the school. And through SOC we had met a large number of radical kids. But gaining new converts and keeping our own morale up was difficult. When we described a new school, we spun its outlines from our imagination. We had no building, no money, no definite curriculum—in short none of the things that most people associated with a school. If somebody was the slightest bit timid or conservative, he was not likely to stay with us for long. I remember asking myself what I would do if the school never got off the ground. Should I have another job waiting in case we failed, should I keep my options open? I plunged ahead into the unknown and threw my anxieties to the wind; in that sense the school helped me a great deal. The kids faced even greater risks. They were leaving the traditional route that led to college, career, and a secure life style, and they had to buck their parents, middle-class people, who never quite believed that we would pull off the project and feared the worst for their kids' futures. In some cases, we, the older people involved, were made the scapegoats for all the tensions that wracked the students' families.

When I look back on these anxious months, I wonder why we kept with it. Analyzing it later, I think I can say that we were all adventurous types; we had all done things before they had become fashionable. Some of the kids had been involved with drugs before they became a fad, had hitchhiked on their own, had already wrested a considerable amount of independence from their parents. One boy, Greg, had been very much influenced by the Beats, when he lived in California, had been moved by Camus and Sartre, had done a lot of acid, and had an intense interest in Eastern religion. I had helped to organize a freedom school in St. Augustine, Florida, during the summer of 1964. Bill Higgs was a white Mississippian who had defended James Meredith when he was trying to enter the University of Mississippi in 1961. I think we felt a need to prove to ourselves and to others that we could create something that no one else thought was possible.

We organized a series of meetings that lasted from mid-February through the summer. Interested high school students, teachers, and parents listened to us try to convince them that we had a serious project. Except for a hard core of eight to ten kids, plus myself, Bill Higgs, and two friends of mine who were teaching in black schools in the District, the faces changed from one session to the next. The fact that our constituency was constantly fluctuating scared us. When would we ever know, we asked ourselves, who was really with us? As it turned out, we would not definitely know until the first week of September, when we had rented a house, and the school had become something of a reality.

In the course of these meetings, at picnics, and at a retreat in the Shenandoah Mountains, we got to know each other very well. Roles of "teachers" and "students" that had previously obstructed communication began to break down in these informal settings. We talked a great deal about what we wanted our school to be—what kind of classes, if any, it should have, how we would finance it, how decisions would be made. These could scarcely be called "planning sessions." We envisioned few of the problems that we were later to face and our vision of the school we hoped to build was vague. One of the things we most often mentioned was that we wanted some kind of community that would break down barriers between teachers and students. One of the ways we planned to do this was by renting houses where those who wished could live together. These houses would also serve as the centers for many of the school's activities. We were also searching for a more "relevant" education than we had been getting. But these were still phrases whose content needed to be filled in. We knew much more what we didn't like about public school education than what we wanted to erect in its place.

These shared experiences were very important in helping to build a feeling of group unity and in fashioning a common educational philosophy, if only a vague and abstract one. We did not want a situation in which the older people would represent the interest of others in the group without their presence. Anyone could act as spokesman at meetings, could recruit new students, and carry out other necessary tasks. The older people at this point handled a lot more of the bureaucratic details (writing to colleges, checking out legal requirements, and the like) but this did not alter the feeling that we were all in this together, that we each had a say in determining the outlines of the school.

Before the school had formally begun, close ties of mutual trust and friendship bound us together. This was to help immeasurably in creating a more organic educational community. Had we simply bought a building, written up a curriculum, and then attracted students, the school would have been a much different place. We all learned as much (and probably more) from the painful struggle of creating our own school than we did from any of the formal classes that we later organized. And what's more each of us had a vital, personal stake in the project. Since we were building it together, there was no one to blame for our mistakes. In a public high school, we could always blame the school administration for all the problems we had; we were now making it impossible for any of us to cop out in this way.

The close relationships we had with each other were like those that developed between Northern college students and young Southern blacks in the freedom schools that the civil rights movement organized in the South during the summer of 1964. There too the process of creating a school from scratch was as important as any formal classes that were held, and the style of the classes was substantially different, much less abstract and impersonal, because of it. Staughton Lynd captures the spirit of the Mississippi freedom schools, the project he directed for SNCC in 1964: "There Northern white college students and Southern black teenagers had first to encounter one another as whole human beings, to establish trust. This happened in the process of finding a church basement together, deciding on a curriculum together, improvising materials together, that is in the context of common work; and it matured in that context too, as those who walked together in the morning registered voters together in the afternoon. . . . What we read together in the mornings was often James Joyce, what was talked about may have been French or algebra as well as Negro history. But I simply testify that the context of shared experience (which meant, too, that teachers characteristically boarded in their students' homes) made all the difference."

I worked in a freedom school in St. Augustine, Florida, in the summer of 1964 and carried back with me very much the same reactions to my experience that Staughton did. It seems strange that it was not until five years later that I became involved in organizing a free school in a white middle-class community. Like many other activists in the movement at that time, traveling South had been something of a vicarious experience for me. I was unhappy and bored by much of what I had studied at Yale and was alienated from many of the students who were preparing themselves for positions in the hierarchies of law, business, and government. It was easier for me to understand the plight of black teenagers than it was for me to understand how repressive my own education had been.

Once they had heard about the school, the Blair administration decided to make things as uncomfortable as possible for me. Some parents had apparently called the school because their children were threatening to drop out of high school and join us. Some of the teachers who taught "honors" classes felt threatened because some of the kids they regarded as their most creative students were talking about leaving. I remember one of my supervisors telling me that the teachers were concerned that we were manipulating kids, encouraging them to leave high school without giving them an honest picture of the risks involved.

Things came to a head when the principal called me into his office ostensibly to talk about my teaching experiences that year. One of the directors of my graduate program and my Blair supervisor were also present. Midway through the conversation they raised the question of whether the work I was doing to organize the school might represent "conflict of interest" with my duties as a teacher. In characteristic fashion, they simply hinted at this possibility. Leaving the question open, they probably felt, would scare me more than a definitive judgment on it. They said they would talk with the central office in Rockville to find out if I was in conflict with Board regulations. If they ever got a ruling from the central office, I never heard about it. But they succeeded in making my days as anxious, as suspense-filled as possible. I never knew from one day to the next whether I would be fired or not. The principal also cautioned me against using my classroom as a forum to proselytize for the school.

When we began to circulate a leaflet in the building announcing the creation of the school, the principal also tried to squelch that, but also unsuccessfully. (We had also gotten these leaflets to other high school students, had spread news of the school by word of mouth, and used the news media.) He again called me into his office and told me that it was customary to get prior approval before circulating leaflets in the school. I told him that this was a violation of free speech. He made no response and then said that since we had circulated a number of leaflets already there was little he could do about it. We did, however, circulate very few leaflets after this, at least not on a large scale, wide-open basis. We were reluctant to confront the anti-leafleting regulations head on. We had sufficient hassles resulting from organizing the school without adding any more. But as I look back on this experience now, I recognize how powerful a weapon the prohibition against free circulation of leaflets and other public notices can be. It enables the public school bureaucracy to define what acceptable speech and opinion is. Parents, teachers, and students who wish to see alternative schools become a reality for a majority of the students will have to overturn these regulations if they are to succeed.

Our announcement that we were going to start a school and the intense interest and enthusiasm this idea inspired in so many kids threatened the faculty and administration. It brought home to them the acute feelings of disaffection that many of the most creative kids in that school felt. And, most powerful effect of all, our school made a number of kids aware that they had an alternative to their daily routine. As long as students were incapable of imagining a life style radically different from the one they were accustomed to, they would tolerate it, no matter how boring it was. If we are ever to make an effective attack on compulsory public education, we must not rant and rave about how bad it is. We must make vivid to large numbers of people the existence of exciting alternatives to that system.

In the meantime, we were attending to the various details that had to be dealt with if we were to begin the school by the end of the summer. We had written to a group of colleges, mostly small progressive schools (Antioch, Goddard, Reed) but also to Yale, Wesleyan, and the University of Chicago asking them what their reaction would be to students graduating from an unaccredited school like ours. We wanted to assure kids and their parents that all their options would not be canceled by virtue of their going to the school. We did not want the school to be a college prep institution and we figured that many of the kids would ultimately decide not to go to college, at least not right away. But we felt that if the responses to our letters were positive, kids could make a more realistic decision about whether to join and about what they would do once they decided to leave the school. The responses we received to our letters were positive. This allayed the fears of the parents of some of the most committed students but others were still skeptical. They wanted a definite assurance from colleges that their kids would get in; or at least they used this as an excuse to hide more basic objections. I was amazed, though, how many people we talked to thought that going to college from a bizarre experiment like ours would be an impossibility. At least, we punctured that myth.

We spent a lot of time talking with the parents of the kids who wanted to go to the school. However, the real initiative on this score came from the kids themselves. Had they not convinced their parents that they were serious, that they had no intention of returning to public school, our arguments would have had little effect. Our presence certainly gave the project a legitimacy, an aura of adult respectability, in the eyes of the parents. At best, we provided reinforcement for decisions that were reached in a struggle between each parent and his son or daughter. With a few exceptions, no parent made any commitment or gave us any specific assurance until the last moment. This fact, of course, added to the general feeling of anxiety we then felt.

We had gone ahead from the beginning, blissfully ignorant of the laws and regulations that might affect our status as a school in the District of Columbia. Bill Higgs had assured us that we would have no difficulties, but we still did not know the hard facts. It was not until late June that two of us decided to sit down with Alex Rode, who had founded an early experimental school in D.C., to find out the legal difficulties we might encounter. Alex told us that since D.C. had no formal accreditation agency our real problems would come from the zoning board. No school, of course, could legally operate in a private residence of the kind we hoped to rent. A school had to be located in a specially zoned commercial area. Moreover, the late-nineteenth-century codes required a school building to have steel doors, fire escapes, stair wells, a parking space for each teacher regardless of whether he has a car. Since we had little or no money, we could not afford the renovating costs that an operation like this would demand. Alex's school had been closed down several times by the zoning people and he had once been taken to court. We decided that we would have most of our activities in the communal houses we planned to rent and that we would try to get a local church (which could pass zoning regulations) to be our official headquarters and mailing address. We hoped that this cover would protect us from harassment by the city. We also decided that we would register as a non-profit corporation and would try to get federal and District tax exemption.

One other important thing came out of these meetings. This was our decision to orient the school toward white middle-class kids. Any illusions we might have had about an integrated effort were dispelled when we spoke to some very savvy black kids from Eastern High School. They said they liked what we were doing but that it was irrelevant to the kind of "freedom school" they wanted. Their advice was that we complement and support each other, not try to duplicate each other's functions.

In late August of 1968 we found a house in an integrated, middle-class area off Sixteenth Street in Washington. Interest and enthusiasm soon began to pick up. Kids began to make the anxious decision to drop out of school, parents began to loosen their grip, and we began to pull our community together. There were twelve of us living in the house. Seven kids and five "teachers." We quickly realized that our project had greater political implications than we could ever have imagined. The landlord, an official from the Indian embassy who wanted U.S. citizenship, began to get uptight and put us on a month-to-month lease. The FBI began to make inquiries among our neighbors. The wife of a government official whose daughter goes to the school received a call over the White House line from an unidentified person saying that she should withdraw her daughter since our house was under surveillance. In the midst of all this, morale was high and our first "classes" got underway. This external threat had a way of helping us build solidarity when it was most crucial. We decided to move, to find a more comfortable landlord.

We now have thirty full-time students. The average age is seventeen. There are from ten to fifteen others who are involved in activities at the school, but who continue to go to their local high schools. There are five of us teaching full time—all except one former teachers in either D.C. or Maryland. We have managed to attract a number of other people—artists, a writer, public-school teachers, etc.—who are volunteering their services to the school.

We offer "classes" in a variety of areas ranging from creative writing and drama to utopian American radicalism. (We have a bulletin board where anyone who wants to get a course going puts up a time for a meeting; times of various local events—lectures, dances, films, government meetings, etc.—also appear.) These core courses, which meet once or twice a week, are intended to complement rather than serve as substitutes for the direct involvement that is central to the school. We aim to explode the classroom, to create the feeling that learning is more than a formal academic exercise, that to be worth anything it must be organically related to the person's most immediate needs and concerns. Students have done a variety of things this year: Several of the kids are working in apprenticeships with local artists—a metal sculptor and welder and a potter, for example. A trip to Baltimore to attend the trial of the Catonsville Nine got us involved in a demonstration protesting the mockery of justice in federal court and in picketing the courthouse. We went to the City Council to hear a friend protest against its avoidance of the police issue and heard the city fathers spend forty minutes discussing the question of civilian escorts for funeral processions. During the fall, classes frequently met in Rock Creek Park and most every weekend we camped out on some land in the Shenandoahs, the site of an old mission. A friend of ours has purchased land there so that we have access to it.

"Classes" in the school have been a very special experience for me after the formality of the public high school. I remember vividly a discussion a group of us had of Gide's *The Immoralist*. It started out with a discussion of our personal reactions to the novel. It soon became a dialogue in which we talked to each other about our own life styles, which ranged from social activism to a kind of religious mysticism. What impressed me was that we felt comfortable enough with each other to speak personally about our concerns—something which is frowned upon in the icy "objectivity" of the public-school classroom. After an hour of conversation, three kids said they felt terribly confused and went off for a long walk.

For myself, the ideal is to become a co-learner. The intimate relationships we have with each other in the community help to make this possible. For many of us the living situation—the communal living—and the learning experience cannot be separated. In fact, much of the richest discussion in and out of class centers on the quality of the relationships we are trying to build.

I have learned many things from my involvement in this project. I have realized how easy it is to bring authoritarian values into an otherwise free and experimental learning situation. The values we have absorbed from our families, our schools, etc., do not vanish just because we begin to organize for radical social change. *Unless we become capable of changing our own lives, of confronting these values, we will have changed nothing at all.* In our school, for example, some of the sharpest debate between the older people has revolved around the use of words like "teacher," "student," "staff," etc.—words which have more than a semantic function, which imply deeply rooted beliefs about the kinds of relationships people ought to have with each other. The younger kids have much better instincts than we do; they have been poisoned less.

We are all familiar with "liberation schools," "free universities," etc., which attempt to change the old curriculum—in the interests, say, of combatting racism or promoting socialism, goals which I heartily support—but which finally do not alter the human relationships which many kids are rebelling against in their homes and schools. It is these human relationships—the attempt, for example, by many teachers to hide their self-interest, their personal values and concerns behind a facade of objectivity—that frequently distort the learning process. By remaining unconscious of this problem, we change course content, but still relate to each other in the same authoritarian way.

The same criticism is applicable to many intentional communities. In our coop a small group is seeking to institute a system of precisely defined roles and responsibilities, being too impatient to let them develop organically. If they were ever to succeed in doing this, our community would have the same hierarchical structure which a year ago our group got together to protest.

All of us have been so badly corrupted by our own education that it is hard to imagine, let alone share, in building a more humane learning and living environment. But this must be done, if we are not to reproduce the same kinds of institutions we so frequently criticize. Political organization and agitation within the schools is just not sufficient. *Contagious examples*—models of learning and living together—are also needed if the public schools are ever to change. This struggle is equally important for ourselves, for we have much to learn—I sometimes think I should say unlearn—if we are to change our own lives, if we are to build a new world together.

- Hypothesize about why other faculty members would not like the close, personal ties that the author says developed between him and his students. Which of your hypotheses seem most probable? Improvise a teachers' lunchroom conversation in which one person assumes the role of Mr. Denker while others play the roles of antagonistic faculty members.

- Obtain and read Jerry Farber's *The Student as Nigger* (New York: Pocket Books, 1969). To what extent do you believe Mr. Farber's remarks apply to students today?

- Brainstorm ways in which "all of us have been so badly corrupted by our own education."

- What are a teacher's legal, moral, and ethical responsibilities to the system when the teacher has accepted a public-school contract?

". . . with proper preparation, it is possible and feasible to provide parents and students with alternatives to the programs and relationships existing in conventional high schools."

Read this article, bearing in mind the opinions expressed in excerpts from the "Seventh Annual Gallup Poll of Public Attitudes Toward Education" (Section One).

A Conservative Community Forms an Alternative High School

Frederick S. Bock and Wanda W. Gomula

Over the past three years educational alternatives within the public schools have emerged with increasing frequency. Unlike most previous attempts at educational reform, alternative schools are not designed to alter existing school characteristics but to offer students, parents, and teachers significant options in the educational process. In a recent *Kappan* column Don Robinson referred to the acceptance of alternatives in education by public schools as "legitimizing the revolution."*

F.S. Bock and W.W. Gomula, "A Conservative Community Forms an Alternative High School," *Phi Delta Kappan* **54**, no. 7 (March 1973). Reprinted by permission.

Frederick S. Bock is director of Academia Cotopaxi, an alternative school in Quito, Ecuador. His experiences include that of classroom teacher, principal, Administrative Director of the Cambridge Pilot School (Harvard University), and Director of the Monroe County Alternative High School, Bloomington, Indiana. Wanda Wallace Gomula has been director of the Monroe County (Indiana) Alternative High School as well as lecturer in education at Indiana University and at the State University of New York-Stony Brook. She served as an instructor and coordinator of a program for drop-outs in the American High School, Kaiserlautern, Germany, and as a teacher of elementary school. Dr. Gomula is a frequent consultant and speaker; she is the author of numerous articles about foreign-language instruction, cultural differences, and alternative-learning approaches.

*Donald W. Robinson, "Scraps From a Teacher's Notebook," *Phi Delta Kappan,* February 1972, p. 400.

Until this year specific programs in public school alternative education have been found almost exclusively in three types of communities: inner-city, urban, and suburban. This fall an alternative school has been established within the public schools of Monroe County, Indiana. This is an area in southern Indiana which, despite the presence of Indiana University, has strong rural influences and is considered conservative. The school board reflects the business and university community as well as the rural population.

The dropout rate among high school students was of concern to county residents, and particularly distressed members of the Monroe County Community Action Program (CAP), who observed that most of the dropouts came from low-income families, thus perpetuating the poverty cycle. CAP, in conjunction with Indiana University and the Monroe County Community School Corporation (MCCSC), mounted a hastily planned attempt in early 1972 to provide a program for about 25 junior high school students. Unfortunately, the group consisted of a homogeneous group of school "failures," in most cases *assigned* to the program by building principals. The results were predictably unsatisfactory, and by late spring the school board and central administration were ready to discard the program.

The problem of dropouts still existed, however, with attention now focused not only on students from low-income families but also on those referred to as "turned-off middle class." Through the cooperation of CAP, the Indiana University School of Education, and the MCCSC, a clearly delineated plan for a nongraded, heterogeneous alternative senior high school was developed by these writers. The plan included specific implementation procedures in such areas as curriculum, staffing, finance, grades and credits, and student recruitment. It was emphasized that participation would be strictly voluntary, with parental approval, and that any boy or girl above eighth grade who would not or could not attend the regular high schools could choose to attend the alternative high school. With strong support from the superintendent, the school board unanimously approved its initiation.

Inherent in the philosophy of the school is the diversity in the socioeconomic backgrounds of the student body. About 75% of the students come from low-income families (as determined by federal guidelines), and 25% come from middle-income environments. This ratio provides a cross-section of the uninterested, disenchanted, and disconcerted students in the area. It also prevents the more articulate pupils with middle-class backgrounds from dominating the heterogeneous atmosphere of the school. Because of space, there is a limit of 70 students, with a number on the waiting list.

The concept of community involvement in the school is emphasized. Parents, students, and staff work together to develop and enhance the program. An advisory board now consists of students, staff, parents, school board members, CAP members, and an Indiana University professor.

The Alternative High School is indeed a joint educational effort among the MCCAP, MCCSC, and the university. Each has devoted considerable energy to making the program successful. CAP has provided 50% of the funding (from the U.S. Office of Economic Opportunity), as well as the support of its agencies in reaching and encouraging the participation of low-income families. The MCCSC has provided the remaining 50% of the funding through Title I, ESEA, and has assisted in such areas as transportation, equipment, supplies and materials, and specialized personnel. Most important, since this school is a component of the public schools, it has school board approval in accreditation for diplomas. Indiana University, nationally recognized as a leader in educational alternatives, provides undergraduate student teachers, master's and doctoral level interns, and the participation of two professors. In addition, students have access to many university activities and facilities.

The student-adult ratio is very low, about three to one, but expenditures for personnel are minimal. The only salaried staff are the director (part-time), the assistant director, a reading teacher, and a mathematics teacher. Other staff members are nine undergraduate students, three graduate students, six part-time counseling interns, and two IU faculty members. There are also a number of community volunteers, especially in the arts and crafts areas.

The school is located in a 3-room building erected in 1906 about 10 minutes from the IU campus, and near one of the large Bloomington high schools. It could be accurately said that the school was formed literally from scratch, for the first phase of the program was the complete, though sometimes crude, renovation of the building by staff, students, and community volunteers. The result is eight learning areas, including a kitchen, darkroom, and combination library-classroom-lounge-meeting area. Perhaps because of the students' identification with the physical development of the school, there has been very little vandalism to the old building.

The two most unusual aspects of this alternative school are, first, that it has been established in a traditional, rural community; and, second, that it provides an opportunity for the involvement of student teachers to a far greater degree than does the conventional 8-week program found in many teacher preparatory institutions. Those who elect to student teach in the Alternative High School do so for either a half year full-time, or an entire year part-time. They are responsible for the development and implementation of their own curriculum and function as advisers to groups of students. They are treated as regular staff members in the decision-making process.

Considerable success has been achieved using an adviser-advisee system that combines the resources of the teachers and the counseling interns in groups of about five students. In some instances the relationships revolve primarily around school matters. In others they are of a more personal nature and require the time and effort of staff well beyond the regular school day and even into weekends. In extreme cases advisers have been able to keep their advisees from serious problems with the law. (It should be noted that a few students have been in legal difficulty and are on probation. There is close cooperation and communication between school staff and the local probation authorities.)

The evolving process of determining the directions of the school has built up-on the joint involvement of students and staff. There are relatively few pre-conceived ideas for curriculum content and methodology or for school rules, except as state law, school board policy, or health and safety considerations may require. A number of avenues are open to give students opportunities to be directly involved in determining the total school program, both academically and in extra-class activities, including governance.

Through the advising groups and individual conferences, students not only select their courses but influence what courses will be offered. Some courses are familiar: creative writing, algebra, local government, a survey of U.S. history. Others are a bit more unusual: "Math Blahs," "Women," "Getting Your Stuff Together," "Playing the Game," and "Hot Rods." Highly individualized assistance is provided for remedial mathematics and reading. Courses are offered in multiples of nine weeks, and with a flexible modular schedule classes vary in length from 45 minutes to two hours.

It is interesting to note the somewhat predictable initial inability of many students to utilize their newly acquired decision-making power. It was not until the second quarter that a larger number, especially the less articulate ones, began to express preferences in curriculum offerings and school policies. Now students even teach courses in such areas as folk guitar, first aid, and leather-craft.

Considerable use is also made of community resources. These include child-care centers, local courts, newspapers, nearby state forests, an Indian reservation, musical concerts, plays, and university athletic facilities. Students have access to the IU library as well as to both high school libraries and the fine Monroe County Library. The school also has its own library, composed primarily of books donated by interested community members.

It may be difficult to evaluate empirically the success of the Alternative High School. Standardized tests were administered last September in reading and mathematics, but there are questions about their validity. They probably serve mainly to reveal the very negative attitudes many of our students have toward standardized tests. We feel that if about two-thirds of the students with us early in the year wish to continue next fall, it will indicate success. There is no doubt that a large number of the students currently enrolled would have dropped out of school or would be in serious difficulty because of truancy. Other indicators of success are absence of the vandalism and serious discipline problems often characteristic of conventional high schools. This can be attributed to the direct in-volvement of the students in the decision-making process as well as the very humane atmosphere of the school. Students are encouraged to voice their opinions about practices they find objectionable, and in some instances peer-group pressure has been quite effective in resolving intraschool problems.

Certainly there are many areas in which the program will improve. To further improvement, students and staff conduct self-evaluations; two university graduate students will formally evaluate the degree to which the school has achieved its stated goals. But there is no question that this school has already affected the dropout rate in Monroe County. It also shows that, with proper preparation, it is possible and feasible to provide parents and students with alternatives to the programs and relationships existing in conventional high schools.

■   Discuss: During teacher training, students should be exposed to traditional as well as alternative schools, and to urban, suburban, and rural schools as well.

■   Compare the authors' comments about "unusual" course titles to item number six on the *Versus* page preceding Section One.

■   Consider this article in the context of Myers' "Alternative Schools: Creative Rebellion Against the Public System," which begins this section, and The Ford Foundation report, "Matters of Choice," concluding this section.

*"Teaching at a school like Murray Road
requires total commitment."*

Compare the attitudes expressed by Clinchy
with reports given by Jane S. Shaw in
"The New Conservative Alternative" and
by Thorwald Esbensen in "Family—Designed Learning: Accountability as
Customer Satisfaction" (both in Section
Two).

Murray Road: Beyond Innovation

Evans Clinchy

To the casual eye it looks like any small, suburban, elementary school—glass,
nondescript, beige stone, slightly modernistic in design for an early 1950s building. Surrounding it is the usual collection of middle-class, suburban homes—not
rich, but by no means poor—each set in the middle of its own small plot of grass.
(This piece of Newton, Massachusetts, happens to be suburbia, even though
Newton *in toto* is really a small city of 92,400 with industry, poor people, and a
national image as the epitome of nonurban educational desirability.)

The casual eye, of course, is all wrong. The Murray Road School is no longer
an elementary school but one of the most unusual high schools in the country. It
houses (on and off) 115 students and eight teachers. Students do not have to be
there unless they actually have a scheduled class or want to be there to use the
facilities or to meet their friends. There is no set curriculum. What "curriculum"

Evans Clinchy, "Murray Road: Beyond Innovation," this article first appeared in *High
School*, eds. Ronald Gross and Paul Osterman (New York: Random House, 1971). Reprinted by permission of the author.

Evans Clinchy is president of Educational Planning Associates, Inc., Boston, and project director for Education in New Communities Project (sponsored by Educational
Facilities Laboratories, Inc, U. S. Office of Education, and HUD), and educational plan-
ner for Chicago 21 Corporation. His articles have appeared in *Saturday Review, The
Boston Review of the Arts, The National Elementary School Principal,* and the *AIA Journal.* In addition, he is the author of *The New Curricula: Revolution for The Schools,*
published by Harcourt, Brace and World. Mr. Clinchy was a Nieman Fellow at Harvard
University.

there is is devised collaboratively by the students and teachers. There are no grades. There is no principal. (The teachers elect one of their number to handle the administrative chores on a rotating basis.)

The students, at the moment, are tenth-, eleventh-, and twelfth-graders, all from the upper, college-bound tracks at Newton High School. Most of the male students sport long hair. Everyone dresses in casual, "hip" attire. Shoes are not much in evidence in warm weather. The atmosphere of the school could hardly be less formal. The halls are filled with students and teachers moving entirely on their own, going about their business. There is no such thing as a "pass" to go anywhere inside or outside of the building. Classes are held in classrooms, in the hall, out on the lawn under trees, depending upon how people feel at the moment (and upon the weather). Classes are also held at night in homes, if they cannot be squeezed into the schedule. (The school is supposed to be closed at 4:30 every afternoon.)

The school's facilities consist of eight largish rooms. Some are typical, 1,000 square-foot, elementary classrooms. Other rooms are slightly larger and are used as: a) a commons room, equipped with a refrigerator, battered old chairs, and a ping-pong table (the school's one piece of physical education equipment); or b) an art studio equipped not so much for teaching as for students doing their own art projects. There is no cafeteria (students bring their own lunches), no auditorium, no gym, no library, no science labs, no language lab, no guidance suite (or guidance counselors), no football team, no cheerleaders, no industrial-arts or home-economics suites. (Each teacher does have his own small office.) It is not an expensive school to operate, despite its roughly 14-1 pupil-teacher ratio.

Indeed, much of the "operating" is done by the students themselves. After the teachers and students have together decided what the "courses" will be for the coming semester, the schedule is worked out by a committee of three students. There used to be a catalogue, atrociously typed, and put together by the students; but that has been abandoned in favor of a floor-to-ceiling cardboard schedule board with courses and times marked in—again, all done by the students. There is a small central office inhabited by the faculty member selected to be the administrator, but inhabited also at all times by students, many of them using the phone at will.

Within this framework of disciplined anarchy the teachers and the students collaborate on all of the important decisions. Since there are virtually no rules, it is difficult to have discipline problems. There are two major requirements—every student must take something called "English" and, at some point, a year of something labeled "American History" (this is a state law). Seventy-five minutes a week of "physical education" is also required, but this is done on the "honor system." Otherwise, students make suggestions about what they would like to study—computer programming, astrology, the origins of man, child psychology, etc. The teachers set forth what they would like to teach—logic, linear algebra, the Alienated Individual in Literature, Comparative Myths, French conversation, etc. The final catalogue is made up of the compromises worked out by students and teachers. Teachers, however, decide how many "credit hours" any particular course is eligible for. All students must end up with a total of sixty-five credits for their three high-school years, the number of credits required for all Newton High School students. At the end of a course, the teacher and student evaluate the student's performance. Usually, the student and teacher will agree on whether credit has been earned, but if there is any disagreement, the teacher's judgment prevails.

If students cannot find a teacher to teach what they want, they are free to set up and "teach" their own course. They can receive credit if a teacher evaluates their work and pronounces it fit. One student, for instance, is offering a course in film-making that meets twice a week, once as a class and once as a three-hour lab period spent shooting and editing film. This same student, Larry Levy, is making a documentary film about the school to be shown to parents, especially parents of would-be students, and to anyone else interested in what's going on.

Another student, Len Goldberg, a tenth-grade student and something of a mathematical whiz, wanted to get a computer-programming course started. Murray Road had no computer, so Len and another student took on the job of figuring out how to solve that problem *on their own*. For four days they worked solidly, going through all of the computer firms in the phone book, trying to find one that would be willing to arrange for time-sharing, etc. All of the laborious details were finally worked out. Len is now the teacher of computer-programming. In a small room off the commons room there is a large and gaudily decorated box with "Mock II—Desk Top Computer" painted on it. Inside the box (if you are foolish enough to look inside) is a telephone. A wire leads from Mock II to a computer terminal beside the desk.

Len came to Murray Road directly from the ninth grade at a nearby junior high school. He had learned from friends about what high school was like. It made him nervous. But when he saw Frederick Wiseman's film *High School*, that finished him. Much of what he saw in the film was exactly what he saw every day at his junior high. He applied immediately for Murray Road, knowing little more about it than it was obviously nothing like the school in the film. He now finds Murray Road very much to his liking. One possible piece of evidence for this is a large sign placed on the huge communications board in the central lobby. It reads:

> Wanted: One total baseball nut—Some guy who as a kid knew everyone's batting average, etc. I am trying to write a fairly realistic computer program to simulate baseball, and I need an idea how the satistics [sic] work. HELP!!!
>
> Len Goldberg, 10th grade

Or, take another example, a black girl who shall here be called Doris and who is not actually a student at Murray Road at all. Doris is enrolled at Newton South High. Last year she was on the verge of dropping out until she heard about Murray Road and began going there whenever she found time (which was, apparently, fairly often at hours when she was supposed to be at Newton South).

School has never been high on Doris' list of favorite pastimes. She grew up in Roxbury, Boston's predominantly black section, and went to her local elementary school. ("I hated it—they were always trying to put us down and telling us how dumb we were.'') She also attended the academically selective Girl's Public Latin School, an institution she found hopelessly rigid and old-fashioned ("like a convent"), but for which she harbors a sneaking admiration. An English teacher, she says, once told her that she did not believe in assigning books less than thirty years old, because "they had not yet stood the test of time."

Although Newton South was considerably better than Girl's Latin, it was still not "free" enough for Doris' tastes. (It is also a large school.) Whenever she can, Doris comes over and takes courses at Murray Road and also takes part in the intense social life. One of her "courses" (completely non-credit) is a small group studying Danish with a teacher who happens to know Danish.

Doris is desperate to gain full-fledged admittance to Murray Road next year. Students are selected by the teachers from those who apply. (There will be thirty places next year, and there are already about one hundred applicants.) The criteria for selection are not completely clear, but one is the staff's estimate of whether the student really wants to come and can handle the considerable responsibility of a basically self-directed education. It is perhaps an uncertainty about Doris' ability to handle that responsibility that keeps the issue in doubt. One effect this has had on Doris is that she is attending Newton South regularly and trying to establish an acceptable record there, but only so that she can earn her way into Murray Road.

Another anonymous student's reaction to Murray Road is recorded in a collection of such reactions put out by the school:

> Unfortunately, I succeeded at the high school and without a great deal of work. Without really pursuing things and without really doing excellent work. It's much harder being at Murray Road and it took me a while to really discover this. At the high school I was able to do a great many things, not really as well as I could have and still pull A's, etc. When I arrived at Murray Road I was very excited by all the options and became rapidly overextended. The standards here, which are self-imposed, are much harder to fulfill. To really fulfill them, one must do a few things excellently rather than many things fairly.
>
> Mathematics still doesn't turn me on, but my dislike isn't quite as acute as it was at the beginning of the year.
>
> At first, I thought I was destined to another hell-raising year in French. But soon I realized that teachers need cooperation from the class, and that teachers have feelings as well—which must sound over-obvious, but I never considered teachers' feelings before.
>
> I am much more involved in everything I do and in the school and give much more of myself and am much less tense. Also, I am making decisions for myself and if I am not satisfied, I am learning to try to change. I know that at Newton High School I would be working hard and getting good grades but that would be all. I am working harder this year because I have my own standards to live up to.

Murray Road is technically not a separate school but an annex to, and therefore a part of, Newton High School. As happens with many such wild experiments, it was not started because of a specific urge to make a radical departure.

Newton High School in the spring of 1967 was badly overcrowded. The Murray Road Elementary School, about two miles away, was offered as a possible way of handling the overflow.

Given this opportunity, the staff of Newton High and its principal, Richard W. Mechem, took advantage of the situation. If a piece of the school was going to be two miles away, there wasn't much point in trying to mesh schedules and trundle students back and forth. It was therefore decided that Murray Road should operate on its own, and that it would consciously and deliberately experiment with new ideas that might turn out to be useful in the programming and design of a new high school to open in the early 1970s. The main point of the experiment was to test out two ideas: that students could take a great deal more responsibility for their own education; and that teachers and students could collaborate on the establishment and development of "curriculum."

The school was planned to open with 150 eleventh-grade, volunteer students who would represent a genuine cross-section of the student body at Newton High. This did not happen. Only 107 students volunteered, and they were all from the college-bound tracks of the school. Most of them, too, were from the "hip" element of the school. Murray Road, right from the start, has had a reputation as a "hippie" haven, and it has been almost impossible to recruit students who are typical, "straight," suburban kids, or students who come from working-class families.

Originally, it was planned that the students would take their eleventh-grade year at Murray Road, and then go back to the high school for their final year and graduation. After the first year of the experiment, the staff argued against this and won. In 1968, the school had eleventh- and twelfth-grade students. This past year it has had tenth-, eleventh-, and twelfth-graders. The staff would like to go back next year to just eleventh- and twelfth-graders, having learned, they say, that the three-grade span is too great for them to handle in such a small school.

Is Murray Road working? How do people—parents, administrators, the students themselves, other students, and the community at large—feel about Murray Road?

There is little doubt in the students' minds that the school is successful. Not perfect, perhaps, but different from and more rewarding than normal "school." The most casual observation of the school gives evidence of that. The atmosphere is one of great warmth and mutual respect between teachers and students. First names are always used by and for everybody. Seldom does one catch a teacher putting on airs and behaving "teacherish." At one point during an impromptu session devoted to painting all the available glass in the front lobby, several of the students decided that one of the men teachers would look better if he had a racing stripe painted down the middle of his face. After being chased all over the school grounds, the teacher returned with a blue racing stripe painted down the middle of his face.

Another example from that same painting session: after spending most of an afternoon covering every glass surface with imaginative designs, the students suddenly remembered that the school was holding a meeting that night for the parents of students who wanted to come to the school next year. In the course of a fairly heated discussion, several things began to become clear. Some of the students—perhaps all of them—were aware that the school has a "kooky" reputation in Newton and that prospective parents, already wary and suspicious, might be turned off if they arrived to find the entrance hall gaudily decorated with bright colors and brighter sayings. Some of the students angrily argued that it would be hypocritical to remove the paint. This is the kind of thing that goes on at Murray Road, they argued, and the uptight suburban parents had better meet it head on rather than find out about it later.

The other side admitted all that, but argued back that it was still the parents who were, by and large, going to decide whether or not the students were to be allowed to come. It was thus better for the school to appear perhaps squarer than it really is, *because it would not be fair to the prospective students if they could not come just because their parents disliked gaudy paint.* The teachers took little part in this discussion. As far as they were concerned, it was all up to the students. At least one teacher sided with the antihypocrites.

But the paint-removers won the argument. Everyone, including teachers and this visitor, was pressed into service to scrape and wash away the paint. It was a painful experience, since much of the work was first-rate.

The students really do seem to *care.* Murray Road is very much *their* school, and they intend to defend it against all comers. Or rather it is a school run by and for students and teachers. There is no organized parents group, nor does anyone seem eager to have one.

The teachers, too, feel that the school is a success so far, not only for the students but for themselves as well. They are a self-selected crew who have really wanted to try something different and who find what they are doing professionally rewarding. Exhausting and often maddening, true, but still professionally rewarding. Although the staff has grown from five to eight, only one teacher has left and gone back to the high school.

The staff as a whole interviews and selects new teachers, whether they be people applying from inside the Newton system or from the outside. They have found that, for the most part, teachers with six or seven years' experience work out best. It takes enormous confidence—both self-confidence and professional confidence—to work in a situation as unstructured as the one at Murray Road. Such teachers, they say with ill-concealed pride, are not easy to come by; and rarely do these qualities show up in brand-new, inexperienced people.

And the parents—what about this neglected group? The evidence seems to indicate that, with the rarest of exceptions, they are pleased by what Murray Road does for and with their children. There have been sporadic complaints, but no serious ones. Getting into college, since almost all Murray Road students are middle-class, suburban and therefore college-bound kids, is uppermost in most of the parents' minds. Eighty percent of last year's graduating class at Murray Road went on to college—exactly the same percent as the comparable group at Newton High. So, apparently, this is not the problem one might have expected it to be.

In addition, many of the parents are actively behind the school and enthusiastic about what it is trying to do. Quoting again from the comments collected and put out by the school, these are parents talking about their own children:

> When my son was unhappy at Newton High School and doing poorly I could never decide whether he was the problem or if perhaps he was right when he said that much of the school did not teach him anything. I feel now he was sincere. This year he cannot get enough of all he is learning—he spends every minute singing the praises of Murray Road, but he does *not* talk about freedom, bull sessions, fooling around and indifference but down-right, genuine desire to make papers perfect, an absolutely amazing love for every teacher, an incentive which has focused his every bit of energy toward doing better today than yesterday and suddenly a hunger for many tomorrows which will enable him to do more. It is a miracle. I can't help feeling such an effervescence could not all be caused by the fact that he is a year older. I am so sure this program has what it takes to make hard study a joy and invites an urge to become more seriously involved in meaningful activity to further a student's ability to make every minute count. With less pressure from school routine that was so great at Newton High, my son has pressured himself more, putting study first, and working to conclusions. I believe his scope has broadened—his desire to absorb more and more. I am aware of the need for organization, and the value of certain lines being met, but I feel this is being done by pupils, on their own.
>
> If he had stayed at Newton High School, I see the possibility of his wings never spreading. I had no idea so much could unfold in so short a time.

Or, less full of enthusiasm:

> She does not seem to spend more time studying at home (if anything less), nor does she show overt signs of more disciplined study habits. What does seem to be the case is that her general satisfaction with the Murray Road program re-enforces the whole learning process. She *seems to learn more in less time.* She has not yet seemed to run into "slumps" as she did habitually two or three times a year when she would be bored with and disaffected by school.

And a final crucial question: has Murray Road fulfilled its original aim of affecting education elsewhere in Newton, particularly at Newton High and the planning for the new high school? Or has it remained a little gem of innovation off by itself, carefully quarantined so that it will not infect anybody? "Yes, to the first question, and absolutely not to the second," says Richard Mechem, Newton High's principal and one of Murry Road's originators and constant supporters. Murray Road, he says, has first and most importantly altered the "attitude" of Newton High teachers and students. It has as yet created no wholesale changes in the school itself, but the fact that Murray Road has survived and prospered has caused many people to rethink what they are doing. Mechem characterizes Newton High as essentially a "conservative" school, although he boggles a bit at using the words. Murray Road, he says, has made everyone more "liberal."

"As far as I am concerned," Mechem says, "Murray Road is a complete success. We sometimes feel that the education we offer at the high school is lifeless.'' What Murray Road has done, he feels, is to demonstrate that education need not be lifeless, that it can have zip and zing, that it can be something that students can respond to.

One direct effect that Murray Road has had on the high school is in Barry House, one of the school's seven houses. Here a group of about 120 sophomores and their teachers have been kept together and given a large block of time in which they organize and schedule themselves. In addition, a group of students all this past year have been agitating and attempting to plan a Murray Road type subdivision of the high school that was to be called the Walnut Street Annex. ''Was'' because it didn't work. The students thought they had the necessary teachers lined up, but at the last minute the teachers pulled out.

Teachers, says Mechem, are one of the big problems in assessing whether or not Murray Road is having an effect. ''Teaching at a school like Murray Road requires total commitment.'' It is not that non-Murray Road teachers lack commitment, according to Mechem, but that they have many other things they are involved in and interested in at the high school. Most of them do not feel they would be comfortable under the intense pressure that Murray Road forces onto teachers.

If teachers are one of the problems with Murray Road's type of education, Mechem feels that an even more serious one is the fact that the school has succeeded in attracting only one type of student—the more liberal, ''hip,'' college-bound student. He refers to this phenomenon as ''psychological stratification.'' He has tried repeatedly, as has Murray Road itself, to broaden the student body and achieve the cross-section that was originally intended. (These efforts have earned him the more or less affectionate title of ''Mix 'em up Mechem'' from the students at Murray Road.) He would especially like to see more children of working-class parents attending Murray Road. But these students are just the ones who are put off by the ''hip'' appearance and the ''liberal'' reputation of the school.

What Mechem—and many other people around the country—is moving toward is a revival of the old-fashioned notion of *pluralism*, the idea that schools—or even pieces of schools—need not all be the same or even all operate by the same rules and aims. There is no particular reason, Mechem says, why schools cannot be shaped to fit students; no reason why there cannot be a wide variety of different kinds of schools from which students (and their parents) can select the most appropriate model.

This notion of pluralism has nothing to do with the concept of tracks or ability grouping along lines dictated by IQ tests or ''academic achievement.'' It has to do with different *styles* of learning, different kinds of students feeling more comfortable with and responding to different ways of becoming involved with the world of knowledge.

This might mean that Murray Road is not necessarily the perfect school for every student. Indeed, it may well not be. But it appears to be one of the most significant alternatives around at the present. And there is little doubt that taking a trip down Murray Road in the moonlight can be quite an experience.

■ Indirectly the author raises the issue of the "need" for materials and facilities for teaching/learning. To what extent, and in what ways, are such things "necessary" in the classroom?

■ What is "teacherish" behavior? What experience—either real or vicarious—can you relate to suggest that teacher behavior in general is or is not changing?

■ Historically, what is the "old fashioned idea of pluralism" in American education? What evidence can you offer to support Clinchy's suggestion that a revival of pluralism is under way?

"...a public day school for people from age three to ninety-three."

Compare the innovation discussed in this article with the one reported in Thorwald Esbensen's "Family-Designed Learning: Accountability as Customer Satisfaction" (Section Two) and with concerns expressed by Alvin Toffler in "The Psychology of the Future" (Section One).

School for All Ages

Gertrude Pemberton, a Philadelphia housewife, has gone back to school with five of her children. While that in itself is quite unusual, the school is even more so. Pemberton and her children attend the St. Agnes School for All Ages, a public day school for people from age three to ninety-three.

"There's no place in Philadelphia I can go to get the education I need besides the School for All Ages," says Pemberton. "I quit school in the sixth grade, went to work at 16, and had six kids. I couldn't even help my kids with their schoolwork before, but now I can. And they can help me. My kids are proud I returned to school."

Actually, the same can be said by nearly all the adult students at St. Agnes: Eight of the nine adults have children in the school. Unlike Pemberton, however, most are only two years away from a high school diploma.

In addition to helping people get a formal education, the School for All Ages (SFAA) is designed to deal with two basic concerns. The first: to increase contact among members of various age groups and of different generations.

"Our society has become age-segregated to an unhealthy degree," explains Henry Kopple, SFAA coordinator in the district's Office of Affective Education. "We believe that learning of standard academic skills and of more general life skills can be promoted through a concerted effort to bring those of different ages together in a situation where mutual teaching and learning can occur." Not only will children and adults be sitting in the same classrooms, he adds, but they'll be tutoring one another as well.

The second major concern, Kopple points out, is to create a cooperative rather than a competitive atmosphere for learning. "This will be done," he says, "through many different kinds of group activities—academic, social and recreational." Many students suffer academically because of the undue pressure they experience in an overly competitive school atmosphere, he explains.

Philadelphia's unique SFAA concept is being implemented in two schools, each of which eventually will have 300 transgenerational students. The first SFAA opened early in February at the Muhlenberg Church in northern Philadelphia and the second early in March at the St. Agnes School in central Philadelphia. Both schools are used exclusively for the public SFAA program.

Currently, St. Agnes has 123 students plus nine adults in grades K to 9, but by next fall, it will have 200 students and three more grades. Muhlenberg Church has 165 students and 9 adults. In their third year of operation, both St. Agnes and Muhlenberg are expected to reach the maximum of 300 students, including some 25 to 50 adults. Kopple established the 300-student maximum because he believes each SFAA must be fairly small to accomplish its goals. By 1976, however, he hopes to open two more Schools for All Ages and, eventually, he plans to have one in each of Philadelphia's eight school districts.

To determine how best to bring the young, older and oldest together, Kopple sought the help of the local Gray Panthers, an "activist" senior citizens group, and visited former teachers of one-room schoolhouses. "These teachers spoke about the family feeling that existed in the room, and about the ways that older children could and did help younger ones," he remarks. "We expanded on that concept, and the School for All Ages was born."

All SFAA students and teachers volunteered to join the program, Kopple points out. Students were recruited through flyers sent home with regular elementary and junior high school students in the areas surrounding the two SFAA schools. Also, local newspapers carried stories explaining the School for All Ages concept. Afternoon and evening meetings then were held for students and parents to hear about the specifics of the program and ask questions.

Final selection of students was based on age spread, racial balance, sex balance, and achievement level spread. St. Agnes' student population is 71.5 per cent black, 23 per cent white, and 5 per cent Puerto Rican, while Muhlenberg's is 80 per cent black, 15 per cent white, and 5 per cent other minorities.

Of the 200 teachers who were voluntarily tested for the SFAA program, 16 were chosen—nine for Muhlenberg and seven for St. Agnes. While four years of experience were required of SFAA teachers, St. Agnes teachers have an average of six years' experience, notes the school's coordinator, James Wright.

Before the two schools opened, teachers took 60 hours of training from the affective education staff. While school is in session, they will attend weekly two-hour inservice sessions, to be followed by an additional 60 hours of training during the summer months.

Regular teachers will be assisted by student teachers and also by adults in the Career Change Program. A unique aspect of the SFAA, the Career Change Program will enable four adult high school graduates in each SFAA community to prepare for new careers in social service. With funds from ESEA Title III, these adults will attend courses at Temple University a couple of days a week and will spend the other days at either St. Agnes or Muhlenberg.

SFAA "days" run from 8:45 a.m. to 3 p.m., normal school hours in Philadelphia. A typical day at the St. Agnes SFAA, for example, begins with a morning "ritual," such as singing or working on a group mural, for cross-age groups. Then students move to their room for instruction in language arts and math from 9:10 to 10:30 a.m. After a short mid-morning break, they return to work on basic skills, participating in the cross-age tutoring program, with adults tutoring children or vice versa.

At 1 p.m., following a one-hour lunch period, cross-age groups of students might continue instruction in science or social studies. Around 2 p.m. they might engage in arts and crafts projects, with instruction offered by adults who teach crocheting or other crafts. Where possible, the day ends with another "ritual," including discussion.

"Adults are not put in separate classes," emphasizes Wright; "they participate in whatever regular school courses meet their needs.

"There is so much that children can learn from the adult generation," he notes. "Children have not shared their grandparents' experiences, primarily because people are so mobile today. We need to bring the first, second and third generations together to provide affective education experiences from different perspectives and to bridge the gap between childhood and adulthood."

Kopple adds that "children with a limited knowledge of and exposure to grandparents or any older people tend to ridicule them, fear them, or consider them 'over the hill' and valueless.

"Because of age segregation," says Kopple, "youngsters have fewer models to emulate for growing and changing. They get locked into their particular stage of development and are frequently unaware of the direction in which maturation and learning will take them.

"And the elderly, when separated into age groups, are likely to lose both the meaning of their past experiences and hope in the future. By establishing relationships with younger people," says Kopple, "the elderly maintain a stake in the future and can purposefully play a role in the present."

- What long-range advantages or disadvantages can you see for "schools for all ages"?

- The article indicates that teachers in the schools discussed took sixty hours of training before the schools opened. With members of your class, brainstorm components of teacher training that you believe would be necessary to successfully function in this type of school setting.

- The SFAA coordinator is quoted as saying that children with little exposure to grandparents and other older people " . . . tend to ridicule them, fear them, or consider them 'over the hill' and valueless." What evidence can you offer to support that point of view?

- List ways in which segregation by age hampers community life.

". . . 'family-designed learning'. . . makes it possible for every family on an individual basis to decide for itself what its children should learn in school."

See excerpts from the "Seventh Annual Gallup Poll of Public Attitudes Toward Education" (Section One) and Frederick Bock and Wanda Gomula's "A Conservative Community Forms an Alternative High School" (Section Two) for contrast and comparison.

Family-Designed Learning: Accountability as Customer Satisfaction

Thorwald Esbensen

"Since there is no evidence that professional educators know appreciably more than parents about what is good for children, it seems reasonable to let parents decide what kind of education their children should have while they are young and to let the children decide as they get older."
—Mary Jo Bane and Christopher Jencks, in "The Schools and Equal Opportunity," *Saturday Review,* September 16, 1972

Reflecting this point of view, a school that is perhaps unique in the country is now in its second year of operation in Duluth, Minnesota. Sponsored by the education department of the College of St. Scholastica in Duluth, the West End Parochial School (grades 1-8) has established a new kind of relationship between parent and educator—one with enormous implications for American formal schooling at all levels, both public and private. Called "family-designed learning," the new partnership makes it possible for every family on an individual basis to decide for itself what its children should learn in school.

This freedom to choose, it must be emphasized, is not the same as choosing the typical course elective. In the traditional school setup, all you can select is the

Thorwald Esbensen, "Family-Designed Learning," *Phi Delta Kappan* **54**, no. 7 (March 1973). Reprinted by permission.

Thorwald Esbensen is Assistant Superintendent, Teaching and Student Services, Edina Public Schools, Edina, Minnesota. A fuller account of the material in this article may be found in Thorwald Esbensen and Phillip Richards, *Family Designed Learning: A Next Step for Individualized Instruction* (Palo Alto, Cal.: Fearon, 1975).

course *title*. Anyone who has ever been a student knows that each teacher has his own ideas of what a course should include. That is reasonable enough, of course. The point is: After you have signed up for a course you have no further say in the matter. You will either learn what you are told to learn or you will flunk. It's as simple as that.

And as maddening. Putting on my parent hat, it appalls me to realize that down through the years neither my wife nor I has ever had a decisive say-so regarding what our children should learn in school.

Consider your own situation as a parent. Your son or daughter, let us say, attends an English class where the teacher is having everyone learn how to diagram sentences. Your offspring thinks this is a waste of time. And so do you. What can you do about it? Look at your options:

1. You can see the teacher. No matter how low-key you attempt to make your visit, chances are the teacher will feel threatened. This is understandable. After all, you are asking that a familiar way of doing business be reorganized—a request which, if honored for other parents as well, could conceivably lead to a classroom where every student would be pursuing his own individualized program. Unless the teacher is in agreement with this approach to instruction *and* capable of managing it, you will no doubt be put down, and quickly. What you will hear may be something to the effect that the present course is in line with departmental policy, is the outcome of a scope and sequence study made by a special curriculum committee, and has the approval of the district board of education. You have just struck out on Option Number One.
2. You can see the school principal. That poor man (or woman) can do nothing for you. Caught between the issue of academic freedom on one side and teachers' organizations on the other, the administrative head of the building cannot cope with your particular problem. Option Number Two is of no discernible use to you.
3. You can go to the PTA. That worthy organization is simply not equipped to deal with the matter of your child's English assignments. It does its share in helping to raise funds for the school library and in sponsoring the yearly school carnival. It cannot help you in your present dilemma. So much for Option Number Three.
4. You can see the superintendent of schools. His job these days is tenuous at best. Bludgeoned by all factions involved with any major issue, he is not likely to be receptive to your child's problem with his English lessons. You'll have no luck with Option Number Four.
5. You can go to the board of education. The function of that body is surely not to concern itself with the details of one student's study program for a single class. No point, then, in pursuing Option Number Five.
6. When all else fails, you can try selling your house and moving to another attendance zone where your child can go to a different public school. Or you can pull your youngster out of the public school system altogether and try a

private school. But note well: Having made this radical decision, your leverage again ceases and you will find yourself taking potluck with your child's new teachers. For all practical purposes, Option Number Six leaves you right where you started.

What it all adds up to is that American formal schooling, given its present structure, is not prepared to respond to your wishes as an individual parent.

OPENING UP THE OPTIONS

Short of deschooling society, is there a feasible way to change this state of affairs? Those of us who have worked for the past two years with the idea of family-designed learning believe there is.

Suppose that you and your spouse have just decided to enroll your 10-year-old son in our program. As soon as you do this, you are given a set of curriculum catalogs containing all of the learning objectives available within the program during the current school year. These catalogs are yours to take home and keep, for you will be using them throughout the year.

The first thing you and your youngster are asked to do is look through the catalogs to see what is presently being offered by the school. You will *not* find general course descriptions and titles but very specific listings of learning objectives that can be chosen for your child. Much effort has been expended to make these as clear as possible. For example, an objective in mathematics might read, "Given a numeral with an exponent, the student will be able to write it in expanded notation and compute the product."

Depending on your relationship with your son, you will give his preferences much or little weight when it comes to choosing the learning objectives that he will try to achieve. We have found that the parents of our upper-division students, grades 5-8, generally give their children a good deal of freedom in this matter. Indeed, out of 160 students who responded to a question on this point, 119 said they felt their own views were allowed to prevail. This has not resulted in a pattern of watered-down, lopsided, or unrealistic choices, in the judgment of our staff. The overall picture seems to be one of relatively conservative decision making with considerable emphasis on the three Rs.

Let us say that, as you and your boy peruse the catalogs, an idea begins to crystalize. You have felt for a long time that a life-skills approach to learning makes more sense than the kind of schooling that emphasizes the recognition and recall of facts. So you resolve to select objectives that seem to stress process rather than product. With this in mind, certain objectives begin to appeal strongly to you. Here is a hypothetical sampling of these:

■ Given a report of an event of doubtful authenticity, such as the account of Pocahontas saving the life of Captain John Smith, the student will be able to cite three historical "facts" that tend to confirm the truth of the report, and three historical "facts" that tend to dispute it. (You respond favorably to this objective, *not* because it has something to do with early American history or, more specifically, with Pocahontas and Captain John Smith—but because it requires the student to come to grips with the problem of *examining evidence.*)

- Given a familiar household object, such as a spoon or an ash tray or a dish rag, the student will be able to list for the object at least five possible uses other than the one ordinarily observed. He will be able to do this within five minutes. (You like this one because it puts a premium on *divergent thinking.*)

- Given the task of describing an object, person, or event, the student will be able to do so using words ordinarily reserved for a different kind of object, person, or event—for example, describing an inanimate object as though it were animate. (You believe that the job of learning to *use ordinary words in fresh, new ways* is an important one, and that your youngster would enjoy tackling it.)

- Given the role of leader for a discussion group, the student is able to elicit verbal contributions from every member of the group regarding the topic under discussion. He is able to accomplish this without himself being the most talkative member of the group. (You've been a member of enough discussion groups to know the value of this kind of *group process* skill.)

- Asked to state his position with regard to a controversial issue, the student will, in the course of setting forth his own point of view, summarize accurately the arguments of others with whom he does not agree. (From what you can see around you these days, *fair-mindedness* is in short supply almost everywhere. Perhaps it always has been. Nevertheless, although formidable to accomplish, it is still a virtue important to acquire.)

This hypothetical sampling does not, of course, address itself to the problem of selecting a constellation of objectives that makes some kind of overall sense, that promises more than a patchwork of unrelated learning experiences. Nor does this sampling indicate how you and your son will work out your various preferences so that a measure of harmony will prevail. But the very fact that a program of family designed learning opens up *opportunities for communication between parent and child* makes the arrangement revolutionary in the best sense of the word.

CURRICULUM BY CHOICE

After your family has made its preliminary decisions concerning the curriculum, a conference is held with each of the teachers who will be offering one or more of the desired objectives. Normally, this takes place at school at the beginning of the fall term. Just prior to these conferences, tests are administered to the students in order to provide staff members with up-to-date information upon which to base recommendations to the families. The family conferences are held throughout the regular school day and into the evening and are generally scheduled over a 3- or 4-day period as needed. A conversation with an individual teacher usually takes about 15 to 20 minutes.

During the conferences the parents and the child hear recommendations concerning the learning objectives the staff thinks appropriate for the child. In other words, the professional educators do have opinions and they express them. *But they do not mandate.* Within the framework of the available curriculum and the state regulations (in the case of Minnesota, at least, this means considerable freedom of choice), each family may choose for itself the learning objectives its children will try to achieve. If, as the result of a teacher's recommendations, a family decides it wants more time to reach a decision regarding a set of learning objectives, the additional time is taken. Conferences are held as needed throughout the year.

Each family is completely free with regard to the number of objectives chosen at any conference. The family may wish to try out a few at a time, or it may wish to make a rather comprehensive selection. It doesn't matter. And, in any case, the family is free to change its mind about its selections at any time. It may add, delete, or substitute objectives whenever it decides to do so. There is complete flexibility in this respect throughout the year. And there are over 1,000 objectives from which to choose within the curriculum, grades 1-8. The grade level indicates only a certain level of difficulty, generally speaking, and no child is restricted by grade level when decisions are made concerning the objectives upon which he will be working.

There does not appear to be any less family interest concerning children's choices at our upper level than there is at the primary grade level. Understandably enough, however, parents allow greater freedom of choice to older children.

A family conference normally ends when a simple decision-making form has been completed and signed by the conferees: the student, his parents, and the teachers concerned. Each student in the program works on the objectives that have been selected by his family, and a *staff-written report on his progress is sent home to his family every week.*

Parents are encouraged to suggest additional learning objectives for the curriculum, and they sometimes do. For example, one mother said that she would be willing to offer instruction in hair styling and skin care. A number of our upper-division girls signed up for these objectives. One first-grade girl also signed up!

We are trying to develop what we may call a *responsive* curriculum, namely, one that evolves in keeping with the expressed desires of our clients. Recently, we have begun developing learning objectives based upon some of the ideas contained in Alvin Toffler's book, *Future Shock.*

We can say as a result of two years' experience that our families (blue-collar workers, for the most part) take great interest in helping to shape the education of their offspring. Indeed, up to and including the present time we have had 100% participation by families. Compared to the usual turnout at PTA meetings or similar gatherings, we believe this is an impressive demonstration of the vitality of family-designed learning.

FULFILLING THE CONTRACT

Physically, our school is an old one with traditional rooms and corridors. But we are not using the building in a traditional way. We have, for example, abolished the self-contained classroom, that time-honored elementary school arrangement where one teacher attempts to teach a number of subjects to a group of children assigned for most of each day to one room with a particular grade-level designation. In its place we have established the learning center. There are upper-division and lower-division centers for each subject. The lower-division centers cater to our pupils in grades 1-4. The upper-division centers are available to our students in grades 5-8. (These grade-level divisions are strictly for convenience, given the nature of our physical plant. They have no other significance.)

Our staff is divided into two teams, one for each division. Each team member in each division works across age and grade levels with all of the children in that division. Each teacher has primary responsibility for one learning center with an emphasis on a particular subject.

The students in our upper division are not separated in any manner by age or grade. They work freely together throughout the day and are almost entirely self-scheduled. Each day every upper-division student plans his schedule of activities for the following day. No bells ring, and the student is free to spend as much time as he needs in any instructional area. The student moves in and out of the various centers as he works on the objectives he and his parents have selected during their family conferences.

Each learning objective has been embedded in what is called a student contract. Figure 1 shows a sample contract.

Whenever a student begins to work on a new contract that he has selected from among the bank of contracts approved by his parents, he must make a commitment as to when he will complete the contract. This is called a bid, and the procedures governing it have been elaborated into a system called the Bid Game.

A student does not need to compete with his fellows in order to be a "winner" at the Bid Game. He need only fulfill his own commitments as a responsible learner. To the extent that he does this, the student accumulates Bid Game points, which he may use to buy time for other activities in which he is interested. For example, there is a chess club that meets one afternoon each week during school hours. It costs 100 Bid Game points per hour to play chess. Other activities include trips to concerts, plays, athletic events, etc. An effort is made to offer as many Bid Game purchase options as possible.

The purposes of the Bid Game are: (1) to improve a student's ability to assess correctly his own capabilities in relation to designated learning tasks, and (2) to increase his level of achievement motivation. The accomplishment of these purposes will, presumably, promote the development of self-directed learning, which is the basic goal of individualized instruction as it pertains to family decision making in our program.

The fundamental question is, of course: Are families competent to choose for themselves from among the many possible aims of instruction?

We believe they are and that they want to do so. We think it is significant that our school is located in a low-income area of the city and that we have had 100% representation at our family conferences. (I suspect that parents with less formal schooling in their own backgrounds tend to make more conservative choices than parents who have had a greater amount of formal education, the latter possibly realizing that a large part of the traditional curriculum may not be worth the powder to blow it up.)

Of course, one of the choices that a family has is to make no choices at all. The family can say, in effect, "Okay, you people are the educators. You decide."

And then we would. After all, that is what we have been doing for lo these many years. So we can, if that is desired, keep on doing it. It turns out, however, that our families don't want to relinquish their newfound authority. To my knowledge, only one family to date has turned its decision-making power back to the school.

Bertrand Russell once remarked that the ultimate reason for democracy is that no *definable* body of persons is wiser in practice than the entire citizenry. On similar grounds, just as I am opposed to literacy tests for voting, I am opposed to any kind of knowledge litmus test for parents. With respect to decision making in American education, we at the West End Parochial School hold that in a democratic society every family ultimately has the right to make its own mistakes.

Figure 1.   A sample family-designed learning contract

Content Classification
Vocabulary development through the use of nonprint media

Purpose
What do you think of when you see or hear words such as *dangerous, rich, love, small, hard, beauty?* Do these words call up any pictures or feelings inside you? Do you think that the meanings these words have for you are the same as the meanings other people get from the same words?

In school you sometimes have lessons that ask you to tell what certain words mean. Often, such assignments ask you to use a dictionary and write down one or more of the definitions that you find there. That is one way to tell the possible meanings of words. There are other ways.

One interesting approach is to use motion pictures, slides, pictures from magazines, etc., to explore the meanings of words. Communication is not limited to the use of written or spoken language. Your work in this area will help you develop your vocabulary through the use of some different audio-visual techniques. This contract is designed to help you discover for yourself (perhaps in moving ways) the richness of the mother tongue.

Performance Objective
Given a list of 10 ordinary words, and shown two films with contrasting settings or points of view, you will be able to assign each word to whichever film the word is applicable, in your opinion. If a word applies to both films, you will assign the word to both films. For each word you will be able to write a sentence or two explaining why you made the choice that you did.

Evaluation
You have now seen two films, and you have been given a list of 10 ordinary words, such as *big, understanding, value, narrow, inside,* etc. Each word is applicable to at least one of the two films and, possibly, to both. Take a clean sheet of paper and divide it into two columns. Put the name of the first film at the head of the first column. Put the name of the second film at the head of the second column. Put each word on your list into *one* or *both* of the columns, depending upon where you think each word fits. For each word, write a sentence or two explaining why you placed the word where you did. Hand in your work. After you have done so, your teacher will discuss the assignment with you and other students assembled for this purpose. Following this discussion, your teacher may ask you to assign another list of words to the same two films, or may assign you two other films to view.

Taxonomy Category
Comprehension

Resources
Nahanni and *The Smile*
The Exiles and *The Lakeman*

- Based on your schooling, to what degree are you able to concur with the remarks by Bane and Jencks which precede this article?

- If you could design you own program for next semester, what would your program include?

- Design a learning contract for yourself in an area of great interest or need. Approach one of your professors or an advisor and attempt to arrange an independent study course for which you could receive credit by carrying through your contract.

"Discipline and achievement are the hallmarks of the Marshall Fundamental School...a new kind of alternative public school...."

Read this article in light of the Ford Foundation's "Matters of Choice" (Section Two) and Mortimer Smith's "Is Common Sense Breaking Through?" (Section Three).

The New Conservative Alternative

Jane S. Shaw

At John Marshall Fundamental School in Pasadena, Calif., the day begins with a flag-raising ceremony, complete with trumpeters. In their classrooms, students pledge allegiance and stand at attention during the ceremony. Ten minutes each morning are devoted to character training, as students discuss the difference between honesty and fairness or recite uplifting poems and aphorisms. Halls and classrooms are quiet. Students concentrate on essential subjects, especially phonics, arithmetic, grammar and social studies. Students who misbehave may be paddled or detained after school.

John Marshall is the kind of school many American adults remember from their childhood. It doesn't look like a school that could cause waves of shock to ripple throughout the country, but it has. For John Marshall is the "school that turned back the clock," as one writer phrased it, the school that turned its back on most of the innovations of the past few decades—on the open classroom, on permissiveness, on self-motivated learning, on casual dress and language. John Marshall's proponents don't consider the school regressive—"I don't think teaching the three Rs is old-fashioned," says one—and it doesn't use such antique symbols as the dunce cap or *McGuffey's Reader*.

Jane S. Shaw, "The New Conservative Alternative." Reprinted with permission from *Nation's Schools & Colleges* (February 1975), copyright © 1975 by McGraw-Hill, Inc., Chicago. All rights reserved.

Jane S. Shaw is a *McGraw-Hill World News* correspondent based in Chicago. She writes about many subject areas in addition to education.

A growing number of schools are adopting its approach. Fundamental schools are being established in such places as Charlotte, N.C., and Jefferson County, Colo., and an increasing number of school districts are weaving elements of the fundamental approach into their programs.

Fundamental schools are a new kind of alternative public school—until recently the term "alternative school" referred to voluntary, relatively unstructured schools which emphasized experimentation, parental and student involvement in decision-making, and self (rather than teacher-initiated) discipline and motivation. The number of alternative schools in the U.S. has increased rapidly over the past few years, from about 60 in 1972 to well over 5,000 this year, according to Robert D. Barr, a director of the International Consortium for Options in Public Education. Nearly always they have been established to meet the demands of parents who were dissatisfied with what the regular public schools provided—and the new fundamental schools are no exception. That is the case with John Marshall, the best known of the fundamental schools.

Discipline and achievement are the hallmarks of John Marshall Fundamental School, which opened in the fall of 1973. Because its enrollment is voluntary, parents who send their children to the school are expected to endorse its philosophy and rules; if they don't, they are expected to transfer their children back to the regularly assigned school. Parents are obviously endorsing the concept; John Marshall's K-8 enrollment of 1,100 was expanded last fall with the addition of grades 9-12, bringing the enrollment to more than 1,600. The increased popularity of the program—and a resulting long waiting list—prompted the district to start a second fundamental elementary school, Sierra Mesa, a K-6 school that opened last fall with an enrollment of 410.

John Marshall and Sierra Mesa each reflect (probably more accurately than any other Pasadena schools) the diverse racial and socioeconomic makeup of Pasadena. The large number of applications for the fundamental schools enabled the district administration to select a diverse student body, and a court-ordered integration plan required it. Both elementary schools are approximately 41 per cent black, 42 per cent Anglo-Caucasian, and 13 per cent Spanish surname. The John Marshall Fundamental High School, however, is 71 per cent Anglo-Caucasian.

Among the "old-fashioned" methods the schools use to enforce discipline and encourage achievement are paddling and detention, letter grades, ability grouping (not yet realized, though still a goal), homework in all grades including kindergarten, repetition of school years if minimum standards aren't met, a dress code, and persistent emphasis on moral standards, courtesy, respect for adults, and patriotism.

But this doesn't mean regimented classrooms, desks bolted to the floor in straight rows, or somber, silent children. "Visitors come expecting a stereotype, expecting rigidity," comments Anna Mary Hession, director of elementary curriculum for the Pasadena district. "But our students are happy; they enjoy school."

"Discipline is the kindest thing you can do for a child," says Henry S. Myers Jr., the school board member who has been the major force in the establishment of the fundamental schools. "Those of us who believe in fundamental education feel very strongly that firm, impartial discipline—a completely controlled classroom—is absolutely essential before effective teaching can take place."

Discipline administered at the fundamental schools seems to be effective. Allan Burt, principal of Sierra Mesa, says that he has paddled some 20 children since school opened in the fall; only two have been sent back to his office for further discipline. Four or five children have had their mouths washed out with soap (a technique not practiced at John Marshall) and none has been back a second time. In spite of Burt's role as disciplinarian, he seems popular at Sierra Mesa. The children are eager to talk with him and greet him as he walks through the school yard. "The children don't seem to be afraid of me," he notes.

Is John Marshall a return to the past? In many ways, Yes, but as its founders see it, the school combines the best of the old and the new. "Some of the techniques of the past have proved to be the best," says J. M. Kellner, principal, and these are used at John Marshall.

What he opposes, Myers explains, is replacing the "well established procedures" with "new untested ones simply for the sake of change."

John Marshall does, however, have its innovations. One of these is an outgrowth of Kellner's belief that parents should not only support the aims of the school but should volunteer time there as well. Ideally, he says, he would like to have each parent spend two hours each semester doing volunteer work at the school. Kellner is also proud of the fact that John Marshall's seventh and eighth-grade classes were the first in California to adopt "The World of Construction," an industrial arts course that emphasizes the practical aspects of modern building and vocational training.

After discipline, commitment to achievement is the major emphasis at John Marshall. "The children have a feeling of security because they are rewarded here for achievement, not for effort. We only succeed as individuals, and the children know this," says Kellner.

Academic results so far have been substantial. In tests given at the end of the first year, John Marshall's elementary school students equalled or exceeded the district median scores in 18 out of 21 tests. Median test scores improved by 12 per cent, more than any other school in the district. (However, in 1974, all the schools' median scores improved, after several years of declining scores.) Peter F. Hagen, research administrative director of the district, says, "Initial indications—after one year of experience—are that John Marshall does appear to be meeting the needs of its very diverse student body." He wants a few more years to observe the results before making a final evaluation of its success.

Myers, however, thinks the students' academic achievement is already apparent—and he's not surprised. "We didn't see how it could be otherwise." The difference between John Marshall and conventional schools, he says, "is like the difference between day and night." Myers speaks caustically about some of the educational strategies he has seen since becoming a board member. He describes some mathematics programs designed to teach "manipulative skills" as "tons of blocks, triangles, clay, toys and gimmicks," and individualized audio reading machines designed to motivate children to read as a "crime" because they waste the children's time, "teaching nothing," in his opinion. Myers is especially critical of an attitude that he feels many educators have toward minority groups. He believes that many minority children fail to achieve because their teachers consider them deprived and don't expect them to learn. He says that some children are promoted year after year without achieving the minimum standards of the grade level, and end up without minimal skills. "It's pitiful to see these kids just go on and on," he sighs.

The apparent success of John Marshall (Sierra Mesa is really too new to be judged) may have been expected, but its impact around the country wasn't. John Marshall has been described widely in national magazines including *Time, Newsweek, McCall's* and *Redbook*, in newspaper columns, on radio talk shows, and in educational journals. As one result, the school has received nearly a thousand inquiries from all over the country. Visitors stream through the school, their number restricted only by the time constraints of the principal and his concern about interrupting classes.

Ironically, the Pasadena fundamental schools resulted as much from an explosive political situation as from educational philosophy. Pasadena, an affluent Los Angeles suburb, has often shifted abruptly between liberal and conservative politics, and these shifts have been reflected in the school board composition. In 1969, the conflict between liberal and conservative became more pronounced as the community began to absorb a growing minority population, and a court-ordered school integration plan went into effect.

The plan included extensive busing and was vociferously opposed by many white parents. It is believed to have precipitated the gradual decline in enrollment that the Pasadena district has experienced since 1969. This trend—total public school enrollment dropped from about 33,000 in 1969 to under 26,000 in 1974—was reversed for the first time last fall.

In 1973, three conservative candidates, including Myers, were elected to the school board by a heavy majority after a campaign in which they promised to "stop forced busing" and advocated a return to stricter discipline in the schools. Once in office, the conservative majority (in addition to appealing the integration plan in the courts) wanted to get rid of the Pasadena Alternative School, an "open" school that epitomized the contemporary educational philosophy opposed by the new board members. "But we knew this would alienate many parents," says Myers, and he suggested instead a "school at the other end of the spectrum—a model school."

The proponents of John Marshall, particularly Myers, seem to have a missionary fervor for what they are doing. Myers believes that he and other educational conservatives are engaged in a "life-and-death struggle" between fundamental and permissive education—a struggle to preserve American values and knowledge created, stored and transmitted over generations. At the same time, Myers (a chemical engineer) and his associates are not fanatics. As the operation of the fundamental schools makes clear, they welcome good teaching; they are explicitly opposed to "harsh and authoritarian" discipline as well as to laxity and permissiveness; and they hope to instill in students a sense of pride and self-worth, as well as a practical grounding in basic education. Their patriotism seems not so much blind devotion to America as an appreciation of its values and heritage.

While other fundamental schools are also committed to the goals of basic education and strict discipline, their administrators and supporters do not seem as fervent as John Marshall's. (For many fundamental schools, declining test scores seem to have been more of a factor in their creation than a concern that civilization is threatened by current trends in education.)

Districts that have fundamental programs include:

Charlotte-Mecklenburg District, Charlotte, N.C. The 500-student Myers Park Traditional Elementary School, a K-6 alternative school, has a structured program in self-contained classrooms and emphasizes discipline, competition, grades and traditional values such as patriotism.

Myers Park became a fundamental school after the Charlotte-Mecklenburg district responded to pressure from parents, partly in reaction to a "progressive" alternative school in the district. And, as in Pasadena, there may have been "underlying motives," Principal Lewis L. Walker admits. The district is under a controversial court-ordered integration plan, and the Myers Park School, located in an affluent white section of Charlotte, offered some parents an opportunity to avoid having their children bused. However, the federal judge overseeing the district's integration plan required that 20 per cent of the Myers Park students be black.

Like John Marshall, Myers Park has received many inquiries from other schools and has had many visitors. Walker remarks, with some humor, "I don't know what people are looking for. They seem to expect old buildings, old classrooms, nothing colorful or pleasing to the eye. Those have nothing to do with being traditional. Our desks are not in rows, we have plenty of supplies, the rooms have lots of artwork." While the school is too new for any assessment of how well the students are doing academically, Walker believes they are progressing well. The only major problem the school has experienced, he says, is the lack of transportation (until recently) to bring black children into the school.

Cupertino (Calif.) Union School District. Dissatisfaction with innovation—"Our district was willing to try almost anything," recalls one disgruntled parent—and distrust of the open classroom were factors in the creation of the Academics Plus (A+) program in Cupertino, a 21,000-student elementary district in northern California. Six classes in Panama School follow the program, concurrent with the regular K-6 program. Academics Plus stresses basic skills, rote and drill, the Golden Rule, friendly competition, teacher-directed instruction, standardized testing, letter grades, and some restrictions on dress.

Lack of bus transportation has prevented expansion of the program beyond classes in a single school, but parental enthusiasm has been high. A survey of parents of 160 students elicited 140 responses, and 93 per cent said they would re-enroll their children the following year. "Accompanying comments were so enthusiastic as to overwhelm us," reports a community leader of the program.

Lagunitas District, San Geronimo, Calif. The Advance Basic Capabilities (ABC) program opened in the fall of 1972 in this semirural San Francisco suburb. Now the district has three programs in its two elementary schools: an open alternative program with 120 students, the ABC program with 95 students, and a traditional educational program with 180 students. Parents are apparently satisfied with the range of educational options, since they generally re-enroll their children in the same program. "We make an effort to give everybody a choice," says an administrator.

Jefferson County (Colo.) Schools. Two fundamental elementary schools, enrolling more than 300 students, were opened last fall in Jefferson County, near Denver. While some administrators, teachers and parents had been discussing the need for a more fundamental approach—and the school district had just formulated a policy endorsing the principle of alternative schools—it wasn't until a clipping describing John Marshall reached them that a concrete proposal was formulated. The two schools stress basic subjects, letter grades, character guidance as well as academic guidance, and enrichment programs only after students have mastered the course content.

Some school districts that haven't established fundamental schools are moving in that direction by designing programs to offer greater choice which include elements of the fundamental approach. Michael Hickey, associate superintendent of the Seattle public schools, reports that "to our amazement" a survey of 10,000 elementary school parents revealed that 20 per cent wanted a school more traditional in philosophy and method than the conventional school. After a group of parents agitated for a return to traditional education, the district opened a school that emphasizes reading and arithmetic, grades, competition and homework, although offering a curriculum that is more interdisciplinary than that commonly found in fundamental schools.

In Quincy, Ill., a high school that offers seven different learning environments includes a traditional curriculum complete with many characteristics of the fundamental schools. In Minneapolis, the Southeast Alternative Program, among its other choices, offers the Tuttle Contemporary School, which stresses the acquisition of basic skills in self-contained classrooms, and by 1976 the entire Minneapolis school system is to be organized to offer parents at least some choice in schools for their children.

Most fundamental public schools are organized as alternative schools, which raises the question of whether future alternative schools will be fundamental rather than "open" or "free" schools. Barr, from his perspective at the International Consortium for Options in Public Education, doesn't think so. He believes that fundamental schools are not a strong movement, but a "somewhat feeble reaction to the drift of things.'' The long-term trend, he believes, is toward a wide variety of educational options that represent a complete spectrum of education philosophies. But he admits he may be wrong: "This may be the beginning of a giant backlash, but I don't sense it. In fact, I sense just the opposite."

On the other hand, Lynne Miller, a staff-member of the National Alternative Schools Program of the University of Massachusetts (the organization that is helping guide and evaluate the Pasadena "open" alternative school) thinks that the fundamental schools may have a significant impact. They have "fostered a split in the whole alternative movement," she says. "There are going to be a lot more fundamental schools." She would "hate to see" such schools replace those that stress internal motivation, self-discipline and less structured atmosphere, but she sees the broadening of options as a healthy development, breaking away from the "traditional school monopoly" which offered no choice.

Another observer, Donald Moore, program director of the Center for New Schools, opposes the "false contrasts" being drawn by proponents of fundamental schools who imply that other, freer, alternative schools do not emphasize skill development. He insists that they do, and points to his own study of Chicago's Metro High School (a school without walls), which showed that students improved their reading skills significantly, compared with a control group.

Even advocates of basic education have a few doubts about the fundamental schools. "If their purpose is to further the cause of basic education, we're all for them," says George Weber, associate director of the Council for Basic Education. This group has given considerable attention to the fundamental school movement and welcomes the increased emphasis on the basics. But, he warns, "They may get hung up on things we don't think are important, such as a particular discipline system or teaching methodology. We're not wedded to any particular design of schools as long as they attain basic educational objectives."

Administrators and teachers at John Marshall seem, so far, to have succeeded in blending methods and curriculums to achieve their clearly defined goals. There is a danger, as Weber suggests, that as fundamental schools proliferate the outward manifestation of the approach could be copied, while the essential goals—development of basic skills, rewarding of achievement, and inculcation of traditional values—could be lost or ignored. Should this happen, it is likely that fundamental schools, instead of presaging a major educational movement, would be merely a "feeble reaction." But right now, they are making waves.

- Summarize the arguments for establishing "conservative alternatives" in public education.

- Debate: "Those of us who believe in fundamental education feel very strongly that firm, impartial discipline—a completely controlled classroom—is absolutely essential before effective teaching can take place."

- Compare discipline procedures explained in this article with related recommendations in the National Commission's Recommendations for Improving Secondary Education (Section One).

- Robert Barr, of the International Consortium for Options in Public Education, comments, "This may be the beginning of a giant backlash, but I don't sense it." What information or experience do you have to support or argue his observation?

- A survey of the schools listed here may be in order. To what degree are the schools continuing to operate in the ways described in this article? To what degree are their programs expanding or being restricted? To what degree are they now supported by their communities?

"The development of optional alternative public schools is probably too minor a move to be called major reform. I prefer to think of it as a strategy for self-renewal."

Compare the ideas expressed in this article with those by Neil Postman and Charles Weingartner in "A History of the Hollering" (Section One) and by Mortimer Smith in "Is Common Sense Breaking Through?" (Section Three).

Optional Alternative Public Schools: New Partners in Education

Vernon H. Smith

In recent years the concept of educational choice (optional schools, alternative schools—call them what you will) has penetrated deeply into the American system of education. It seems likely that in the foreseeable future many different types of schools will exist side by side within the total educational structure, each designed to meet a different set of specified learning and living needs of young people. These schools will not be competitive with nor antagonistic to one another, but rather will be complementary in effort and thrust, helping American education redeem its long-term commitment to the fullest education of every child.

While the standard school certainly will continue to be the major institution in American education, it will not be the exclusive one. Other types of schools will develop, seeking to provide more fully for the total educational needs of the community. Widespread educational options—the coexistence of many types of alter-

Vernon H. Smith, "Optional Alternative Public Schools: New Partners in Education," *The North Central Association Quarterly* **49**, no. 3 (Winter 1975). Reprinted by permission.

Vernon H. Smith is professor of education and director of the Center for Options in Public Education at Indiana University. He is currently serving as co-director for the International Consortium for Options in Public Education and as editor of the Consortium's newsletter *Changing Schools*. Dr. Smith has been a teacher and supervisor in public schools. He is the author of over one hundred publications in education and English education; three of his books deal with optional public schools.

native schools and programs—should strengthen American education as a whole.[1]

The development of optional alternative public schools is based upon four simple concepts:

1. In a democratic society people should have choices about all important aspects of their lives. Our present monolithic structure for public education, in which children and youth are assigned without choice to a public school, evolved more by accident than by intent. Students, parents, teachers, and administrators should all have options among a plurality of schools.

2. Different people learn in different ways. This is all too obvious, but remember the psychology of learning is much newer than the organizational structure of the public schools. If we know that different people learn in different ways and at different times, what sense does it make to assign all the eight-year-olds in the neighborhood to one school and one classroom within that school?

3. Learning in schools should not be isolated from the world outside the school. Four national reports on secondary education published within the last year are unanimous in their criticism of the schools for isolating youth from society and for segregating youth from adults and from other age groups in the schools.

4. Those closest to the action, the individual school, should have the biggest share in the decision making. The local community, the families involved, and the teachers and administrators should all have a share in decisions that affect their lives.

Today it is no longer necessary to justify the need for alternative public schools. Since 1970, at least a dozen national reports on education have recommended the development of optional alternative public schools. Recently the *Report of the National Commission on the Reform of Secondary Education* urged that, "Each district should provide a broad range of alternative schools and programs so that every student will have a meaningful educational option available to him."

The North Central Association has already recognized the development of optional alternative public schools with the publication of *Policies and Standards for the Approval of Optional Schools and Special Function Schools*, which were approved in March 1974.

Over two thousand optional alternative public schools are in operation today, and at least several thousand more are being planned and developed throughout the country. These alternative public schools provide options for stu-

---

[1]North Central Association Task Force on Non-Standard Schools, *Proposed Policies and Standards for the Accreditation of Optional Schools and Special Function Schools*, revised first draft (December 1973), p. 1.

dents, parents, and teachers within their communities. When I describe some of the types of alternative public schools in existence, many of you will nod to yourselves, "Oh yes, we have that." You do not have the kinds of options that we are considering here unless every family in your school district has choices among different schools in the community at no extra cost.

When a community has several optional alternative public schools available, the conventional school itself becomes one of the options. And as you might expect, it is usually the most popular option. Obviously, the advantage that the optional schools have over the earlier reforms is that they do not require consensus. The families who are satisfied with the conventional school still have that option. For those families who opt for something other than the conventional, the risk is low. If the alternative proves to be unsatisfactory for some students, they can return to the conventional school. The alternative schools will not replace the conventional or standard school. They will be complementary to it so that coupled together, the alternatives and the conventional will be able to provide educational programs that are more responsive to the needs of more students.

TYPES OF OPTIONAL ALTERNATIVE PUBLIC SCHOOLS

Because alternative public schools usually develop as responses to particular educational needs within their communities, there is no single model or group of models that would encompass their diversity. We can identify at least a dozen different models today, but the great majority would fit into the following types or into combinations of these types:

Open schools with learning activities individualized and organized around interest centers scattered throughout the building.

Schools without walls with learning activities throughout the community and with considerable interaction between school and community.

Learning centers with a concentration of learning resources in one location available to all of the students in the community. These would include such facilities as magnet schools, educational parks, and career education centers.

Continuation schools with provisions for students whose education in the conventional schools has been (or might be) interrupted. These would include dropout centers, re-entry programs, pregnancy-maternity centers, evening and adult high schools, and street academies.

Multicultural schools with emphasis on cultural pluralism and ethnic and racial awareness, and usually serving a multicultural student body.

Free schools with emphasis on greater freedom for students to determine their own educational goals and to plan appropriate learning experiences. Although this term is more frequently applied to nonpublic schools, a few are available by choice within public school systems.

Schools within schools with a small number of students and teachers involved by choice in a different educational program. This would include the *mini-*

school within the conventional school building and the *satellite school* at another location but with administrative ties to the conventional school. The school-within-a-school would usually belong in one of the six categories above.

A recent development has been the school that is a *complex of mini-schools.* Haaren High School in New York City, Quincy II in Quincy, Illinois, the New School in Cleveland Heights, Ohio and Ravenswood High School in East Palo Alto, California, are all large high schools that consist of a number of mini-schools. As far as the educational program is concerned, there is no longer an identifiable conventional school or program.

Not all alternative public schools would fall into these types. There is at least one school in which all learning activities are based on behavioral modification (Grand Rapids, Michigan) and another that is a nongraded continuous progress school (Minneapolis, Minnesota).

Many alternative schools operate as voluntary integration models within their communities—in Louisville, Kentucky; St. Paul, Minnesota; Philadelphia; and Chicago, for example.

Special function schools that serve students who are assigned or referred without choice would not be included. A school for disruptive students may be highly desirable in some communities, but it should not be confused with optional alternative public schools.

WHAT DO THESE SCHOOLS HAVE IN COMMON?

Whereas each alternative public school has been developed in response to needs within its community, most of them share some or all of the following characteristics:

1. As previously stated, the school provides an option for students, parents, and teachers. Usually the choice is open to all within the community, but there must always be choice for some so that the alternative school has a voluntary clientele. The school population should reflect the socioeconomic and racial makeup of the entire community. There is no need for public alternative schools that are elite or racist.
2. The alternative schools has as its reason for existence a commitment to be more responsive to some educational need within its community than the conventional schools have been.
3. The alternative school usually has a more comprehensive set of goals and objectives than its conventional counter-part. Although most alternative secondary schools are concerned with basic skill development and with college and vocational preparation, they are also concerned with the improvement of self-concept, the development of individual talent and uniqueness, the understanding and encouragement of cultural plurality and diversity, and the preparation of students for various roles in society—consumer, voter, critic, parent, spouse....

4. The alternative school is more flexible, and therefore more responsive to planned evolution and change. Since the alternatives are being developed in today's age of accountability, they rely more on feedback and formative evaluation in the development and modification of their curricula.
5. The alternative schools tend to be considerably smaller than our comprehensive high schools. The median enrollment in alternative public schools would be around two hundred. Because they are smaller, the alternatives tend to have fewer rules and bureaucratic constraints on students and teachers.

The size of both elementary and secondary schools has been increasing for the past twenty years. Critics are now suggesting that schools cannot be large and humane too. Proponents of alternative schools suggest that when students choose their school, there is a stronger loyalty to that which is chosen over that which is compulsory. Alternative schools report less vandalism and violence, less truancy, and fewer absences on the part of students (and teachers) when compared with other schools at the same level in the same school district. This may be partly because the students in the smaller school have a bigger share in determining the rules and regulations. Shared decision making is another characteristic of many of the alternative public schools.

DEVELOPING MORE RESPONSIVE SCHOOL SYSTEMS

The development of optional alternative public schools is probably too minor a move to be called major reform. I prefer to think of it as a strategy for self-renewal. The development of optional public schools within the system is a simple and effective way to provide a total educational program that is more responsive to the needs of more families within any community.

Within every community and every public school system, the development of optional alternative schools should be considered. Many communities will find that alternatives are needed immediately; many will not. Dialogue within the community is critical so that parents, teachers, and students will understand the availability of options. After such dialogue, a decision that the community has no need for alternatives at this time is just as healthy as a decision that the alternatives are needed.

Earlier I stated that the alternative schools would not replace, but would be complementary to, the conventional schools. Let us look at some of the ways in which these options will complement the standard program within a community.

Of course, the first and most obvious way is that these alternative schools will be responsive to the needs of some students that are not currently being met by the existing programs. Some kids need schools that provide for their different styles of learning. Some kids need small schools. Some kids need schools in which they have more opportunities for self-determinism and decision making; some kids benefit from more learning experiences in the community, including work experiences.

The alternative schools can provide an exploratory or pioneering function. We can try out innovations in the smaller school that might be resisted in the larger school, particularly if they were to involve all students and all teachers.

The alternative schools will encourage the conventional schools to look at themselves more carefully. In many communities, there are long waiting lists for admission to the alternative schools. This creates a healthy self-examination on the part of the faculties in the conventional schools.

The alternative schools provide for more community involvement in the educational process—first, through exploratory dialogue on the need for optional alternatives; second, by offering families choices and thus compelling them to make decisions; and third, by involving community members in the regular function of the alternative school.

The alternative structure provides a simple mechanism for continuous change and improvement. Already in some communities we are seeing the development of alternatives to the alternatives. The alternatives provide a structure that is more responsive without additional layers of bureaucracy.

The alternative schools provide opportunities for exploring and trying a wide variety of learning facilities. They are already making use of the different kinds of space available within their communities. However, the smaller, more flexible school could become a proving ground for new concepts in school design, new combinations of hard and soft facilities, and new approaches to matching learning environments with learners and teachers.

The alternatives provide new opportunities for the cooperative development of better teacher education programs. They provide a field base for new cooperative ventures between the public schools and the teacher education institutions.

However, most important of all, the alternatives will provide educational choice within the community. Attitudes of the community toward the schools will become more positive when they see real options available. Students and parents will feel a stronger loyalty to that which is chosen. Teachers and administrators will benefit from a clientele that comes by choice, rather than compulsion.

The alternative schools provide an additional level of accountability to the school system. When alternatives are available by choice, you have a consumer market in education. When thousands of families place their children on the waiting list for a few hundred openings in the alternative schools, as is the case in several communities today, those alternatives must be meeting a perceived educational need. Community control of the schools is a highly controversial topic. Here we are talking about consumer choice, with or without community control.

I have intentionally omitted cost because there is little to say. Some alternative schools cost more; many cost less. In general, however, they operate on the same per pupil budget cost as the other secondary or elementary schools within their communities. Sometimes modest funds are necessary for planning and development; sometimes they are not. Anyone planning an alternative school should plan to operate on the regular per pupil cost of education within the community, and should avoid the use of external funds in the basic operation of the school. As a district moves to alternative schools, there may be transitional expenses just as there are minor added expenses each time a new conventional school is opened.

AN IDEA FOR WHICH THE TIME HAS COME

> As for me, I see unity through diversity. A diversity in educational design that will permit parents moving from Houston, New York, or Los Angeles to find a curriculum program and an organizational pattern amenable to their thinking. I see absolutely no need for uniformity of organization or standardization of design. There is room in this sprawling system for alternatives and there is a place for the varied educational philosophies of both educator and patron.
>
> To pretend that administration or supervision of these alternatives is an easy task is to display managerial ignorance. Flexibility and diversity are difficult to manage but, to me, the alternative to diversity is educationally untenable. The alternative is standardization and comformity. It is untenable because now in education we speak of uniqueness, of individuality. This mandates alternatives.[2]

Five years ago, I doubt if we could have found a single reference on the optional alternative public school. Today we can find hundreds if not thousands. To my knowledge no one was really pushing them, but here they are. To me, the most powerful and most impressive aspect of the current development of alternative public schools is the unbelievably widespread support that they have gained in such an incredibly short time, as educational changes go. I am forced to conclude that the alternative public school is ''an idea for which the time has come.''

- In what ways does this article summarize issues, descriptions, or problems discussed in preceding articles of this section?

- Support or attack the "four simple concepts" on which Smith says optional alternative schooling is based.

- How many of the types of optional alternative public schools exist in your community? If you have not been a student in one or visited one, make arrangements to do student aide work or to observe in as many such schools as possible.

- Assume that a teaching position becomes available to you in a community where the concept of alternative public schooling exists (including, as Smith points out, traditional schooling). In which type of school described in this article would you wish to teach? For what reasons?

---

[2]Bruce Howell, *Superintendent's Bulletin* **44**, no. 2 (Tulsa Public Schools, September 4, 1973):1.

"...alternative school students perform at least as well as their counterparts in traditional school programs, and usually better."

Also consider the articles by Mortimer Smith, "The Reforms Most Needed in Education" (Section one) and "Is Common Sense Breaking Through?" (Section Three) in order to contrast the educational philosophies expressed.

Matters of Choice: A Ford Foundation Report on Alternative Schools

Public education is evolving from a system of schools to a network of options. The educational system will become an umbrella of alternatives: free schools, traditional schools, camps, job corps centers, ethnic programs. When I first started speaking of a "network" to the Berkeley Board of Education, they were terrified of the idea. Now they're beginning to use the term themselves.

Richard I. Foster, Former Superintendent,
Berkeley Unified School District

There have always been alternatives to traditional public schools, ranging from private schools, religious schools, and reform schools to the ultimate alternative of no school at all. In the 1960s parent-controlled "free" schools proliferated around the nation, providing alternatives for some middle-class dropouts. Storefront schools and street academies, supported by businesses and philanthropic organizations, provided alternatives for some inner-city youth who had given up on—or been given up by—the public schools. Despite these alternatives, the idea of providing schooling options had low priority among educational reformers until the early 1970s.

Reprinted by permission of the Ford Foundation, 320 East 43 Street, New York, New York 10017.

The Ford Foundation was created in 1936 by Henry and Edsel Ford for administering funds "...for scientific, educational, and charitable purposes, all for the public welfare."

Today, the range of alternative schools is wide and diverse. Private academies like Harlem Prep send inner-city dropouts to major universities.* Within public systems, schools-without-walls like the Parkway Program in Philadelphia use an entire city as a classroom. Publicly-supported community schools like the Morgan School in Washington, D.C., actively involve parents in the education of their children. Alternative schools take such forms as mini-schools, multicultural schools, ethnic schools, student-directed schools, parent-directed schools, open schools, and units within traditional schools.

Some alternative schools are part of federally supported experiments—for example, the system of twenty-three alternatives in Berkeley, California. The Massachusetts Experimental School System is a state-supported effort to provide a model for alternative education. Many alternatives are tax-supported schools that depart from traditional educational methods while remaining part of the local public school system. Other alternatives are privately supported schools that barely survive by scrambling for corporate and foundation dollars.

ORIGINS

The alternative school movement has many roots, including the "free school" movement and experiments with more effective educational approaches. Voucher programs, performance contracts, and community control have also contributed to the development of alternative schools.

Most *voucher proposals* call for granting each child in a community a "chit" or "voucher" worth a specified amount of education—for example, one year's worth of schooling. The parents can then spend their voucher on any educational activity they choose, including traditional public schooling. Most voucher programs assume that several educational alternatives will be available to parents. If certain alternatives are more popular with parents and students than others, then the former will grow and the latter decline. *Performance contracts* generally entail hiring an agency outside the school to teach a specified subject or skill to the students. In theory, the agency is paid only if the students reach an agreed level of performance in that subject or skill, thus fulfilling the contract.

Both vouchers and performance contracts are based on the premise that schools and school systems should be accountable for the quality of education they provide. If the schools don't provide quality education, then parents should be able to discard them and choose other methods of education or other schools that will perform better. *Community-supported* schools often spring from the same desire for accountability: if the public schools can't teach their children, then parents have a right to operate schools which can. In short, the idea of alternative schools is based on the right to choose.

Alternative schools have also risen from the ashes of past attempts at school reform. In the 1960s the federal government, private foundations, corporations,

---

*Harlem Prep has now become part of the publicly supported New York schools.

and community groups poured massive amounts of money and energy into efforts to change the public school system. The gloomy statistics documenting the shortcomings of public schools in the education of minority students highlighted the poor fit between school offerings and the needs and goals of many students.

These large-scale efforts failed to produce large-scale changes, partly because it is so difficult to make a dent in the public school system. It bends, absorbs, and springs back into its original form. Moreover, many of the reforms attacked the problem from the top down. They sought to change teachers and curricula without focusing enough on the day-to-day political and community life of the school. Even these modest reforms threatened some educators. "We use to train teachers and then bring them back into the schools," said former Berkeley Superintendent Richard Foster, "and they wouldn't be allowed to try out the new techniques they had learned. The schools prevented them from making changes. They were afraid."

Beginning in the late 1960s, the Ford Foundation assisted efforts at a new kind of reform involving smaller, more experimental, more tentative efforts to improve education. At first, these efforts centered on privately financed alternative schools. However, private alternative schools are often unstable. Even though they spend a disproportionate amount of time raising money, their average life-span has been only eighteen months. Although no Constitutional barrier exists to spending public funds of private nonsectarian schools, legislative and political inhibitions usually prevent such expenditures. Because the overwhelming majority of children attend public schools, private schools have little political constituency to assist in gaining tax dollars.

The Foundation's efforts at assisting alternative schools have therefore focused on public schools or on providing seed money to new alternatives designed for public support. These experiments are testing a variety of ideas in structural arrangements, curricula, and parent and student involvement. Some Foundation-assisted alternatives are still struggling for survival. Just as privately supported alternatives are at the mercy of foundation and private grants, so publicly supported alternatives are subject to changes of political climate. Some educators fear that the mood is increasingly hostile to experimentation. "It's easy to kill an alternative," said Byron Stookey, former project director of one alternative agency in New York, the Committee for a Comprehensive Education Center. "If somebody wants to show that you've screwed up, they probably can—because you probably have." Traditional public school programs too fail to bring many students to respectable achievement levels, but alternatives are more vulnerable because their mistakes are more visible.

It is precisely because of their ability to correct mistakes and to respond rapidly and directly to the needs of their constituencies that alternatives have gained strength and cohesion. Although much of this report addresses the common problems and failures that alternatives share as innovative social forms, the overall record is of success and vitality in providing a wide range of educational experiences and options.

QUESTIONS AND OUTCOMES

Alternative schools are unique experimental laboratories which are beginning to address some of the most profound questions in education. What is a "learning experience," and how does one evaluate it? Can parents play a meaningful role in their children's education, and if so, what is it? How much freedom and responsibility can students handle? How important is the study of a child's cultural and ethnic heritage to his learning? How important are teacher training, facilities, materials?

Alternatives must struggle with these questions more intensely than most public schools because their survival depends on their ability to attract and hold students. The alternatives have given validity to a new kind of grass-roots educational reform. People not only choose alternatives, but tune them to community needs through an often agonizing process of experimentation.

Some critics contend that the school alternatives hardly constitute a movement because so few students are involved. In New York, for example, a few thousand students are enrolled in alternative programs out of a total city enrollment of more than 1.1 million. However, in Berkeley, California, one-fourth of the children attend public alternative schools. The Philadelphia public school system offers more than sixty experimental alternative programs. In California, the state legislature recently passed a bill authorizing the conversion of four school districts into networks of alternative schools. This year, the New York City Board of Education organized an Independent Alternative Schools Committee, composed of the directors of the city's eleven independent alternatives. In addition, New York is setting up a resources and information center for the city's thirty "mini" alternatives that operate within regular high schools. Almost every large high school in the city has requested funds to support an alternative school within or associated with the school.

Supporters of alternative schools include the National Institute of Education, local community groups, and education reformers of almost every philosophical bent. The National Consortium for Options in Public Education, with headquarters at Indiana University, estimates that alternative schools are being planned, developed, or operated in more than one thousand U.S. communities. The number of alternative public schools in operation may be as high as 1,200 with a total enrollment of 100,000. While these numbers are small compared to total enrollments in our public schools, they testify to a growing movement, not a languishing experiment.

How do the students who attend alternative schools fare? Where standard measures of achievement such as test scores and college admissions are applicable, they show that alternative school students perform at least as well as their counterparts in traditional school programs, and usually better. Attendance rates almost without exception exceed those in regular schools.

Even alternative schools that cite better student-teacher rapport as their major achievement cannot be considered failures. They give many students a second chance to get the education they missed in traditional public schools, whether they were fast learners who were bored with traditional school or slow learners who were left behind. Thus, if alternative schools are, as some educators contend, dumping grounds for students the traditional public schools don't want, they are also refuges where the dumped can learn.

- The Ford Foundation study suggests that the total enrollment in alternative schools in the United States may be as high as 100,000 students. How many students are enrolled in American schools? What percentage of students is enrolled in alternative schools?

- The study observes that "attendance rates almost without exception exceed those in regular schools." What reasons can you suggest to account for this?

- Comment on the statement that alternative schools are "refuges where the dumped can learn."

Annotated Bibliography

"Alternatives in Public Education," *Bulletin of the National Association of Secondary School Principals* **57** (September 1973), whole issue.

    Twenty brief articles which discuss various aspects of alternative education available to secondary-school planners. Several interesting experiments are reported.

ARGYRIS, CHRIS. "Alternative Schools: A Behavioral Analysis." *Teachers College Record* **75** (May 1974), pp. 429–452.

    The author examines alternative schools in terms of how Americans are socialized to behave, which has important implications for the success or failure of an innovative school. The ideas presented here may help one understand why a given school has survived while other new models have not.

AYERS, BILL. "Travelling with Children and Travelling On." *This Magazine Is About Schools* (1970), pp. 110–130.

    Describes the author's efforts to develop a "free school" for children, and his eventual defeat. Are community reactions against this kind of radical education justified or not?

BANE, MARY JO. "Essay Review: Education Vouchers." *Harvard Educational Review* **41** (February 1971), pp. 79–87.

    The considerable controversy surrounding the idea of issuing educational vouchers to parents who could then use these to select public or private schools for their children is discussed in relation to three different statements.

BENNETT, H. *No More Public School.* New York: Random House/The Bookworks, 1972.

    A "do-it-yourself" handbook for people who want to start an alternative school. Includes practical advice on how to meet legal requirements, how to finance such a school, and examples of the kinds of supplies and equipment needed. An unusual feature is the samples of contracts and agreements a new school director should be familiar with. (137 pp.)

BHAERMAN, STEVE, and JOEL DENKER. *No Particular Place to Go: The Making of a Free High School.* New York: Simon and Schuster, 1972.

    The personal story of two radical professionals who moved from standard public-school education to the founding of their own school community, through many trials and difficulties both within and outside the school. Fascinating and illuminating story. (222 pp.)

BORTON, TERRY. *Reach, Touch and Teach: Student Concerns and Process Education.* New York: McGraw-Hill, 1970.

A personal approach to the development of "new" educational practices. The author includes descriptions of what he does with samples of student work, and also discusses some other alternative programs in experimental schools across the country. The films produced by Borton of his Philadelphia program might prove illuminating. (213 pp.)

CARSON, RICHARD O. *Adoption of Educational Innovations.* Eugene, Oregon: The Center for the Advanced Study of Educational Administration, University of Oregon, 1965.

When a new program is suggested, what kinds of school systems are most likely to adopt the innovation? Why are some administrators more eager to find and support change? A fascinating study.

DENNISON, GEORGE. *The Lives of Children.* New York: Random House, 1970.

A compassionate account of the author's work in inner-city classrooms and his efforts to develop a "free school" to release the potential of seemingly stunted children. Has inspired many commentators, imitators, and critics. (308 pp.)

FRYMIER, JACK R. *et al. School for Tomorrow.* Berkeley: McCutchan, 1973.

This is not a description of what *the* school for tomorrow might be like, but what *a* school could be like if it were designed to meet the needs of children as desired by some educators and other planners. (307 pp.)

GLATTHORM, ALLAN A. *Alternatives in Education: Schools and Programs.* New York: Dodd, Mead, 1975.

A former director of an alternative high school provides in this volume a practical review of the various kinds of programs which may be developed, all considered "alternatives" to the typical secondary school. (240 pp.)

GRAUBARD, ALLEN. *Free the Children: Radical Reform and the Free School Movement.* New York: Pantheon Books/Random House, 1972.

Describes for the general public the free-school movement and offers assessment of its successes and failures. A valuable introduction to what the free-school movement is all about. (306 pp.)

GROSS, BEATRICE, and RONALD GROSS, eds. *Will it Grow in a Classroom?* New York: Delta, 1974.

This collection of articles stresses some innovative classroom practices. Which ones would be likely to fit into the typical public secondary school? Why might some of these interesting teaching ideas be considered too radical? (316 pp.)

HOLT, JOHN. *The Underachieving School.* New York: Pitman, 1969.

The books by Holt, *How Children Learn* and *How Children Fail*, together with this one are excellent sources for the ideas that permeate the writing and thinking of proponents of alternative schooling. Critics have claimed that his views are elitist and come from his experience with private, select schools. (209 pp.)

HOLT, JOHN C. *What Do I Do Monday?* New York: Dutton, 1970, pp. 293–303.

> This is John Holt's vision of learning based on a Gestalt rather than a logical model. The reader is provided with information sources and aids to assist teachers in changing the system congruent with Holt's vision.

JENNINGS, FRANK G. "Alternative Schools: A Behavioral Analysis." *Teachers College Record* 75 (May 1974), pp. 429–452.

> An analysis of the assumptions underlying various approaches to alternative educational practices, with emphasis on decision-making among those participating in developing innovations.

LA NOUE, GEORGE R., ed. *Educational Vouchers: Concepts and Controversies.* New York: Teachers College Press, Columbia University, 1972.

> An excellent collection of important statements, studies, and documents exploring the issues revolving around the development and use of vouchers as an alternative to standard pupil assignment in schools. (176 pp.)

LEONARD, GEORGE B. *Education and Ecstasy.* New York: Delacorte Press, 1968.

> Do students really want to learn? This author believes that curiosity is a prime motivator, and schools which accept this idea would not only be radically different from those we have today, but all students would learn—with joy. (234 pp.)

LICHTMAN, JANE. *Bring Your Own Bag: A Report on Free Universities.* Washington, D. C.: American Association for Higher Education, 1973.

> A well-documented report of the "free university" or "open university" movement in the United States. The innovative aspects of these programs were more in the subjects considered than the methods utilized; most were the traditional seminar-discussion type, with little or no use of technology. (128 pp.)

MURROW, CASEY, and LIZA MURROW. *Children Come First: The Inspired Work of English Primary Schools.* New York: American Heritage Press, 1971.

> The authors describe in detail how the day is organized in the "new" English open schools. They include an interesting section on school reform. These schools have been widely praised by American educators—can they fit into the American school atmosphere? (271 pp.)

PFEIFFER, JOHN. *New Look at Education: Systems Analysis in our Schools and Colleges.* New York: Odessey Press, 1968.

> The school system is amazingly resistent to the methods of business, yet in each generation new efforts are made to rationalize the schools. In this small book the author describes a number of efforts to apply systems analysis to schools. (162 pp.)

POSTMAN, NEIL, and CHARLES WEINGARTNER. *The Soft Revolution.* New York: Delta Books, 1971.

> The authors of *Teaching as a Subversive Activity* present a practical guide to school reform. The subtitle "A Student Guide for Turning Schools Around" is appropriate. (183 pp.)

RASBERRY, SALLI, and ROBERT GREENWAY. *The Rasberry Exercises.* Freestone, California: Freestone Publishing Co., 1970.

Another example of the "new wave" in educational reconstruction which hopes to reach students and their parents "imprisoned" in today's schools and to inspire and help them develop new free schools as alternatives to the standard public-school program. (125 pp.)

SAYLOR, GALEN, ed. *The School of the Future Now.* Washington, D. C.: Association for Supervision and Curriculum Development, 1972.

Outstanding educators present their views of what education ought to be like, from early childhood through the adolescent years. Case studies of school systems that are attempting to meet these ideals are included. (130 pp.)

SCHOENHEIMER, H.P. *Good Schools.* New York: Behavioral Publications, 1972.

Brief descriptions of outstanding schools from all over the world. Shows the great variety of "good schools," each reflecting different cultural values and educational patterns. (128 pp.)

SCHRANK, JEFFREY. *Teaching Human Beings: 101 Subversive Activities for the Classroom.* Boston: Beacon Press, 1972.

A generous collection of interesting and different kinds of activities suitable for innovative classrooms. Provides a specific look at what many of the advocates of alternative education are talking about. (192 pp.)

SCIARA, FRANK J., and RICHARD K. JANTZ, eds. *Accountability in American Education.* Boston: Allyn and Bacon, 1972.

Selections provide excellent background for the discussion of accountability, with consideration of some methods used to provide solutions: national assessment, voucher plans, performance contracting, and others. (410 pp.)

SCOTT, JOHN ANTHONY. *Teaching for a Change.* New York: Bantam Books, 1972.

Directed particularly at social-studies teachers, this volume suggests ways teachers can develop innovative practices to help students deal with both contemporary and future problems. (242 pp.)

SNITZER, HERB. *Living at Summerhill: A Photographic Documentary on A. S. Neill's Pioneering School.* New York: Collier, 1968.

Originally published in 1964, these photographs provide vivid evidence of what the first of the "free schools" was like, interspersed with brief paragraphs and verbatim dialogues from children and staff. (143 pp.)

TROOST, CORNELIUS J., ed. *Radical School Reform: Critique and Alternatives.* Boston: Little, Brown, 1973.

This collection of essays on school reform and commentary regarding the feasibility and/or desirability of such reform includes familiar names, as well as some that are less familiar. Section on teaching of values stresses a conservative position. (314 pp.)

TURNER, JOSEPH. *Making New Schools: The Liberation of Learning.* New York: McKay, 1971.

The author describes many specific instances of new approaches to learning; the illustrations are a useful addition to a literature that is often heavy on theory but relatively thin in specific examples. Most of the material reports existing programs in ordinary public-school classrooms. (302 pp.)

UMANS, SHELLEY. *The Management of Education: A Systematic Design for Educational Revolution.* Garden City, New York: Doubleday, 1970.

A particularly interesting volume since the author is Director of the Center for Innovations of the New York City Public Schools. Her observations indicate that it is possible to plan innovations and carry them out even in a large bureaucratic system. The variety of innovations described is interesting: Which of them are still alive and being utilized? (226 pp.)

UNRUH, GLENYS G., and WILLIAM M. ALEXANDER. *Innovations in Secondary Education.* New York: Holt, Rinehart and Winston, 1970.

Excellent and comprehensive review of the many kinds of changes suggested and being tried out in secondary-school curriculum, organization, and staffing. (247 pp.)

VON HADEN, HERBERT I., and JEAN MARIE KING. *Innovations in Education: Their Pros and Cons.* Worthington, Ohio: Jones Publishing Co., 1971.

A compendium of recent innovations in public education. The authors briefly describe each, giving pros and cons, raising questions and issues about the practice advocated. The questions posed would be useful guides for assessing an innovative practice in a field observation. A bibliography of additional sources is included. (184 pp.)

WEINSTEIN, GERALD, and MARIO D. FANTINI, eds. *Toward Humanistic Education: A Curriculum of Affect.* New York: Praeger, 1970.

Provides a theoretical framework and specific details of the "Elementary School Teaching Project," designed to change ways of teaching and the content of instruction so that students are directed toward humanistic intellectual styles of thinking and learning. Intriguing ideas of innovative classroom strategies with emphasis on feeling first and thinking about it later. (228 pp.)

vs.

The belief that a highly industrialized society requires twelve or twenty years of prior processing of the young is an illusion or a hoax.[1]

A school system like the one we got today is just training people for welfare.[2]

All too often we are giving children cut flowers when we should be teaching them to grow their own plants.[3]

Of all issues in education, the issue of relevance is the phoniest.[4]

Virginia education officials are considering a proposal to deny high school diplomas to students who cannot read, write or perform basic arithmetic computations.[5]

At the Parkrose High School near Portland, Oregon, a marriage course "using the lab approach, starts with mock [marriage] ceremonies complete with flowers, wedding bands and receptions...." ...the young marrieds, after pretending to get jobs, prepare a budget, rent an apartment, and have a baby, end by getting a divorce. Good old life-adjustment education is not dead.[6]

"Well it finally happened! The new curriculum we have developed is the same one we gave up 15 years ago."

SOURCES FOR VERSUS

1. J.H. Plumb, "An Epoch That Started Ten Thousand Years Ago Is Ending....," *Horizon*, Summer 1972.

2. A student writing in *Chicory: Young Voices from the Black Ghetto*, ed. by Sam Cornish and Lucian W. Dixon (New York: Association Press, 1969).

3. John Gardner, former U.S. Commissioner of Education, speaking in the film *Make a Mighty Reach*, National Education Association, 1966.

4. Wendell Barry, *The Last Updated Whole Earth Catalog* (Baltimore: Penquin Books, Inc., 1975).

5. Paul G. Edwards, "Virginia Wants Diploma Link to Reading, Writing, Arithmetic," *The Washington Post*, 4 October 1975.

6. *Council for Basic Education Bulletin*, October 1974.
7. Ford Button, *Today's Education*, September–October 1975.

Judgments: Galatea or the Monster?

Preceding sections have considered issues regarding "the need to create something different" and efforts that have been made to reorganize already existing schooling, as well as efforts to start anew. In this section, an array of commentators offer their conclusions about ideas, programs, and movements that have served to create change. While judgments offered range from aye to nay, with room in the middle for a little of both, the discussion that emerges is both lively and thoughtful.

Once more, the *Versus* page presents some contrasting and provocative ideas that may help you to generate pertinent discussion prior to reading the articles. To what extent do you agree with your classmates, for example, about items one, four, and five? What's wrong, if anything, with the course described in number six? Discuss the validity of the cartoon's statement with teachers who have worked in schools for a number of years.

As you read, it may be helpful to make an imaginary lineup of opposing writers. If you could assemble them in person for a debate, on whose team would you want to be a member? What judgments would you add to the ones already presented here? Sidney Hook, Jonathan Kozol, B.F. Skinner, Mortimer Smith, and Robert F. Havighurst have written widely in the field of education—presenting both theory and relating practical experiences. It would be wise, as a potential or practicing educator, to be familiar with their writings since their varied philosophical positions usually are represented by some members of any school's community. An examination of their views—regardless of persuasion—will also assist you in clarifying the philosophy governing your own teaching approach.

The annotated bibliography concluding the section can be helpful in further evaluating judgments made by the experts represented here. How many of the references in all the bibliographies of this book would you be interested in adding to your own professional library? What books already known to you would you want nearby for ready reference or inspiration?

As you examine the article titles and the excerpts that precede each selection, what overall ideas do you formulate about the content of the section? Do the excerpts elicit positive or negative reactions from you? Can you be specific about why you feel a certain way? Leafing back through the entire book, in what way do you see the titles and excerpts as expressing a range of opinions about the nature of education? If you were to write an article putting forth your attitudes toward alternative schooling, what would one good quote or excerpt from your article be?

As you read this concluding section, some questions that may be helpful are:

- To what extent do schools *really* effect the lives of students?
- Beyond the basics, are twelve or thirteen years of schooling necessary for most people?
- What merit is there in "continuing education" throughout life?
- If you had it all to do over again, what form of schooling would you select for yourself?
- If you have children, what type of school would you like them to attend?

Returning to the first *Versus* of the book, page 1, you will find excerpts from the stories of Pygmalion and Frankenstein which suggest comparisons between these tales and educators' efforts to find alternatives in schooling. You may recall that once Pygmalion's statue of Galatea was brought to life, the two lived "happily ever after," and that, after wreaking much havoc in the lives of all he encountered, Dr. Frankenstein's monster was destroyed. After reading the articles in this text and relating the viewpoints expressed to your knowledge of alternatives, what word do you predict will be used most often in the future to pass judgment on alternative schooling: "Galatea" or "monster"?

*"The school will not achieve a changed
society when nothing around it changes."*

Examine Greer's comments in relation to
those of Robert Havighurst in "Requirements for a Valid 'New Criticism' " (Section Three) and of Neil Postman and
Charles Weingartner in "A History of the
Hollering" (Section One).

Romanticism, Rheumatism, and Public Education

Colin Greer

"It is, no doubt, impossible to prevent his praying," Screwtape advises his
nephew, the junior devil Wormwood, "but we have means of rendering the
prayers innocuous. Make sure," the senior devil cautions, "that they are always
very 'spiritual,' that he is always concerned with the state of her soul and never
with her rheumatism."[1] From C.S. Lewis to Jonathan Kozol and Herbert Kohl,
an expanding core of writer-teachers are telling "the way it spozed to be."[2]

This is by no means to impugn the honesty of what has become a new literary
genre in America nor to demean what Frank Jennings calls the "moral nerve"
they lay so bare; it is rather to complain that too often these first hand, often
moving descriptions of the oppression and irrelevance of the public schools tend
simply to set the writer apart from his colleagues and fail to confront "the abid-
ing problems of the urban schools." These works are not simply the memoirs of a
teaching career as was *Up the Down Staircase,* some six years ago; they are the
work of men who were all, to some degree, writers before their books on schools
were published. They are pointedly critical and self-exonerating in the face of
well-known failure in the process of public education and among the people who

Reprinted by permission of the publisher from Colin Greer, *Cobweb Attitudes* (New
York: Teachers College Press, copyright 1970 by Teachers College, Columbia University),
pp. 21–30.

Colin Greer is the author of *The Great School Legend: A Revisionist Interpretation of
American Public Education.* He is Director of the University Without Walls in City University of New York and is senior editor of *Social Policy.*

173

work within it. This body of literature has popularly established the chronic breakdown in public education across the nation, but it does little for the rheumatism in the bones, and tends to sanctify wholesale condemnations of professional educators as though this were indeed your creaking joint.

To say, as Edgar Friedenberg has in reviewing some of this literature, that the nation's schools are being run by people without "good intentions" is the unfortunate but logical conclusion of these works. Teachers are neatly bundled together and made the collective scapegoats for the troubles of the city. Kozol is anxious to accuse his former colleagues of racism without softening the charge with any mention of the teachers' subjection tŏ, or responsiveness to the multiple pressures being brought to bear on the schools. This is the logic which permits the firing of New York teachers on vague charges. It is the logic which, again in New York City, disguises the futility of a two-week postponement of school in order to quick-train slum area teachers with the pretense that there existed dependable knowledge of what was necessary, or that a teacher retrained in a two-week program guaranteed improved pupil performance. This wonderfully simple solution offers an attractive explanation for school success and school failure but places a burden on teacher potency way beyond any demonstrable data yet acquired through manifold analyses of the complex problems of urban education.

Tried and tested in pushing most middle-class children (and the exceptions from lower down the ladder) from grade to grade, and on to college, city school systems have not been nearly so efficacious for the greater part of the urban mass. In the hitherto middle-class, high-achieving schools, a general increase in the free lunch program has invariably gone hand in hand with diminished levels of school performance. High mobility, language difficulty, and low income, impediments in negotiating the complexities of urban life which have always warranted a helping hand, now become gigantic obstacles to the establishment of school success in a society rapidly discarding muscle power for brain power. Puerto Ricans, Poles, Italians, Israelis, Haitians, recent decades' arrivals to the nation's cities and the remainder of earlier ones, perform a notch or two less well, are a degree or two less motivated, and will do increasingly less well in society given existing opportunities. Among these poor one finds, too, a body of the more pathologically poor—the "under-class," as Gunnar Myrdal calls them—who often get lost in the national bookkeeping which is particularly and belatedly sensitive to Negro deprivation. To neighboring communities, as well as to those individuals who come in to help, these people warrant a level of scorn, abuse, and pity, which cuts right across the heterogeneity of component ethnic parts. School personnel record daily, with varying degrees of frustration, the high correlation between abject school failure and environmental despair.

While it is true that in some cities the educational apparatus can still be characterized by the "semi-barbarism" Superintendent of Schools Maxwell found in New York at the turn of the century, in all cities public education faces the contemporary challenge of different rates of change in school and society, and an unprecedented need to succeed with those it has traditionally failed to teach. This is not to offer a bland whitewash for the nation's teachers. Most assuredly there are teachers who have no right to have the intellectual growth, or even physical care, of children entrusted to them; but there are also those, in unfortunately underestimated numbers, I believe, who are dedicated to this task.

As a profession numbering millions, they are representative of all that goes to make up this nation, urban and rural. Buck passing is a tradition in public education, it has run and re-run the gamut from *awful* pupils and *awful* teachers to *awful* parents and *awful* finances; one, two, all, and more of these factors have been held blameworthy at least since 1900. We can readily accept that dedication on the part of less than all teachers is not enough, that dedication to teaching is not the only reason men and women enter the profession (there are teachers honest enough to admit they don't like students), and that the narrow vision of political and economic pressure determines our direction and our path: but by the same criteria these writers are indicted too.

Even when Kozol describes the gross inhumanity displayed by some horrific figure with rattan in hand, we read only of the occurrence, never of the battle against the legitimacy of such procedures. To be fired for reading a poem does nothing for the questions at issue, and only emphasizes the bind in which the most well-meaning may be caught. Similarly, the presumption that depicts Kohl doing what other teachers cannot do with the brightest class in the grade is neither a reason for blaming later failure on other teachers, nor for quitting the field oneself. It is not a convincing reason for quitting, but a quite understandable one, and that again is the bind, is it not? How, in fact, can we keep the talent which is the master teacher in the classroom?

I am uneasy with glib slurs against colleagues unless the slurs are presented in the true muckracking tradition—as the spearhead to amelioration through exposure of the evil. But what is the evil here, beyond the "death at an early age" maxim? There are no labor laws to be passed, no tenements to be reconstructed in response to the complaint. Unless Kozol and Kohl are the answers, packagable and marketable, (and one sincerely feels for the work with *36 Children*) we have been told little more than that the structures of public education in the nation's cities are consistently failing to reach the Negro child in the ghetto slum, and that someone should do something about that and about the brutality some teachers perpetrate on their pupils.

We are not, however, told of the classroom teacher who has been teaching for three years in the ghetto school; we are not told of the teacher who offers gifts to pupils who come poorly clothed and hungry; who loves some of the children who come unloved and washes some of those who come unbathed and smelling badly. Nor are we told of the teacher who cannot get more than four pairs of scissors or enough paper to aid in her efforts to make the day brighter even if reading does not always follow. The indictment somehow neglects the fact that other teachers reach pupils too, they know defeat and victory year after year, and the system does not reserve its punishments for Negro children alone. Teachers generally, and pupils generally, "die" a little every day, and they "die" a little more with every year. So, too, do the principals and their assistants, the men and women I met in three months of interviewing and observation: they do not all breathe flames at their students, though there are those who do, and they are not all rude and disrespectful to parents. There are those whose office door is ever open, and who keep a supply of warm winter clothes for the needy.

This concept of charity may be outmoded and even useless in the face of huge societal anomalies, but still, these are the people who cry for the pain of their children, and their spirit will be needed, whatever the design of our solutions. These are the men and women from whom Bayard Rustin asked understanding in the daily confrontation with frustration and aggression. He predicted that urban violence will be most directly aimed against the teacher because "there is no economic dependence on him." In the final analysis, however, it is the dignity and self-respect of the teacher, or the lack of it, which will set the tone for the classroom experience and the relationship between school and community. Whether the educator is Negro or white, he will be equally susceptible to bureaucratization and equally frustrated by failure. The question of racism is real because it is real in American society, but the problem in the classroom does not begin or even end there.

As early as 1928, in his presidential address to the Progressive Education Association, John Dewey chastised his fellow educators for destroying better than they built. At another Progressive Education Association conference four years later George Counts found Progressive Educators "fundamentally, realistically, and positively" unprepared to deal with the American social situation because they were on the whole, "romantic sentimentalists" with no elaborated theory of social welfare. Dewey agreed with Counts on the need for changes in education "departing from present educational procedures very widely." In fact, "a revolution from top to bottom" would have to follow any attempt to take account of the constantly readjusting "mobile phases" of contemporary culture.

"We are entering a new world" said William Russell of Teachers College, Columbia University, "the world of the machine age." It was the Depression which finally confirmed these theorists in their belief that education in the form of public schooling must free itself from its dependence on the ethic of rugged individualism. In Counts' view, it was this middle-class ethos which branded the thinking and defeated the hope for change among traditional and Progressive educators alike. The relationship between socio-economic status and school achievement confirmed by dozens of studies in the following decades attested to what these men perceived. More and more, the breakdown of economic relevance for the public school in the slum, as it became an increasingly long stopover in the cycle of poverty, required special attention. President Hoover's White House Conference on Child Health and Protection considered the large numbers of students who were totally missed by the educational process; but in the major cities, meanwhile, schoolmen still faced ever new urgencies with drastically inadequate funds.

Study after urban study from the 1920's on mourned the inability of public education to reduce the high rates of school drop-outs and school failure in the "less favored" parts of the city. As time went on, the lament increased in frequency as in urgency, taking on a racial and thereby more morally inspired aspect, but school failure remained much more tolerantly distributed among black and white school children. It was, in fact, the emphasis on failing children which Counts considered so middle-class in its orientation. According to him, it was not that the children of the poor did not need to have education made more relevant to their lives but that the problems lay not so much in deficiencies among poor children which impeded school learning but were rooted in education as a public institution. School did little to benefit the more favored school child. The retained and the successful pupil prospered in spite of, rather than because of, school attendance. Economic demands generally determined the changing average in school-leaving age, not school attractiveness, and success came as a result of pupil motivation and natural ability. Dean McConn of Lehigh told a Rollins College Conference in the early 1930's that "good" public education in America was attained largely "by accident." Constance Warren, President of Sarah Lawrence, remembered the teaching she had experienced through school to have been of the "stupidest." Educators at the conference generally agreed that American education, at the public school and college levels, more than deserved this chastisement because it had totally failed to "foster a hunger and an interest in knowledge." Students with such motivation learned in spite of the school, although many suffered through the limitations imposed by it. The school was a relatively useless instrument for those who seriously needed its mediation, and the bright pupil got precious little stimulation from it.

In this setting teachers were rather like immigration inspectors at Ellis Island before whom new arrivals were docile and quiet, afraid to offend those on whose decisions their future depended. Those who learned well, learned by themselves—the school merely broadened their vocabularies, so to speak. Evaluative studies have been eloquent in describing the extent to which the poor were denied privileges in school and society but progress in modifying the disadvantaged has in no way challenged the market for such studies. Very little progress has been made toward the development of professional skills in line with the gaping needs which exist. The kinds of new questions which are necessary for changing understanding and expectation of school success in ways which will deal ethically and with promise for those whose opportunities are severely limited by their capacities have hardly begun to be asked. There are less bright and even stupid people, just as there are ugly people, all of whom deserve access to the good life without classification on new levels of social undesirability and abberation. Meantime, the racial and ethnic biases through which all social considerations are approached make it impossible to deal with these far more radical issues.

There has been a great deal of talk about bringing the city into the classroom and the need to promote the freedom to learn in a society so fraught with rapidly changing skill needs and so desperate for changes in the structure of society itself, but there has been little progress in providing school practitioners with relevant procedure to draw upon. Teacher training institutions must be held guilty for the "careerist ambition" which Theodore Roszak finds in the "academy." "Small scale research backed up large scale grants" has welcomed public response to the discussion of public education with defensible, unimaginative programs.[3] Reading progress has become the most sought-after measure of school performance as the sociology of education was "transformed from social ideology to an empirical science," as the Harvard School of Education bulletin proudly notes. But such scores remain largely a measure of school performance under the pressure of public demands. This too often leads to an intensification of the drilling which takes place in many a classroom caught in the thrall of the "success society" and the "Ph.D octopus" which William James and Veblen feared were stifling imagination and passion among teachers and pupils alike. The product orientation of the educational process, with its demand for delayed gratification, readily acknowledged as totally outside the framework of the less than middle-class, perpetuates the overall failure to make the process itself a meaningful daily experience. One should not, for instance, have to mortgage ten years in order to become a doctor because that is the point at which a "real" living can be earned but rather one should be aware of satisfaction, of being now, all along the way. Meanwhile many a lower class child drops out of school and the middle-class child from college. Together with the retained pupil, they combine to reinforce the schema while educators aspire to knowing how to teach the revered savings bank quality, deferred gratification.

It is the same line of ignorance and concern which links Dewey's *How We Think* in 1910 with John Holt's *How Children Fail* and *How Children Learn* in the 1960's. Indeed, Holt too has taken the position "that our 'best' schools, whether urban or suburban, public or private, are no good."[4] It is the subject of more popular urgency now, because at the height of national prosperity, it is no longer even tenable to confirm the highly selective, highly competitive economic system to which Ellis Island led.

Holt's complaint, shared and vigorously expressed by Edgar Friedenberg and Paul Goodman, has to be differentiated from the general criticism of the writer-teacher discussed in the first part of this chapter. Holt's attack is broadly-based and looks to freeing the schools from "old ways" which impede innovation and flexibility. This is a child-centered attack, sympathetic to the pain of the socially oppressed, but primarily concerned with the oppressed individual in the classroom and the quality of society itself, not the redistribution of social privilege. Not content with the application of psychological and sociological labels to explain the plight of the Negro poor, or even of the poor in general, these men are concerned with the high divorce rate, juvenile delinquency, and moral inertia in the prosperous suburbs which seem to go hand in hand with the extreme competitiveness which is a criterion of normalcy in modern psychology, treading an uneasy line between the child guidance center and childhood pleasure.

In a sense these men have gone to the heart of the problems of public education: it simply does not work, neither as a mechanism for instruction nor as a challenge to the established order of poverty and affluence. But American schools will continue to be open as long as they succeed in fulfilling those unspoken purposes by which the nation has traditionally defined public schooling. There has been a cleavage between education and public schooling in the United States closely analogous to the "classic cleavage between industry and business": that

Max Lerner finds in Veblen's economic thought.[5] In both instances, the latter force imposes a pecuniary value on the former. Its role in the body of national institutions has led to the sabotage of education conceived in terms of the individual and his potential and of culture in the sense of cultivation and growth, the agricultural origin of the word. It has stood against inordinate and insufficient productivity by keeping its confirmation of abilities highly selective. If the ends and means of public education are antiquated now that public schooling from elementary school through university monopolizes wider opportunies, if this is really a period of transition (a comfortable cushion of a phrase for a great many), it does not by any means follow that out of the transition will come a system defined by different purposes. "What we believe," writes E.B. Castle, "determines what and how we teach."[6] Although it presents as many ethical problems as it answers, it is a sobering reflection on the good intentions of American educators to note that in Russian and indeed in Jesuit schools, a deliberate effort is made to teach the child through concrete experience and uniform method the values and behaviors most consistent with Communist or Catholic ideals.

The version of society characterized by American public schooling is one on which the individual proceeds up the social hierarchy by himself. Public schooling is the apparatus by which the ladder is scaled. In such a system, the very expansion of prosperity which it has gradually permitted creates different rates of change. The functional relation of proletarian groups in school and in society is no longer relevant but at the same time the experience of rising in the lower classes has been missed by those caught at the bottom in the change from a "functional" to "an acquisitive" society. "The conscious need to learn...is not easily imposed in anyone" Raymond Williams maintains. He argues that if we view public schooling as a medium of mass communication and understand that communication depends on common experience we can then appreciate that the communication is only confounded when it encounters a contradictory, formulated experience. We have become hamstrung on the process of transmission and are only just beginning to give consideration to the levels and elements of shared experience which promote learning in the middle-class child.[7]

In effect, our problems exist in the image of the ladder itself. The poverty which is so much a part of the nation's affluence testifies to the fact that we do not know how to force people, by a system which has produced defensive vested interests, up a ladder built to take a few at a time. While automation and cybernation might increase numbers among the upwardly mobile, the "acquisitive" society will continue to take its heavy toll. As we replace a hierarchy of birth and money with a hierarchy of merit, poverty (albeit benign in comparison to poverty in Bombay) will retain its partnership with affluence. Job training programs make one very dubious as to the potential employment benefit obtained from the temporary care-taking of the less fortunate members of society—a society for the description of which de Tocqueville coined the word "individualism."

The arena of public debate has been used to distort seriously the place of the school as an instrument of change. Misleading predictions surround the discussion, mindless of G.B. Shaw's challenging remark that "there is no way out through the school master," and mindless of the relatively inconsequential place of the school in the truly critical problems of our time—nuclear survival, racial prejudice, and poverty. The school will not achieve a changed society when nothing around it changes. If the "schools are accountable" as numbers of schoolmen have believed, it is only to the extent that problems may be approached through the school. The questions of reading, delinquency, and school withdrawal are the immediate questions the school must face up to. And it can do so only if it is sensitive to the fact that children are the objects around which the debate is raging.

The complexity intrinsic to such child-centered procedures as individualized instruction and the freedom to learn are quite unresolved in the present rediscovery of them. Atrophy in so-called experimental schools, and paralysis in the public institutional set-up, promote only studies of and extended critiques of the inadequacy. Contemporary concepts such as individual growth, spontaneous creativity and learning how to learn as a force in the classroom would represent more than a change in educational know-how, they would have to go hand in hand with a radical change in the values of society itself. This brand of egalitarianism has, with a few exceptions, been diffused into the well-wishing but intensely pragmatic affluence of an expanding middle-class America; an America which hides its homework as though knowledge were merely a possession to be guarded jealously. This is the rheumatism which has rendered well-intentioned changes in administrative structure innocuous. Grandiose programs and hardware have generally brought more of the same, ensuring that more of the same will result at the end of the educational process.

As universal public schooling adds more and more years to minimum required attendance, so higher education, too, has become an integral part of the joint popularization-standardization process. Ironically, "school" is an American idiom for college. The compulsion escalator (the hard core of popularization) requires school attendance, it does not require school success. As a result, new proletarians have had more years of schooling than ever but the phenomenal rates of failure they used to sustain at the elementary school level have been shifted to the high school and college levels where the familiar forty to sixty per cent of all entrants fall behind, fail, and drop out.

And yet even if it were true that children from all classes benefitted instructionally from public education this would not necessarily do anything to diminish the inequalities of either economic class or social status distinctions between groups. Whatever the benefits for the odd individuals, schooling heightens the inequalities as it becomes more efficient in monopolizing the selection of winners and losers. The United States Office of Education is now considering possible contracts with large companies such as IBM to act in the name of public education and transmit the skills required by their expanding enterprise. Such efforts might well succeed in reaching larger numbers of the disadvantaged. But having reached them says nothing about the readiness to pump them into the economy or how else the relative differences in social and economic standing will be reflected. In the formal education process the machine may teach reading; even tampering with reading scores might replace failure with success if that was simply what was needed. But would there be, as Friedenberg fears, "unemployed IBM operators and technicians hanging around, the way India and Africa have lawyers?"[8]

The contradition I have discussed, the cleavage between education as public schooling and education as a regenerative agent is fundamentally the root of the problem. It is this contradiction which leaves social scientists and educators locked into a knowledge base originating in socio-economic relations, reducing them to paralysis in the search to do things differently. Despite their notions of personal growth, affective expression, and individual human potential as criteria of effective action, they do not have the slightest inkling as to how public education can contribute to the creation of a better future society. This monumental ignorance notwithstanding, however, they look to smaller and larger bureaucracies, more and less poverty—the same old questions hiding the same old priorities—for solutions to social problems through the school with a surprising freedom from the realization that theirs is basically a subservient institution which is in business primarily to protect people against each other according to a hierarchy established elsewhere in the pluralistic society. How then can the essentially negative content of schooling in and for a divided society be restructed while continuing to be functional for the existing society? Only when the divisiveness itself is no longer functional can this happen.

NOTES

1. C.S. Lewis, *The Screwtape Letters* (New York: Macmillan, 1943).

2. Jonathan Kozol, *Death at an Early Age* (Boston: Houghton Mifflin, 1968); Herbert Kohl, *36 Children* (New York: New American Library, 1968); J. Herndon, *The Way It Spozed to Be* (New York: Simon & Schuster, 1969).

3. "On Academic Delinquency," in Theodore Roszak, ed., *The Dissenting Academy* (New York: Pantheon Books, 1968).

4. John Holt, *How Children Fail* (New York: Pitman, 1964).

5. Max Lerner, *The Portable Veblen* (New York: Viking Press, 1958).

6. E.B. Castle, *Ancient Education and Today* (London: Penguin Books, 1961).

7. R. Williams, *Culture and Society, 1780-1950* (London: Pelican Books, 1966). Describes "ladder" and "communication transmission" in his conclusion.

8. Edgar Z. Friedenberg, "An Ideology of School Withdrawal" in Daniel Schreiber, ed., *Profile of the School Dropout* (New York: Vintage Books, 1968).

■ Assume and defend a position regarding Greer's contention that the schools are, and will continue to be, viewed as rungs on the success ladder rather than revolutionary in impact.

- What are the implications of the words "romanticism" and "rheumatism" in the title of this article?

- Greer takes exception to the arguments of writers such as Kozol, Kohl, and Herndon who imply, according to Greer, that there are no humane and effective teachers and administrators in the public schools. What instances, personal or vicarious, can you enumerate to support Greer's indications that "good" individuals and programs exist?

- In what ways has your education to date fostered a "hunger [for] and an interest in knowledge"?

*"...the moral failings of the professed
followers of Dewey are graver than those
of his critics...."*

Read B.F. Skinner's "The Free and Happy
Student" and Robert Havighurst's "Requirements for a Valid 'New Criticism' "
(both in Section Three) for ideas related to
this article.

How the Insurgents Misinterpret Dewey
Sidney Hook

During the last few years there has been an open season on the American school system from the most elementary to advanced levels. It has been indicted not only for its failure to teach the rudiments of the traditional disciplines, but for its repressive attitude towards the spontaneous activities and the outreaching natural curiosity of the child and student as learning animals. The schools have been compared to penal institutions not only because of the physical conditions that exist in some ghetto areas but even more so because of the manner, spirit and methods of instruction.

Such criticism comes from those who regard themselves as libertarians and humanists and who either profess themselves inspired to some degree by the thought of John Dewey or are commonly regarded as continuing his influ-ence—writers like Paul Goodman, Ivan Illich, John Holt, Jonathan Kozol, George Dennison, Edgar Friedenberg, George Leonard. Their criticisms are exer-

Sidney Hook, "How the Insurgents Misinterpret Dewey," *Change Magazine* **3**, no. 7 (November 1971). Reprinted by permission of *Change Magazine*, NBW Tower, New Rochelle, New York 10801.

Sidney Hook's educational experiences are wide-ranging: he has been a secondary-school teacher, a college instructor, a lecturer, and a professor of philosophy. He is head of the department of philosophy at New York University. Dr. Hook has been a Guggenheim Fellow and a fellow of the Academy of Arts and Sciences and of the National Academy of Education. His books include *The Paradoxes of Freedom; John Dewey: Myths and Democracy; The Metaphysics of Pragmatism;* and *Education for Modern Man.*

cising a surprising influence on educators and teachers: they are partly responsible for a phenomenon observable in liberal arts colleges from one end of the
country to another, viz., the abandonment of required courses and even area
distribution studies as unendurable forms of faculty paternalism and violations
of the "student's autonomy, his moral freedom and responsibility." Since the
student, in this conception, is the best judge of his own educational needs, it is a
tyrannical imposition from without to require him to take any courses that he
thinks he does not need.

I am concerned here with the ways in which such views misinterpret the
thought of John Dewey. It is an open question whether Dewey's educational
philosophy has been more flagrantly distorted in the accounts given of it by some
of his latter-day disciples than by the criticisms of his vociferous detractors. Both,
it seems to me, have been intellectually irresponsible in disregarding his plain and
easily available texts. But the moral failings of the professed followers of Dewey
are graver than those of his critics: first, by the very virtue of their allegiance,
which should impose a greater conscientiousness upon them, and second, because
the fundamentalist critics of Dewey have as a rule seized upon their formulations,
as professed followers of Dewey, as evidence of the validity of their fundamentalist reading of him.

NEED FOR AUTHORITY

The first misconception of John Dewey's philosophy stems from the notion that
because he stressed the importance of freedom, he was therefore opposed to
authority. Nothing could be farther removed from his true teaching. "The need
for authority," he wrote, "is a constant need of man." (*Problems of Men,* p.
169) It is a constant need because conflicts, differences, incompatible desires, perspectives and possibilities are ever-present features of existence and experience.
Some authority is therefore necessary, and for Dewey the supreme authority is intelligence. It is "the method of intelligence, exemplified in [but not identical with]
science, [that should be] supreme in education." (*Experience and Education*, p.
100) Intelligence recognizes that not all forms of conduct are possible or
desirable, that restriction and negation are as central to any discipline as affirma-
tion and that the growth which prepares the way for further desirable growth can
be achieved only through a limitation of possibilities. Freedom outside the context of the authority of intelligence is the license of anarchy. The democratic idea
of freedom, Dewey tells us again and again, is not the right of each individual to
do as he pleases; instead the "basic freedom is that of freedom of mind and of
whatever degree of freedom of action and experience is necessary to produce freedom of intelligence," (*Problems of Men*, p. 61).

The second misconception of Dewey's philosophy—one more fateful because of its educational corollaries—is the equation drawn between education
and experience. From this equation it is inferred that experience itself is educative, and that any series of experiences—the more direct and dynamic the better—can be substituted for formal schooling, which is often disparaged as an

artificial experience. Experiences of travel and living away from school are often considered as appropriate substitutes for study. In short, *having* an experience is identified with knowing or understanding it.

Dewey, however, makes a central distinction between experiences that are "educative" and experiences that are "non-educative" or "mis-educative." The first are those that result in increased power and growth, in informed conviction, and sympathetic attitudes of understanding, in learning how to face and meet new experiences with some sense of mastery, without fear or panic or relying on the treadmill of blind routine. The second may give excitement but not genuine insight, may result in a mechanical training or conditioning that incapacitates individuals when the situations encountered in life change and must be met by intelligent improvision.

But is it not true, some critics counter, that Dewey believes that we learn by doing? And does not that mean that anything a child or student desires or decides to do inside or out of schools is *ipso facto* educational? No, emphatically, no! Doing is part of learning only when it is directed by ideas which the doing tests. Doing in Dewey's sense is the experimenting that is guided by an hypothesis, not the blind action that never reaches the level of an experiment. It is true that we learn by doing: it is not true that all doing is a form of learning.

CURRICULAR ABUSE

The fallacy that converts Dewey's statement that "all genuine education comes about through experience" into the belief that "all experiences are genuinely educational" is reflected today in two kinds of curricular abuse in our liberal arts colleges. The first is the tendency to assume that any subject matter is as good as any other subject matter for educational purposes and that all intellectual standards or hierarchies or grades of achievement and excellence merely reflect traditional prejudices that must be swept aside from the standpoint of the egalitarian ethic of a democratic education. This is a point of view held unfortunately not only by students eager to reform or reconstitute the curriculum but by some members of the faculty. One recent college reader titled *Starting Over*, apparently making a fresh start to get away from the prejudices, of the past, declares in its preface to these selected readings: "We don't rule out the possibility that Lenny Bruce may have more to teach us than Alfred North Whitehead." They do not indicate *what* we can learn from Lenny Bruce that is of such moment that it dwarfs the many things that one can learn from Whitehead. Dewey, on the other hand, insists that "the central problem of an education based on experience is to select the kind of present experiences that live fruitfully and creatively in subsequent experiences." (*Experience and Education,* p. 17)

Dewey has two basic principles which still provide the direction for continued criticism not only of existing practices but of any proposed reforms: first, an equal concern that *all* children in the community develop themselves by appropriate schooling to the full reach of their powers and growth as persons; and second, a reliance upon the best available scientific methods in the psychology of learning to discover the means, methods and materials by which this growth can best be achieved in the case of each individual child.

It should be obvious how absurd it is to attribute to Dewey a belief that only the child is important in the teaching process and not the subject matters that he is taught, and that therefore it is relatively unimportant what he is taught or what his present experiences are so long as they are enjoyed. What Dewey is saying simply is that unless we take into account that "powers and purposes of those taught," their needs, capacities, attention spans and related phenomena, we cannot rely on the alleged inherent education value of any subject to become meaningfully acquired in the child's present experience. Enjoyment, of course, is an aid, not a drawback to learning, but it should come from interest and growing absorption in the tasks and problems to be mastered. He does not believe we can substitute for a sound psychology of learning a set of hunches, intuitions and impressionistic anecdotal accounts of what has occurred in teaching highly selected children in special circumstances without any objective controls. But the latter constitute the stock in trade of much of the recent writing of our school critics, who totally disregard the danger of extrapolating techniques and methods from episodic learning situations to a public school system that must provide structured and sequential courses of study.

Their familiar assertion that because children learn to speak and walk without formal schooling they can learn almost anything else they need to know in the same way, is evidence of how dogma can put out the eyes of common sense. It is not even true in most cases for learning how to read and write, divide and multiply. There are some skills which if not acquired when young by formal schooling are rarely completely mastered in later years.

The greatest damage of the new dogmas that equate experience and education is apparent not only in what students are offered in the way of courses, and materials within courses, but what they are often permitted to do in fulfillment of their academic responsibilities. Much of this is covered by the euphemisms of "field work" or "independent study." These must be sharply distinguished from the clinical experience that is essential to the acquisition of knowledge and skills in many scholarly and professional areas. Genuine clinical experience is related to a definite body of knowledge or set of techniques that the student tests or applies in concrete situations continuous with those he will subsequently face; it is carefully supervised, the student's progress checked and evaluated so that he knows in what direction to continue. "Field work" today often means no field except what the student professes an interest in, and work means whatever he chooses to do.

"CREATIVE CANDLE-MAKING"

The *New York Times* (April 26, 1971) revealed the kind of "field work" done at the New York State University College at Old Westbury under the presidency of Harris Wofford. According to this uncontested report, the independent study which students were allowed to pursue embraced:

"Almost any project that was neither illegal nor hazardous. Among selected topics were 'Migrant Camps and Workers,' 'Liberation of the Ghetto Through Economics,' 'Film Study,' 'Guitar—Country Blues,' 'The Craft of Sewing'. . .One student's project was called 'Creative Candle-Making—learning how to (appreciate) and making candles.' The professor's role in this five credit project was 'to look at my candles when I make them and receive several as gifts'. . .The project of one woman student, for five credits, was called 'Poetry of Life.' Her project description reads as follows: 'Now I hear beautiful music. Then I paint, a mind picture. Later I walk in the wood. Reverently I study my wood, know it. Converse with a poet meaningful to me'."

These oddities undoubtedly are not representative of all institutions that offer "field work," although the chief architect of this curriculum was rewarded by being offered a post at a more prestigious educational institution. But Old Westbury marks a growing tendency to substitute a period of mere lived experience for a period of academic study. Unless undertaken in connection with a structured course of study and intelligently supervised by faculty it would be far better to terminate academic study at the point where the student is ready "to do his own thing," and hopefully earn his own living.

The issues I am discussing are raised in a fundamental way when any general requirements are proposed for educational institutions. The new critics of education are against all requirements on the ground that needs are personal and that students are the best judges of their educational needs. I find a threefold confusion in this point of view: the tendency to assume that, first, desire and impulse are synonymous with need; second, when not synonymous, desire is an unfailing index of need; and third, because needs are personal, they are unique and necessarily subjective.

- Impulse and desire may sometimes be an expression of need, and desire is often a consequence of frustrated impulse. But our common experience shows that we sometimes desire things we don't need and that we sometimes, especially in an educational context, discover what we really need only when we have ascertained what our purposes are. One may need to acquire certain skills and knowledge in order to achieve a purpose. Therefore, as Dewey put it, "the crucial educational problem is that of procuring the postponement of immediate action upon desire until observation and judgment have intervened." (*Education & Experience*, p. 81). Like Hume, Dewey believes that desires are the ultimate moving springs of action, but unlike Hume, he holds that we need not be enslaved by our desires, that they can be governed, modified, sublimated.

- If this is true, desire is not always an unfailing index of genuine need. It depends on how and when the desire is expressed and whether our intelligence has disclosed the price to be paid in present and future for acting on it.

- Finally, even if it is true that human needs are personal and individual, it doesn't follow that the student is the best judge of them or is even always aware of the needs required by his purposes. One can draw an analogy here with the medical needs a person has who wishes to live a healthy life. It does not follow that because they are *his* needs, they may not also be common to others. Nor does it follow that he necessarily is the best judge of them. They are objective needs even if they are personal needs, and the physician is usually the better judge of them than the patient.

Let us apply this to the educational scene, particularly since the new progressive critics of education encourage the present student generation to assert itself against its "exploiters." Students demand the right to select their own courses on every level, and with a kind of democratic belligerence inquire: "Who are *you* to tell me, a grown person of 16 or 18 years of age, what my educational needs are? How can you prate about democracy in education? After all, I am neither an infant nor an idiot!" To which I believe we can reasonably answer:

"We are qualified, professional educators who have been studying the educational needs of our students and our culture for many years. We gladly indicate what we believe your educational needs are and are prepared to set forth the grounds on which we select them, inviting your critical response. For example, we believe that you and your fellow students have a need to communicate clearly and effectively, to acquire a command of your own language oral and written, no matter what your subsequent educational experience or career will be. You have that need whether you are presently aware of it or not. We believe you have a need to understand the essentials concerning the nature of your own bodies and mind, for what you don't know about these matters—as the current drug culture indicates—may hurt you, even kill you. Again, we believe that you have a need to understand something of the history of your own society, the political and economic forces shaping its future—all the more so because you have already indicated that you are aflame with reformist and revolutionary zeal to alter society.

"Surely you must understand the conditioning social, political, and technological factors of any social change that hopes to improve on the past. Your unwillingness to learn about these crucial matters would cast doubts on the sincerity of your professions. It was Karl Marx who pointed out to William Weitling that ignorance is not a revolutionary virtue. We believe that you have other intellectual needs that are requisite to the proper, performance of your function as a citizen, especially now that you are or will soon be of voting age. These needs you have in common with all other students, and the courses we require are those designed to meet them. We welcome your suggestions. Of course, you have other educational needs that are not common but personal and reflect your own special aptitudes, interests and aspirations. Here we are prepared to guide you, and help you fashion your own educational purposes and curriculum. Gradually you must take complete responsibility for your own education. When you do, your decisions are more likely to be sensible if they are informed."

Most of the criticisms the new progressive critics make of the educational establishment have been launched from what they declare to be democratic and humanist premises. I want to say a few things about the roles proposed for students and teachers in the democratic reconstitution of institutions of higher learning. Does a commitment to democracy require or justify the recent demands that students have almost as great an influence as the faculty in deciding the curriculum and operating the university?

POLITICAL DEMOCRACY

We must make some crucial distinctions. In the first instance democracy is a political concept. In a political democracy, however, it does not follow that all the major social institutions can or should be run on politically democratic lines according to which each individual counts for one and no more than one, and where a numerical majority makes a decision that binds the entire community. In a political democracy the army, the church, the museum, the orchestra, the family and the school cannot be organized in a *politically* democratic manner if these institutions are to perform their proper specific functions. There is, to be sure, a sense in which we can speak of a democratic family, of a democratic army, orchestra or university. This is the moral sense. This requires in the family, for example, not that children have an equal vote on all questions affecting them but that they be treated with respect, listened to, given rational answers to their questions and not humiliated by arbitrary decisions. In a school or university the spirit of democracy can prevail, without students functioning as citizens do in the larger political community, by devising modes of participation that will make their educational experience more meaningful and without establishing a preposterous equation of intellectual authority between the learned and the unlearned, the mature and the immature. Such an equation is never drawn between masters and apprentices in any field, and in the field of education the overwhelming majority of students, except on advanced graduate levels, cannot be realistically regarded as apprentices.

Without vesting students with educational power equal to that of the faculty, they are always to be treated as persons, always consulted, always listened to, and given responsibilities commensurate with their growth and maturity in those areas where they have competence until they can take over their own education.

This brings me finally to the role of the teacher in education. Only those unfamiliar with Dewey's work can believe that he rejects the active role of the teacher in planning the classroom experience by properly organized subject matters. The teacher must have, he writes, "a positive and leading share in the direction of the activities of the [classroom] community." (*Experience & Education*, p. 66.) Because he eschews the role of a drill master and refrains from imposing adult demands upon the growing child, the teacher's task is more difficult, requiring more intelligence and consequently more subtle and complex planning than was required in the days when pedagogues ruled with loud voice and big stick.

Some of the recent critics of education give the impression that all that is required for good teaching is a loving heart, that most courses in preparation for teaching are a waste, and that not only in teaching, but in all other vocations and professions, individuals learn best by the apprentice method or on the job. That anybody can teach something is probably true, but that anybody can become a *good* teacher merely by teaching on the job is demonstrably false. We may not be preparing teachers properly, but the remedy is not the abandonment of preparation and greater reliance upon volunteers and paraprofessionals but in the improvement of that preparation.

In assessing and selecting teachers, whatever other qualities and skills are sought, one should look for a sense of concern on the part of teachers, especially on the lower levels of instruction, and a sense of mission on all levels. By a sense of concern I mean something stronger than interest and less than affection. A teacher cannot love all children, and most children, except those that *are* genuinely preferred and loved, can see through the pretense of the profession, for they know that genuine love is disciminatory. Paul Goodman asserts that one must either love students or resent them, but this is typical of his false disjunctions. The good teacher respects all of his students, is concerned about them and recognizes his equal responsibility for the educational growth of all of them.

INDOCTRINATING ZEAL

The teacher's sense of mission is troublesome, because it can easily be transformed into an indoctrinating zeal that uses the classroom for purposes foreign to the process of learning. Dewey was unalterably opposed to indoctrination, political or otherwise. He was aware of the great social reforms and reconstructions that were necessary in order for the schools to realize the moral ideals of the democratic society, and as a citizen he was always in the forefront of the battle for reform. But all the schools could legitimately do was "to form attitudes which will express themselves in intelligent social action." This, he says, "is something very different from indoctrination" (*Problems of Men, p. 56*) *because* intelligence; alone of all virtues, is self-critical. Only those indoctrinate who are unable or unwilling to establish their conclusions by intelligent inquiry. Dewey was confident that if his views about man and society had merit they would be recognized as valid by those whom the schools—in the proper exercise of their educational function—had taught to study and deal with the social world and its problems responsibly, i.e., intelligently, scientifically, conscientiously. He would have regarded any attempt to indoctrinate students with his own doctrines and proposals as an arrant betrayal of his educational philosophy.

The effort today to politicize schools and universities from within is foolish for many reasons, the most obvious being its counter-productive character. For nothing is more likely to bring about the politicizing of the university from without, and from a perspective extremely uncongenial to that of the new progressive critics of education. In combatting this internal politicizing, one of the most formidable problems is coping with the teacher who regards his class as a staging ground for revolutionizing society or for disrupting the local community if its norms of social morality fall short of his notions of the good society. In pursuit of a political commitment, he is often led to abandon elementary principles of professional ethnics, and sometimes to deny in an apology for his political mission that any distinction can be drawn between objective teaching and indoctrination.

PARTISANS OF REVOLUTION

The following passage appears in a publication of Teachers College (*Perspectives in Education*, Fall, 1969), where John Dewey formulated the principles of education for a free society:

"It is the task of the teacher to educate—to educate for change—to educate through change. To educate for orderly planned revolution. If necessary to educate through more disruptive revolutionary action."

John Dewey would have been the first to repudiate this travesty of the role of a teacher in a free society. The task of the teacher is to educate students to their maximum growth as perceptive, informed and reflective persons so that they can decide intelligently for themselves what is to be changed, *where* and *how*. It is not the teacher's function to indoctrinate his students in behalf of any cause no matter how holy, to brainwash them into becoming partisans of revolution or counter-revolution. To declare as this teacher does—and unfortunately he is not alone—that students are to be educated for and through "disruptive revolutionary action" is to declare oneself morally and pedagogically unfit to inhabit the academy of reasoning.

John Dewey's philosophy is not understood in many of the places where he is honored as well as in many of the places he is denounced. He is not the father of permissiveness, nor the prophet of life adjustment. We can still learn from him without assuming that he said the last word about our problems in school or out. For him democracy was not merely a set of political mechanisms but a way of life in which we use all the arts of intelligence and imagination in behalf of human freedom.

- The "new" critics of the schools seek to legitimize their insurgency by alleging inspiration from John Dewey, says Sidney Hook. How does Hook take exception to this attempt to identify with Dewey?

- In what ways is Hook concerned with the simplistic extension of Dewey's belief in political democracy?

- John Dewey's writings on education should be read if you have not already done so. A panel presentation in which individuals present material directly from Dewey's books and from writers who have adapted or extended his ideas could be instructive. A final assessment should raise Hook's concern: Are the extensions simplistic? Do they "misinterpret" Dewey?

*"...it is unwise for young white teachers
to attempt to impose their version of the
counterculture upon poor children and
their families."*

Compare and contrast Kozol's remarks
with those of Mortimer Smith in "The Re-
forms Most Needed in Education" (Section
One) and of Joel Denker "Boredom,
Utopia, and 'Unprofessional Conduct' "
(Section Two).

Free Schools Fail Because They Don't Teach
Jonathan Kozol

The average life span of the free schools has been nine months. Why do they fail
so often?

Unfashionable and unromantic as it may appear, the major cause for failure
in the free schools is our unwillingness or inability to teach the hard skills.

This is the kind of square and rigorous statement that you do not often encounter in the free-school literature. It is something that we had better speak
about, however. If we do not, these schools will not survive.

In the free schools, as in the public schools, there are always a certain number of children who learn to read in much the same way that they learn to tell
time, navigate the streets of their own neighborhood or talk and play games with
each other. For these children, formal reading methods are a waste of time. They
tend merely to mechanize and to devitalize the child's own creative power. In

Jonathan Kozol's experiences as a teacher in a ghetto school in Boston led him to write
Death at an Early Age, for which he received the National Book Award. Mr. Kozol is a
graduate of Harvard College and was a Rhodes Scholar at Oxford. He continues to work
with children of the ghetto in the Newton (Massachusetts) Public Schools. He is the author
of numerous articles as well as the novel *The Fume of Poppies.* This article is taken from
his book *Free Schools.* Mr. Kozol's most recent work is *The Night Is Dark and I Am Far
From Home.*

most cases, however, it is both possible and necessary to teach reading in a highly conscious, purposeful and sequential manner.

Teach. I believe today as strongly as I ever did that all education should be child-centered, open-structured, individualized and unoppressive. This point of view inspired me and others in our struggle for reform within the Boston public schools, and it led eventually to the creation of the free schools. There is no question now of going back to a more circumspect position. There *is* a question, however, about the naive, noncritical acceptance of the unexamined notion that you cannot *teach* anything. It is just not true that the best teacher is the grownup who most successfully pretends that he knows nothing or has nothing to suggest to children. It is not true, either, that the best answer to the blustering windbag teacher of the old-time public school is the free-school teacher who attempts to turn himself into a human version of an inductive fan.

Some of the young white persons who come new into the free-school situation are surprisingly dogmatic and, ironically, manipulative in their determination to coerce the parents of poor children into accepting their notions about non-manipulative education. In his book about Bill Ayers and Diana Oughton, *The Making of a Terrorist*, Thomas Powers tells the history of one of the original free schools, established in 1966 in Ann Arbor, Michigan. The school went under for a number of reasons, but Powers notes: "The single most important failing of the school, and the one on which it foundered in the end, was the fact that no one learned to read there."

Collapse. In the jargon that pervades part of the free-school movement, *the child will ask someone to teach him to read as soon as he really wants to read.* Powers observes that, in the three-year history of the school, "that time never seemed to arrive." The school ended on a bitter note. The participants claimed that harassment by public officials caused the school's collapse. In fact, however, it collapsed because parents were taking their children out of it. The founders of the school were committed to helping black children, but according to Powers, they "rejected the terms on which the black parents wanted their children to be helped." In turn, the parents rejected the school.

This is a classic sequence. White men and white women who come in to teach and work alongside black and Spanish-speaking people in the intense, committed atmosphere of the urban free school have to learn to exercise their ideologies and their ideals with great sophistication. Poor people will never reach political consciousness and power by adopting the values of the upper-class elite. These elite ideologies and ideals do not meet the actual needs of the specific, real and nontheoretical children who are sitting here before us.

Weave. It is a bitter pill for many young white persons to swallow, but in many cases the very rewards and skills that we—who possess them—now consider rotten and corrupt are attractive and often irresistible to poor people. Often enough it is not material greed that motivates them—it is the more immediate matter of survival. There's not much that a poor, black 14-year-old can do in cities like New York or Boston if he cannot read and write enough to understand a street sign or to read a phone book. It is too often the rich college graduate who speaks three languages with native fluency, at the price of 16 years of high-cost, rigorous and sequential education, who is most determined that poor kids should make clay vases, weave Indian headbands, play with Polaroid cameras, and climb over geodesic domes.

In the matter of reading, there is no reason why the free school must adhere to either of two irresponsible positions. It is as much an error to say that learning is never the consequence of conscious teaching as it is to imagine that it always is. The second error belongs most often to the public schools; the first to many of the free schools. The truth of the matter is that you *can* teach reading. Lots of people do. I have taught children to read in many situations in which they very likely would not have learned to read for several years if I had not taken a clear initiative. George Dennison has done the same. So too have the people at the New School for Children in Boston. It is true, as I have mentioned, that it is not always necessary. When it is not necessary, it obviously is ill-advised. When it *is* necessary, but when, in the name of joy and freedom, it is not undertaken, the parents have very good reason to be angry.

Shock. Frequently, a child who comes into the free school after a number of years in public school will associate the printed word with pain and intimidation. He is shell-shocked and numb, afraid of anything that has to do with books and with black ink. If he is ingenious and sophisticated, as many 14-year-olds in Boston's South End are, he may be able to disguise his fear of words and, in this way, deceive the young white teacher.

"He's beautiful," the young utopian volunteer will say. "He just likes cinema and weaving more than books. . . . When he's ready for books. . . when he senses his own organic need. . . he'll let us know."

The horrible part of this is that the young volunteers really mean this and, moreover, often believe it with a dedication that precludes any possibility of self-correction. It is too much like looking into the windows of a mental hospital and making maniacal observations on the beautiful silence of the catatonic patients. Children who are in psychological shell shock over reading are not beautiful and are not in the midst of some exquisite process of organic growth. They are, in the most simple and honest terms, kids who just can't do a damn thing in the kinds of cities that we live in. There must be a million unusual and nonmanipulative but highly conscious ways to free children from this kind of misery. There is only one thing that is unpardonable. This is to sit and smile in some sort of cloud of mystical, wide-eyed, nondirective and inscrutable meditation—and do nothing.

How do we teach reading? George Dennison offers many good ideas in *The Lives of Children.* Sylvia Ashton-Warner, James Herndon and Herbert Kohl also recommend a number of specific approaches.

I have had the most success with a mixture of approaches; in one case I even made profitable use of a sequential, rather rigorous, old-fashioned phonics method, but tying it in with a lot of good, intense, uninhibited dialogue with students. In dialogue, the children could find words that carried high intellectual voltage or great sensuality. Certainly, words like *sex* and *cops* and *cash* and *speed* and *El Dorado* are far more likely to stir the passions of the 14-year-old children that I know than *postman, grandmother* or *briefcase*. I also find that many children who think they cannot read, and who are afraid to begin from zero, are excited to find that "GTO," "GM," "GE" or even "CBS-TV" are at the same time words and letters that they already understand quite well. They do not think they have the right to call this reading.

Some of the most intelligent and inspired writing on this subject has been done by the Brazilian scholar, Paulo Freire. The heart of his method has to do with the learner's recognition of a body of words that are associated with the most intense and potentially explosive needs and yearnings of his own life. Freire calls these words *generative*, because they generate thirst, consciousness and motivation in the learner, and also because they can be broken down and reassembled to generate new words. Freire's methods are inherently political. I doubt, therefore, that they can be applied in public schools without immediate repercussions. They are, however, ideal materials for use and application in the free schools.

Impose. The issue of reading opens up the larger question of the purpose and function of a free school in the neighborhood that is economically cheated and politically disenfranchised. In my belief, it is unwise for young white teachers to attempt to impose their version of the counter-culture upon poor children and their families. It is especially dangerous if they do this while they neglect certain obvious survival matters.

Frequently a young newcomer to the free-school movement refuses to recognize that to a very considerable degree his own risk-taking attitudes and antisystem, antiskill, anticredential confidence is based upon the deep-down knowledge that in a single hour he can put on shoes, cut his hair, fish out an old but still familiar piece of plastic from his wallet, go over to Brattle Street, go into Brooks Brothers, buy new clothes, and walk into a brand-new job.

Some of us do not like to admit that we have this sense of intellectual and financial back-up. The parents of poor children, however, recognize this sort of thing quite clearly. They also recognize, with equal clarity, a) that their own children do not have this kind of protection, b) that, if they do not adapt to the real conditions of the system they are fighting, they will not survive, and c) that much of the substance of the white-oriented counter-culture is no real help in that struggle.

I have twice visited Cuernavaca to talk with Ivan Illich and Everett Reimer. Twice I have returned to Boston to confront the hard realities that still must shape decision-making here. It is a luxury, at 2,000 miles' distance, to consider an educational experience that does not involve credentials or curriculum or long-term sequential labor. In immediate terms, in cities such as Boston and New York, it is unwise and perhaps destructive to do so. Instead, we must face up to the hard truth that these credentials and measured areas of expertise and certified ability constitute, *as of now,* the irreducible framework for our labor and our struggle.

In speaking of this issue, I find myself in the difficult position of one who admires Ivan Illich and respects Everett Reimer, but who also lives in Boston in the year of 1972. I try to find the meeting place between these widely separated points of reference in something that I think of as waging guerrilla warfare with credentials.

I would like to join in court suits as co-witness or co-plaintiff, to confront the racist, stupid, pernicious character of College-Board Examinations. I would like to join in obstructive, meddlesome and—wherever necessary—illegal civil disobedience in the offices of the men who govern and control the Educational Testing Service. I would like to join in the campaign of words that John Holt and Ivan Illich are waging against illegal job-discrimination—not just on grounds of race, religion, sex, or years, but also on grounds of previous years of certified domestication and indoctrination in the public schools. I would, moreover, like to go beyond the war of words and take specific action that would make people aware of how unjust this credential apparatus is.

There are also some less-public, but no less-important guerrilla activities. The most obvious way to show up the flimsiness of the 12-year public-education interlock is to short-circuit these sequential obligations. Twelve years of lock-step labor in math or language manifestly waste a child's learning energies. Freire teaches basic literacy in 40 days. Few children need six years to learn to write 10 consecutive, reasonable, cogent and powerful sentences. Ivan Illich and the U.S. State Department both have developed methods by which students can master three years of high-school French or Spanish in three months. Several free schools now are thus short-circuiting the accepted sequences of public school. This is, however, a very different thing from turning our backs and acting as if the system of credentials will just go away. The citadel does not need to be revered or loved in order to be stormed and conquered. It is insane, however, to behave as though it were not there.

Scorn. Many of the poor parents I know are anguished, angry or uneasy when they are with young white women and white men who appear to scorn the credentials-curriculum interlock. Too often, these teachers do not recognize the real needs and the specific agonies that poor people in this country must cope with.

Social insult, hunger, sickness, physical alarm, the siren's scream and the blue light spinning in the neon sky, the desperation of a mother in the back-street clinic of a miserable urban slum—these are the metaphors of truth and pain that still must shape our judgments and decisions.

In my neighborhood, one family of four, who have been my friends now for six years, live on an annual income of 3,000 dollars. Another family, to which I have been drawn through friendship with two of the oldest children, has survived some recent 12-month periods on 1,800 dollars (there are 10 children in the family). Men and women who are locked into such lives will inevitably be unsettled by white persons who tell them that their children do not really need degrees, do not need math or English, do not need to find out how to psych-out an exam, do not need college, do not need money, do not need ugly, contaminated, wicked, middle-class success. The issue for these children is not success. It is survival.

Lag. Black and Puerto Rican children in this neighborhood of Boston live in a medical, economic and educational disaster area. Children whose basic competence is the equal of any child in Palo Alto or in the wheatfields of Nebraska are, statistically, by fifth-grade level, at least one year behind their white suburban counterparts in such basic coding and decoding skills as math and reading; by seventh-grade level, they are two years behind; by ninth-grade level, three years; by 12th-grade level (if they ever get there), four or five years.

Ninety percent of the Puerto Rican kids in Boston drop out of school before they get into the 10th grade. Their odds, first on surviving the attrition-rate, then on being able to go on to higher education, are one 20th the odds of kids in ordinary white suburban schools, one 30th the odds of kids in places such as Evanson and Greenwich, one 50th the odds of kids at St. Paul's, Exeter and Groton.

Decree. The medical odds with which these children live are even more alarming. On the national average, 20 children out of 1,000 die during the first 12 months of life. In all-white neighborhoods outside the cities, the figure is much closer to 15 per 1,000. In black communities like Harlem, Watts and Newark, the figure seldom runs lower than 30 or 35 and often runs as high as 50. Northern liberals like to remind each other that some of the most catastrophic health conditions still exist primarily in rural sections of the Deep South. In the event that we feel smug, however, H. Jack Geiger of Tufts University points out that there are a number of Northern ghetto census-tracts in which the infant-death rate exceeds 100 deaths for every 1,000 children. In these sections of the United States we have come very close to the level of the Biblical plague in the Book of Exodus.

For poor black, poor white and poor Puerto Rican people, the risk of death before age 35 is four times greater than the average for the nation as a whole. In certain neighborhoods of the United States the childbed death-rate for black women is now six times the rate for white women. The excess mortality figure for poor people in New York City is 10,000 to 15,000 yearly. The figure for newborn infants nationwide is estimated to be as high as 40,000. These infant-deaths occur primarily in the rural slums and in the Northern ghettos. These 40,000 infants are the victims of social, professional and institutional murder.

Poison. Those children who survive the hour of imperfect birth encounter equally formidable dangers in the first few years of life. The crumbling plaster in many slum dwellings is covered with sweet and sticky lead paint that poor children eat or chew as it flakes off the walls. The lead paint poisons the brain-cells of young children. Infants become blind, are paralyzed, undergo convulsions, and sometimes die, if they chew it over a long time.

The forces of the law in Boston do not compel a landlord to replace, repair or cover over the sweet-tasting crust of paint that paralyzes children. The law *does* allow a landlord to take action to evict a family if the mother or father misses one rent payment by as much as 15 days. Even in those cases in which the letter of the law supports the tenant, judges often will not penalize or publicly embarrass rich and powerful owners of slum properties who are their friends or are financial benefactors of politicians to whom the judges owe their court appointments.

Rage. It is in this context, then, that sane and sober parents, in such cities as New York and Boston, draw back in fear or anger at the condescending, if often idealistic, statements of young teachers who tell them to forget about English syntax and the Mathematics College Boards, but send away for bean seeds and for organic food supplies and get into grouptalk and encounter.

It seems to me that the parents of poor children are less backward and more realistic than some of their white co-workers are prepared to recognize. Survival skills are desperately important for the children of the powerless and the poor within this cold, efficient nation; they must not be sarcastically and ignorantly scorned by rich young white boys in blue jeans and boots with good degrees from Princeton, Oberlin and Yale.

Harlem does not need a new generation of radical basketweavers. It does need radical, strong, subversive, steadfast, skeptical, rage-minded, and power-wielding obstetricians, pediatricians, lab technicians, defense attorneys, building-code examiners, brain surgeons. Leather and wheat germ may do the trick on somebody's radical estate 10 miles east of Santa Barbara or 16 miles south of Santa Fe but it does very little good on Blue Hill Avenue in Boston on a Sunday night when a man's pocket is empty and his child has a fever and the buses have stopped running.

I cannot draw a perfect blueprint for passionate, angry, realistic education. I know, however, that it is within our reach and that some of the free schools come extremely close. I also know this is the kind of goal that is most worthy of our pursuit. There has to be a way to find pragmatic competence, internal peace, and ethical passion all in the same process. This is the only kind of revolution that can possibly transform the lives of the people in the land in which we live and in the time in which we are living.

- How does Kozol, by arguing that free schools don't teach, undercut a fundamental perspective of learning fostered by the free-school movement?

- What does Kozol offer as essential to a realistic schooling for the poor clientele enrolled in free schools?

- Kozol's remarks in this article take on greater significance when they are viewed against his earlier writings, especially *Death at an Early Age* (Boston: Houghton Mifflin, 1967). Compare the major points of this article with those presented in that book.

- Discuss the implications of Kozol's complaint about "...condescending...statements of young teachers who [say] forget about English syntax and the Mathematics College Boards...."

> *"His name is Emile. . . . His father was Jean-Jacques Rousseau, but he has many foster parents, among them Pestalozzi, Froebel, and Montessori, down to A.S. Neill and Ivan Illich. He is an ideal student. . . . Unfortunately, he is imaginary."*

Compare the comments by Skinner with those of Jerome Bruner in "The Process of Education Revisited" (Section One) and of Joel Denker in "Boredom, Utopia, and 'Unprofessional Conduct' " (Section Two).

The Free and Happy Student

B.F. Skinner

His name is Emile. He was born in the middle of the eighteenth century in the first flush of the modern concern for personal freedom. His father was Jean-Jacques Rousseau, but he has had many foster parents, among them Pestalozzi, Froebel, and Montessori, down to A. S. Neill and Ivan Illich. He is an ideal student. Full of goodwill toward his teachers and his peers, he needs no discipline. He studies because he is naturally curious. He learns things because they interest him.

Unfortunately, he is imaginary. He was quite explicitly so with Rousseau, who put his own children in an orphanage and preferred to say how he would teach his fictional hero; but the modern version of the free and happy student to be found in books by Paul Goodman, John Holt, Jonathan Kozol, or Charles Silberman is also imaginary. Occasionally a real example seems to turn up. There are teachers who would be successful in dealing with people anywhere—as states-

B.F. Skinner, "The Free and Happy Student," *New York University Educational Quarterly* (Winter 1973). Reprinted by permission of the author.

B.F. Skinner is world-renowned for his research, writing, and teaching as a behavioral psychologist. His name has become part of the language with such terms as "the Skinner Box", and he is well known for his invention of the Air-Crib. Associated with Indiana and Harvard Universities, he has written *The Behavior of the Organism, The Science of Human Behavior, The Technology of Teaching, Beyond Freedom and Dignity,* and *About Behaviorism.* His novel, *Walden Two,* an exposition of his conditioning principles, remains a best-seller.

men, therapists, businessmen, or friends—and there are students who scarcely need to be taught, and together they sometimes seem to bring Emile to life. And unfortunately they do so just often enough to sustain the old dream. But Emile is a will-o'-the-wisp, who has led many teachers into a conception of their role which could prove disastrous.

The student who has been taught *as if he were Emile* is, however, almost too painfully real. It has taken a long time for him to make his appearance. Children were first made free and happy in kindergarten, where there seemed to be no danger in freedom, and for a long time they were found nowhere else, because the rigid discipline of the grade schools blocked progress. But eventually they broke through—moving from kindergarten into grade school, taking over grade after grade, moving into secondary school and on into college and, very recently, into graduate school. Step by step they have insisted upon their rights, justifying their demands with the slogans that philosophers of education have supplied. If sitting in rows restricts personal freedom, unscrew the seats. If order can be maintained only through coercion, let chaos reign. If one cannot be really free while worrying about examinations and grades, down with examinations and grades! The whole establishment is now awash with free and happy students.

DROPPING OUT OF SCHOOL, DROPPING OUT OF LIFE

If they are what Rousseau's Emile would really have been like, we must confess to some disappointment. The Emile we know doesn't work very hard. "Curiosity" is evidently a moderate sort of thing. Hard work is frowned upon because it implies a "work ethic," which has something to do with discipline.

The Emile we know doesn't learn very much. His "interests" are evidently of limited scope. Subjects that do not appeal to him he calls irrelevant. (We should not be surprised at this since Rousseau's Emile, like the boys in Summerhill, never got past the stage of a knowledgeable craftsman.) He may defend himself by questioning the value of knowledge. Knowledge is always in flux, so why bother to acquire any particular stage of it? It will be enough to remain curious and interested. In any case the life of feeling and emotion is to be preferred to the life of intellect; let us be governed by the heart rather than the head.

The Emile we know doesn't think very clearly. He has had little or no chance to learn to think logically or scientifically and is easily taken in by the mystical and the superstitious. Reason is irrelevant to feeling and emotion.

And, alas, the Emile we know doesn't seem particularly happy. He doesn't like his education any more than his predecessors liked theirs. Indeed, he seems to like it less. He is much more inclined to play truant (big cities have given up enforcing truancy laws), and he drops out as soon as he legally can, or a little sooner. If he goes to college, he probably takes a year off at some time in his four-year program. And after that his dissatisfaction takes the form of anti-intellectualism and a refusal to support education.

Are there offsetting advantages? Is the free and happy student less aggressive, kinder, more loving? Certainly not toward the schools and teachers that have set him free, as increasing vandalism and personal attacks on teachers seem to show. Nor is he particularly well disposed toward his peers. He seems perfectly at home in a world of unprecedented domestic violence.

Is he perhaps more creative? Traditional practices were said to suppress individuality; what kind of individuality has now emerged? Free and happy students are certainly different from the students of a generation ago, but they are not very different from each other. Their own culture is a severely regimented one, and their creative works—in art, music, and literature—are confined to primitive and elemental materials. They have very little to be creative with, for they have never taken the trouble to explore the fields in which they are now to be front-runners.

Is the free and happy student at least more effective as a citizen? Is he a better person? The evidence is not very reassuring. Having dropped out of school, he is likely to drop out of life too. It would be unfair to let the hippie culture represent young people today, but it does serve to clarify an extreme. The members of that culture do not accept responsibility for their own lives; they sponge on the contributions of those who have not yet been made free and happy—who have gone to medical school and become doctors, or who have become the farmers who raise the food or the workers who produce the goods they consume.

These are no doubt overstatements. Things are not that bad, nor is education to be blamed for all the trouble. Nevertheless, there is a trend in a well-defined direction, and it is particularly clear in education. Our failure to create a truly free and happy student is symptomatic of a more general problem.

THE ILLUSION OF FREEDOM

What we may call the struggle for freedom in the Western world can be analyzed as a struggle to escape from or avoid punitive or coercive treatment. It is characteristic of the human species to act in such a way as to reduce or terminate irritating, painful, or dangerous stimuli, and the struggle for freedom has been directed toward those who would control others with stimuli of that sort. Education has had a long and shameful part in the history of that struggle. The Egyptians, Greeks, and Romans all whipped their students. Medieval sculpture showed the carpenter with his hammer and the schoolmaster with the tool of his trade too, and it was the cane or rod. We are not yet in the clear. Corporal punishment is still used in many schools, and there are calls for its return where it has been abandoned.

A system in which students study primarily to avoid the consequences of not studying is neither humane nor very productive. Its by-products include truancy, vandalism, and apathy. Any effort to eliminate punishment in education is certainly commendable. We ourselves act to escape from aversive control, and our students should escape from it too. They should study because they want to, because they like to, because they are interested in what they are doing. The mistake—a classical mistake in the literature of freedom—is to suppose that they will do so as soon as we stop punishing them. Students are not literally free when they have been freed from their teachers. They then simply come under the control of other conditions, and we must look at those conditions and their effects if we are to improve teaching.

Those who have attacked the "servility" of students, as Montessori called it, have often put their faith in the possibility that young people will learn what they need to know from the "world of things," which includes the world of people who are not teachers. Montessori saw possibly useful behavior being suppressed by schoolroom discipline. Could it not be salvaged? And could the environment of the schoolroom not be changed so that other useful behavior would occur? Could the teacher not simply guide the student's natural development? Or could he not accelerate it by teasing out behavior which would occur naturally but not so quickly if he did not help? In other words, could we not bring the real world into the classroom, as John Dewey put it, or destroy the classroom and turn the student over to the real world, as Ivan Illich has recommended. All these possibilities can be presented in an attractive light, but they neglect two vital points:

(*a*) No one learns very much from the real world without help. The only evidence we have of what can be learned from a nonsocial world has been supplied by those wild boys said to have been raised without contact with other members of their own species. Much more can be learned without formal instruction in a social world, but not without a good deal of teaching, even so. Formal education has made a tremendous difference in the extent of the skills and knowledge which can be acquired by a person in a single lifetime.

(*b*) A much more important principle is that the real world teaches only what is relevant to the present; it makes no explicit preparation for the future. Those who would minimize teaching have contended that no preparation is needed, that the student will follow a natural line of development and move into the future in the normal course of events. We should be content, as Carl Rogers has put it, to trust

> the insatiable curiosity which drives the adolescent boy to absorb everything he can see or hear or read about gasoline engines in order to improve the efficiency and speed of his "hot rod." I am talking about the student who says, "I am discovering, drawing in from the outside, and making that which is drawn in a real part of me." I am talking about my learning in which the experience of the learner progresses along the line: "No, no, that's not what I want"; "Wait! This is closer to what I'm interested in, what I need." "Ah, here it is! Now I'm grasping and comprehending what I need and what I want to know!"[1]

Rogers is recommending a total commitment to the present moment, or at best to an immediate future.

---

[1] Carl R. Rogers, *Freedom to Learn* (Columbus, Ohio: Merrill, 1969).

FORMAL EDUCATION AS PREPARATION FOR FUTURE REWARDS

But it has always been the task of formal education to set up behavior which would prove useful or enjoyable *later* in the student's life. Punitive methods had at least the merit of providing current reasons for learning things that would be rewarding in the future. We object to the punitive reasons, but we should not forget their function in making the future important.

It is not enough to give the student advice—to explain that he will have a future, and that to enjoy himself and be more successful in it, he must acquire certain skills and knowledge now. Mere advice is ineffective because it is not supported by current rewards. The positive consequences that generate a useful behavioral repertoire need not be any more explicitly relevant to the future than were the punitive consequences of the past. The student needs current reasons, positive or negative, but only the educational policy maker who supplies them need take the future into account. It follows that many instructional arrangements seem "contrived," but there is nothing wrong with that. It is the teacher's function to contrive conditions under which students learn. Their relevance to a future usefulness need not be obvious.

It is a difficult assignment. The conditions the teacher arranges must be powerful enough to compete with those under which the student tends to behave in distracting ways. In what has come to be called "contingency management in the classroom" tokens are sometimes used as rewards or reinforcers. They become reinforcing when they are exchanged for reinforcers that are already effective. There is no "natural" relation between what is learned and what is received. The token is simply a reinforcer that can be made clearly contingent upon behavior. To straighten out a wholly disrupted classroom something as obvious as a token economy may be needed, but less conspicuous contingencies—as in a credit-point system, perhaps, or possibly in the long run merely expressions of approval on the part of teacher or peer—may take over.

The teacher can often make the change from punishment to positive reinforcement in a surprisingly simple way—by responding to the student's successes rather than his failures. Teachers have too often supposed that their role is to point out what students are doing wrong, but pointing to what they are doing *right* will often make an enormous difference in the atmosphere of a classroom and in the efficiency of instruction. Programmed materials are helpful in bringing about these changes, because they increase the frequency with which the student enjoys the satisfaction of being right, and they supply a valuable intrinsic reward in providing a clear indication of progress. A good program makes a step in the direction of competence almost as conspicuous as a token.

Programmed instruction is perhaps most successful in attacking punitive methods by allowing the student to move at his own pace. The slow student is released from the punishment which inevitably follows when he is forced to move on to material for which he is not ready, and the fast student escapes the boredom of being forced to go too slow. These principles have recently been extended to college education, with dramatic results, in the Keller system of personalized instruction.[2]

THE RESPONSIBILITY OF SETTING EDUCATIONAL POLICY

There is little doubt that a student can be given non-punitive reasons for acquiring behavior that will become useful or otherwise reinforcing at some later date. He can be prepared for the future. But what *is* that future? Who is to say what the student should learn? Those who have sponsored the free and happy student have argued that it is the student himself who should say. His current interests should be the source of an effective educational policy. Certainly they will reflect his idiosyncrasies, and that is good, but how much can he know about the world in which he will eventually play a part? The things he is "naturally" curious about are of current and often temporary interests. How many things must he possess besides his "hot rod" to provide the insatiable curiosity relevant to, say, a course in physics?

It must be admitted that the teacher is not always in a better position. Again and again education has gone out of date as teachers have continued to teach subjects which were no longer relevant at any time in the student's life. Teachers often teach simply what they know. (Much of what is taught in private schools is determined by what the available teachers can teach.) Teachers tend to teach what they can teach easily. Their current interests, like those of students, may not be a reliable guide.

Nevertheless, in recognizing the mistakes that have been made in the past in specifying what students are to learn, we do not absolve ourselves from the responsibility of setting educational policy. We should say, we should be *willing* to say, what we believe students will need to know, taking the individual student into account wherever possible, but otherwise making our best prediction with respect to students in general. Value judgments of this sort are not as hard to make as is often argued. Suppose we undertake to prepare the student to produce his share of the goods he will consume and the services he will use, to get on well with his fellows, and to enjoy his life. In doing so are we imposing *our* values on someone else? No, we are merely choosing a set of specifications which, so far as we can tell, will at some time in the future prove valuable to the student and his culture. Who is any more likely to be right?

The natural, logical outcome of the struggle for personal freedom in education is that the teacher should improve his control of the student rather than abandon it. The free school is no school at all. Its philosophy signalizes the abdication of the teacher. The teacher who understands his assignment and is

---

[2]*P.S.I. Newsletter*, October 1972 (published by Department of Psychology, Georgetown University, J. G. Sherman, ed.).

familiar with the behavioral processes needed to fulfill it can have students who not only feel free and happy while they are being taught but who will continue to feel free and happy when their formal education comes to an end. They will do so because they will be successful in their work (having acquired useful productive repertoires), because they will get on well with their fellows (having learned to understand themselves and others), because they will enjoy what they do (having acquired the necessary knowledge and skills), and because they will from time to time make an occasional creative contribution toward an even more effective and enjoyable way of life. Possibly the most important consequence is that the teacher will then feel free and happy too.

We must choose today between Cassandran and Utopian prognostications. Are we to work to avoid disaster or to achieve a better world? Again, it is a question of punishment or reward. Must we act because we are frightened, or are there positive reasons for changing our cultural practices? The issue goes far beyond education, but it is one with respect to which education has much to offer. To escape from or avoid disaster, people are likely to turn to the punitive measures of a police state. To work for a better world, they may turn instead to the positive methods of education. When it finds its most effective methods, education will be almost uniquely relevant to the task of setting up and maintaining a better way of life.

- How does Skinner support the idea that freedom *from* school is merely the illusion of freedom?

- What major flaws does Skinner find in the "real world as educator"?

- Skinner emphasizes one effort of the educational reformers as valid. What is that effort, and how does he verify its compatibility with his own beliefs?

- Draw parallels between Skinner's view of the teacher as controller and the view held by educational reconstructionists that the teacher is a social reformer.

"In some 'innovative' schools...it is possible to become the well-rounded man by studying macrame, tie-dying, revolutionary theory, wilderness survival, yoga, or Black Women I and II."

Smith's points of view in this article should be viewed in relation to excerpts from the "Seventh Annual Gallup Poll of Public Attitudes Toward Education" (Section One) and to Lawrence Cremin's "The Free School Movement—a Perspective" (Section Three).

Is Common Sense Breaking Through?

Mortimer Smith

As we have pointed out before in these pages, there are reformers and reformers in education. One group is concerned with what it believes to be the primary function of schools, skills and knowledge, and concentrates therefore on strengthening the curriculum and on better preparation of teachers. Then there are the radicals of reform who are less concerned with academic accomplishment than with making the school an agency for the reform of society and for producing people who will be humane, loving, and noncompetitive.

The effort to use the schools for social and personal regeneration has resulted in some rather bizarre programs and practices, especially in the high schools. In some "innovative" schools there are only the loosest of requirements and the students may for the most part choose their own courses. It is possible to become the well-rounded man by studying macrame, tie-dying, revolutionary theory, wilderness survival, yoga, or Black Women I and II. In some schools

---

Mortimer Smith, "Is Common Sense Breaking Through?" *The Council for Basic Education Bulletin* 16, no. 1 (September 1971). Reprinted by permission.

Mortimer Smith is a social historian, biographer, and writer on education. One of the founders of the Council for Basic Education, he was editor of the *CEE Bulletin* until 1974. Author of numerous articles in magazines and anthologies, he is also author of *A Consumer's Guide to Educational Innovations, A Citizen's Manual for Public Schools, The Dimished Mind,* and *And Madly Teach.*

students sit on the floor in the halls, playing cards or strumming on guitars. The "musts" are love and relevance and calling the teacher by his first name. Mass cutting of classes is a commonplace and the truant officer is a quaint historical figure, like the lamplighter.

There are not too many of these free-wheeling schools but because conventional schools are often willing to adopt parts of the innovative programs their influence is greater than their numbers. But in the last year or so there have appeared faint intimations of dissatisfaction with the radical reforms. For one thing, that spineless wonder, the average American parent, is beginning to think that the PTA should be something more than a place to discuss Saturday's baked goods sale and uniforms for the band, and so this hitherto bland forum now often rings with demands to know what's-going-on-here. This has happened at the John F. Kennedy High School in Montgomery County, outside Washington, D.C., a school considered to be one of the most innovative and independent in the East. Last fall members of the PTA registered strong protests against the school's lack of structure, its exotic course offerings, and its policy of never entering failure on a student's transcript. Some parents did not think the school could be proud of the fact that the number of students taking National Merit Scholarship exams had dropped in two years from 170 to 40. The parental revolt resulted in the resignation of the principal and present indications are that John F. Kennedy High is headed for more confrontations and further reexaminations of its program. (See "Innovation and Discord at a Model High School" by Peggy Thomson in *Washington,* the weekly magazine published by *The Sunday Star,* August 15.)

Not only parents, but some of the teachers and administrators who have been most enthusiastic about the new programs, are beginning to look soberly at what they have wrought. In this connection we refer our readers to five articles about the John Adams High School in Portland, Oregon, which appeared in the May issue of *Phi Delta Kappan.* Adams has a national reputation as a model innovative school.

The five articles are written by staff members of Adams, including the principal. Naturally the writers are committed to the program but their remarkably candid discussion suggests that they not only see some flaws in practice but may have uneasy philosophical doubts. Before quoting some of these comments, let us state briefly the Adams pedagogical credo. The central experiment at Adams is the General Education program, described in one of the articles as "a means to learn about a society in flux, one in which the only constant is change." General Education is based on the study of contemporary problems such as air and water pollution, slum conditions, urban renewal, etc. (Students may also take electives, such as math, science, and foreign languages.) The planners of the programs are generally sympathetic to the ideas of John Holt, Paul Goodman, and Herbert Kohl. They think learning is best in an unstructured, free setting with the students involved as fully as possible in determining the program. The teacher "tells the student neither what he is to do, what he is to learn, nor how."

Perhaps the frankest of the five articles is the one by Allen L. Dobbins, who heads the instructional division at the school. He points out that not all students are happy with freedom, especially those with "severe skill limitations" (and this includes many who are "very bright"). These students simply cop out by roaming the halls or dancing in the lounge. The staff was pained to discover that these students thought "they weren't learning anything, that teachers didn't make them do any work." The solution was to create a basic skills department, highly structured and with much tighter constraints—that is, the solution was to revive what the program was originally designed to get rid of. Says Mr. Dobbins: "The popularity of basic skills with students has presented all of us with undeniable evidence that many students were not adequately served in these areas elsewhere." He has much to say about the difficulties of reaching any agreement about aims and program. Many parents, teachers, and not a few administrators, he says, would like a return to a more traditional school. A number of teachers "and some of our more radically oriented students" want an even more loosely organized school. He says that the majority of parents, teachers, and students are somewhere between these two poles.

Another staff member at Adams, Patricia A. Wertheimer, agrees that many students feel they are not learning much and that they want more direction from teachers and more organization of class work. She says: "By spring 1970, it appeared to many of us that the school was characterized to far too great an extent by a pervasive restlessness and lack of commitment to the effort required to achieve excellence." She believes Adams needs to offer alternative modes of learning: that is, alternatives to the free, unstructured program which is the heart of the Adams plan.

It should be remembered that the two writers quoted above, and the authors of the other articles, are part of the original Adams innovative team. They are zealots, but obviously honest zealots who are facing up to the fact that there is in this case a great gulf between promise and reality. While it is true that the article by Robert B. Schwartz, the school's principal, hints that success might be achieved if only more money was available, all of the articles exhibit a becoming modesty about Adams' achievements and a reluctance, as Schwartz suggests, to accept the verdict of visiting experts that Adams is "the most important invention since sliced bread."

We urge our readers to get hold of the May *Phi Delta Kappan* and read these appraisals of a leading innovative program. Here we have been able to merely suggest the genuine doubts expressed by those who are advocates of the program. Their honest and realistic evaluations, together with parental examination of innovative programs, suggest that common sense may indeed be breaking through. The doubts of parents and teachers about some of the more far-out programs may be harbingers of better things to come in educational reform. Perhaps we are entering a period when romantic reform will gradually give way to realistic and realizable reform.

- Review some of Mortimer Smith's descriptions of current criticisms and misgivings held by the public.

- The emphasis on traditional curricula and basic skills is welcomed as educational "good news" by Smith. Based on your experience as a secondary-school student, and perhaps as a school employee, indicate ways in which you agree or disagree with Smith's position.

"I find the situation far from desperate. It is encouraging, but rough in spots, and the rough spots are most clearly seen in the big-city slums. We are learning to do the job for disadvantaged children, but making a good many mistakes in the process."

Apply Havighurst's comments to Max Rafferty's "American Education: 1975-2000" and to the National Commission's "Recommendations for Improving Secondary Education" (both in Section One).

Requirements for a Valid "New Criticism"
Robert J. Havighurst

On November 2, 1967, the New York City School Board reported the results of school achievement tests that had been given the preceding April to all pupils in the second and fifth grades. *The New York Times* reported the results in a page of tables and headlined the story on page one with "City Pupils Losing Ground in Reading and Arithmetic." Let us examine some of the test results.

The national average reading scores for these grades in April were 2.7 and 5.7 respectively. New York City school children averaged definitely below these levels, and there was some evidence that the New York City average was lower than it had been the year before.

The New York Times did not point out the fact that almost 300 of the 650 elementary schools had reading averages for their second grades of 3.0 or higher—that is, three-tenths of a year above the national average. Nor did *The Times* report that 44 elementary schools had reading scores for their fifth grades averaging 7.0 or more—1.3 of a year above the national average.

Robert J. Havighurst, "Requirements for a Valid 'New Criticism'," *Phi Delta Kappan* **50**, no. 1 (September 1968). Reprinted by permission.

Robert J. Havighurst is Professor of Education and Human Development at the University of Chicago. A leader in educational research, Dr. Havighurst is the author and co-author of over twenty books, including *American Higher Education in the 1960's, Comparative Perspectives in Education,* and *Adjustment to Retirement: A Cross-National Study*.

During that same month of November, the New York State Board of Regents called for "a concerted effort to reform urban education." The "Bundy Report" of the Mayor's Advisory Panel on Decentralization of the New York City Schools, which was published November 9, commences with the statement, "The New York City school system, which once ranked at the summit of American public education, is caught in a spiral of decline." *The Times* on that date referred in an editorial to what it called "the deterioration of New York's gigantic school system."

The Saturday Review for November 18 carried the following headlines on its front cover—*Requiem for the Urban School* and *Education in Washington: National Monument to Failure.*

The unwary middle-income parent, with several school-age children, is very likely to read these pieces in *responsible* newspapers and journals, and to decide to move to the suburbs, where he is assured by the same press that the schools are good. This person may live in Queens District 27, where 20 out of 27 schools are well above average in reading achievement, or in Queens District 26, where every one of the 24 elementary schools averaged at least .4 of a year above the national average at the second grade and at least one year above the national average at the fifth grade. But if he follows the *responsible* press, unless he explores the fine print, he is misled to suppose that he cannot find "good" public schools in the city.

Although these examples are taken from New York City, they can be duplicated in every large city. In some areas of the city, where the people of average and above-average income live, school achievement is above the national average, and about the same as it is in the "better" suburbs. In the low-income areas, school achievement is low.

How bad is education in our big cities? Does a dispassionate examination of the facts justify such widely publicized statements and slogans as "our children are dying," "requiem for urban education," "the end of the common school," "death at an early age," all applied to the work of the public schools in large cities?

We spend much more on education now than we did in 1955, much more per child, and a great deal more of our gross national product. Yet we are not making much headway with the education of disadvantaged children.

The children who are doing so poorly in our public schools constitute about 15 percent of the total group of children. They come predominantly from the homes of parents who are in the bottom quarter of the population in income, educational level, and occupational status. An equal number of children in such homes do fairly well in school—hence we cannot simply say that the children of the poor do poorly in school. Many of them do very well. But about 15 percent of children come from poor families *and* do poorly in school. We call these children "socially disadvantaged" because there is ample evidence that their home environments give them a very poor preparation for success in school.

Since World War II the families that produce these children have collected in large numbers in the slums of the big cities. Before World War II the majority of these children were living in rural and relatively isolated areas, and consequently their failure in school did not create an obvious social problem.

The other 85 percent of American children are doing quite well in school, according to the ordinary standards of judgment applied by most Americans to the schools.

I find the situation far from desperate. It is encouraging, but rough in spots, and the rough spots are most clearly seen in the big-city slums. We are learning to do the job for disadvantaged children, but making a good many mistakes in the process.

The criticisms of urban education.

What are the criticisms? There are two major themes of criticism of urban education, and they are quite different. The first and most general is that the schools are failing to educate the children of the poor, and it is the fault of the schools rather than the fault of the slum culture and home environment to which the children of the poor are subjected.

The second criticism is that the educational system is doing a poor job for the middle-class child and youth. The argument is that the present middle-class establishment is failing to govern the country effectively and failing to solve the country's international and domestic problems, and at the same time attempting to train the next generation to carry on this pattern of civic failure. One of the leading critics, writing an article entitled "In Praise of Populism," says "Indeed, the essential idea of this resurgent populism, in my opinion, is that the powers-that-be in the world are incompetent, their authority is irrational, they cannot cope with modern conditions, and they are producing ultimate horrors."

Who are the critics?

There is a group who appear at this time to have easy access to the responsible newspapers and journals. These include Paul Goodman, Edgar Friedenberg, Nat Hentoff, John Holt, Herbert Kohl, and Jonathan Kozol. These are not irresponsible people. On the contrary, they feel a tremendous moral responsibility to report their perceptions of the schools and their hypotheses for the betterment of the schools.

There are certain personal characteristics of these critics which are relevant to their criticisms. I do not propose to psychoanalyze them, and I have shared these qualities at one time or another in my own career. All of these characteristics do not apply equally to all of the critics. For one thing, they tend to be anarchists. That is, they do not like rules and institutions set up by society to regulate the conduct and development of its members. For another, they tend to be hostile to authority and therefore critical of the Establishment. A third characteristic is that some of them are young men agonizing in public over their discovery that the world is a difficult place.

To this group of critics should be added another group who are especially concerned with one or another disadvantaged minority group, and claim that the schools are failing to educate properly the children of these groups either by discriminating against them or by offering them inappropriate forms of schooling. The principal minority group on whose behalf these critics speak is the Negro group, though there are similar arguments on behalf of Puerto Ricans, Spanish-Americans of the Southwest, rural whites of the Appalachian-Ozark mountain area, and American Indians.

What is wrong with the schools?
The critics tend to attribute the shortcomings of the schools to the fact that they are operated by "the Establishment." The Establishment consists of the bureaucrats who administer the schools and who in turn are supported by the political leadership of the big cities, backed by a middle class satisfied with the school system in its present form. Thus Jason Epstein, writing on the Bundy Report that recommends decentralization of the public schools of New York City, says,

> ...the urgent matter is to wrench the school system away from the bureaucrats who are now running it and whose failure now threatens the stability of the city itself. As a practical matter the children of the ghetto, who now comprise nearly half the total public school enrollment, are largely without a functioning educational system at all, and the present school administration has shown that it is incapable of supplying them with one.

Related to this criticism is the contention that the size of big-city systems makes them bad. When a single school board and a single superintendent and his staff have to take responsibility for more than about 50 schools or 50,000 pupils, it is argued that the school system becomes rigid, unable to adapt to the various educational needs of various subgroups and sections of the city.

Third, there is the criticism of the common school, or the system of public education. Thus Peter Schrag, editorializing in *The Saturday Review* for April 20, 1968, on the subject "The End of the Common School," says,

> Although criticism of schools and teachers has always been a great national pastime, there is something fundamentally new in the declining faith in the possibilities of reform, and particularly in the kind of reform that can be accomplished within the existing school structure. The characteristic view, reflected in pressures for decentralization and for the establishment of competing institutions, is that school systems tend to be self-serving, bureaucratic monsters that need replacement rather than reform. Although these demands have arisen during a time when the schools can attract more resources and more sophisticated staffs than ever before, they also coincide with the moment when the schools have achieved a near-monopoly position as gatekeepers to social and economic advancement: Where the schools were once considered benign, happy institutions for the young, they are now increasingly regarded as instruments of power.

Schrag says that there will have to be a number of alternative forms of education that may replace the single public school.

A few such competing institutions have already been established. In the large cities there are a few community schools, storefront academies, and programs for dropouts. Most of these operations are considered in some measure remedial and temporary. Most of them are inadequately financed and do not begin to meet the problems of miseducation, even in the communities where they are located. Yet the problems that led to the establishment of such institutions are going to be with us for a long time, and unless the public schools begin to accommodate far more diversity and to offer far more choice than they now do, the desperate need for alternatives will continue.

What do the critics propose?

As one would expect from critics who tend to be anarchists and who are hostile to the forms of authority, the positive proposals for educational improvement tend to be few and weak. There are three broad approaches.

1. Abolish the present school system and allow new institutions to emerge. This kind of proposal tends to be supported by critics who believe that there is too much bureaucracy with consequent rigidity in the present school system. They are not much concerned with the nature of the new institutions, since they tend to distrust institutions. With John Holt in *How Children Learn,* they follow Rousseau in their belief that children will learn best if allowed to initiate their own education. Paul Goodman writes, "We can, I believe, educate the young entirely in terms of their free choice, with no processing whatsoever."

2. Experiment widely and freely with new procedures, looking for teachers with enthusiasm, creativity, and iconoclasm. New ways of working successfully with disadvantaged children and youth will emerge from such experiments.

3. Require the schools and their teachers to do a much better job of teaching disadvantaged children. This is the proposal especially of some Negro educators, who believe that the school system at present, both North and South, tends to *reject* Negro children, to assume they cannot learn well, and to avoid the effort of teaching them effectively.

There are two principal weaknesses in the positions taken by the critics. First, many of them, and especially those who speak for minority groups, are ignoring the basic research on the importance of the pre-school years in the preparation of a child for success in school. They ignore the following basic proposition.

The child's cognitive and social development in the years before age five are extremely important in his readiness for school work and his achievement in school. This proposition has been established by the empirical work of Bernstein in London, Martin Deutsch in New York, Robert Hess and his co-workers at the University of Chicago, and Skeels and Skodak at the University of Iowa. This proposition is widely discussed and amplified in the writings of J. McVicker Hunt, Benjamin Bloom, and Jerome Bruner.

Second, they ignore the post-war work on methods and materials of teaching mathematics, science, social studies, and foreign languages which has effectively reformed the curriculum of the intermediate and high school grades, and vastly improved the education of the majority of children and youth who do average and superior work in school.

Nevertheless, the critics serve a valuable purpose in contemporary education. They are sensitive people, aware of the needs for improvement in our society and in our education. They are especially useful as our social conscience.

II. WAYS OUT OF THE EDUCATIONAL MESS

Granting the proposition that major changes must be made in big-city education, how shall we decide what changes to make, and how shall we make them? There are three groups of people with something to say on this topic—the establishment, the anarchists, and the activists. All are prepared to talk about changing, though all are not equally prepared to take actual responsibility for changes.

The establishment as a change agent.

It is customary to describe the Establishment as a bureaucratic organization wedded to things as they have been in the past. The national organization of school superintendents and the organization of school principles have been accused of standing athwart the path of progress.

Yet some city school systems have been remarkably ready to exercise leadership in the making of changes. For instance, the New York City system which has been pilloried in *The New York Times* as a deteriorating system has been one of the most flexible, most experimental, and most responsive of all big-city systems to the social situation and the social needs of the big city. A list of outstanding changes in the New York City schools in the past 30 years would include:

- The establishment of a system of specialized high schools serving the entire city with outstanding programs for the ablest students.
- A long history of special programs for gifted elementary school children, centered at Hunter College.
- Programs in certain high schools to meet the local community needs of a particular ethnic group, such as the program at the Benjamin Franklin High School when Leonard Covello was principal there.
- Science teaching programs in the intermediate grades and the high schools that led the way to the improved science courses which swept the country after 1960.
- The Statement on Integration adopted by the New York City Board of Education in 1954, shortly after the Supreme Court decision on segregation. This was not only the first policy statement on integration to be adopted by a big-city board of education, but one of the strongest; and it was put into effect by a positive open enrollment policy and by a vigorous rezoning program during the first years, when these measures could be fairly effective.

- The Demonstration-Guidance Project in Junior High School 43 and the George Washington Senior High School. This was the first of the attempts by the big-city systems to enrich their programs for socially disadvantaged children.
- The Higher Horizons Project in a large number of elementary schools, which was carefully and critically evaluated by the Research Bureau, and was the first big-city project for the socially disadvantaged to warn us that the job was not going to be easy. While other cities reported rosy but carelessly compiled results of their projects, New York City forced educators to face the facts.
- The More Effective Schools Program, a carefully designed project to improve the education of the socially disadvantaged, which has been evaluated carefully and critically by an independent research agency.
- The study of Puerto Rican children in New York City schools made by J. Cayce Morrison in the 1950's, which helped the school system to recognize and go to work on this special problem.
- A series of experiments in delegating responsibility for the conduct of schools to local district school boards, stretching over the last 70 years. Notable in this series was the project in the Bronx headed by Joseph Loretan in the late 1950's, when he was district superintendent there.
- A set of current experiments in the delegation of responsibility to local community committees for choosing administrators and teaching staff and for adapting the curriculum to local community conditions. This is a radical and controversial experiment which no other big-city school system has been able to try. Whatever becomes of it, it will give us valuable knowledge on the problem of relations between the school system and local communities.

It is a curious thing for the critics to proclaim the proposition that New York City schools are failing, when these schools are leading the country in working at the problem of educating socially disadvantaged youth, defining the problem, and studying it scientifically and experimentally.

During this period of the last 30 years, the great majority of books on the problems of education in the big city have come from New York City. These have been written by a wide range of people with a wide range of motives and experience.

Still, many of the great cities have been slow to innovate, and there certainly is a problem in all big-city systems where a bureaucratic structure stretching from the office of school principal to that of superintendent tends to perpetuate practices to which the organization has already grown accustomed. An example is the use of federal funds under Title I of the Elementary and Secondary Education Act to supplement educational services in schools located in poverty areas. The tendency has been to use these funds to support "more of the same" rather than to innovate. That is, the money has been used to pay teachers for an extra hour of classes after school, for Saturday morning instruction, for summer instruction, and to reduce the size of classes. This has not worked very well, and has given rise to criticism of big city systems for failure to try bold new experiments.

The anarchists as change agents

The anarchists have been strong on criticism and weak on constructive proposals for change. They are, of course, opposed to the creation of a new set of organized and institutional practices, since, as anarchists, they mistrust procedures which tend to become rigid and confining. They proclaim "the end of the common school" and tell us that we are killing off the minds and spirits of children, but they are wary of writing proposals that could be put into an organized educational system. They favor experimentation of many kinds, but do not argue for careful evaluation of such experiments. For instance, Peter Schrag, writing in *The Saturday Review* of June 15, 1968, on "Learning in a Storefront" makes the following approving statement:

> The East Harlem Block Schools, which operate nursery and primary classes in four locations, have discovered no new pedagogical secrets, operate according to no rigid theory, and have conducted little validating research. What they are doing, however, is to demonstrate that educational programs directed by parents and often staffed by parents are not only effective—at least in the judgment of those same parents—but that they represent a community focus and center of interest limited only by the financial resources their sponsors can attract.

He notes in passing, as though it were not an important matter, that there is no validating research on these schools. He also notes that the project costs $2,000 per child per year for 135 children, but he gives no indication that such a program would have to be supported by a thorough research validation if it would have any chance of gaining the public support that could spread it to cover one hundred times as many children. It would have to do this to produce a significant impact on the education of disadvantaged children in New York City. Instead, Schrag points out the importance of getting the schools into the hands of parents. "It is the parents who are minding the store," he says. It is this kind of anti-institutional and anti-organizational emphasis which is both the strength and the weakness of the anarchist position.

But the ablest of the anarchists recognize the need for new institutionalized procedures. Thus Paul Goodman, who calls himself an anarchist, also says explicitly that new institutions are necessary. After speaking of the present educational establishment as a hoax on the public and calling for an end to it, he says in the letter which appears in this *Kappan*, "Of course our society would then have to re-open or devise other institutional arrangements for most of the young to grow into the world; and in my books I propose many of these, since this is the problem."

To see the anarchist position most ably stated, and stated in most positive terms, one should read more of Goodman's writing. His article on "Freedom and Learning: The Need for Choice" in *The Saturday Review* for May 18, 1968, expands the ideas expressed in the above-mentioned letter. Here he argues that the educational system which has developed into such a large and expensive set of operations since 1900 is a hoax on American society. It tends to force conformity on the younger generation, and conformity to a set of adult institutions which are bad for everybody. He calls for more free choice in learning and says, "Free choice is not random but responsive to real situations; both youth and adults live in a nature of things, a polity, an ongoing society and it is these, in fact, that attract interest and channel need. If the young, as they mature, can follow their bent and choose their topics, times, and teachers, and if teachers teach what they themselves consider important—which is all they can skillfully teach anyway—the needs of society will be adequately met; there will be more lively, independent, and inventive people; and in the fairly short run there will be a more sensible and efficient society."

Up to age 12, Goodman says, there is no point to formal subjects or a prearranged curriculum. Teaching should be informal, and should follow the child's interest. If let alone, a normal child of 12 will, Goodman believes, learn most of what is useful in the eight-year elementary curriculum by himself.

However, Goodman recognizes that some families do not provide an adequate setting for their children to learn the elementary school curriculum, and he has a proposal for a kind of school to serve these disadvantaged children. He says,

> Since we have communities where people do not attend to the children as a matter of course, and since children must be rescued from their homes, for most of these children there should be some kind of school. In a proposal for mini-schools in New York City, I suggested an elementary group of 28 children with four grownups: a licensed teacher, a housewife who can cook, a college senior, and a teen-age school dropout. Such a group can meet in any storefront, church basement, settlement house, or housing project; more important, it can often go about the city, as is possible when the student-teacher ratio is 7 to 1. Experience at the First Street School in New York has shown that the cost for such a little school is less than for the public school with a student-teacher ratio of 30 to 1....The school should be located near home so the children can escape from it to home, and from home to it. The school should be supported by public money but administered entirely by its own children, teachers, and parents.

Looking at the positive suggestions of the more constructive anarchists, of whom Goodman is a good example, we see that they want education to be institutionalized to minimal degree, with a wide variety of small school and college units in which pupils and teachers work as far as possible on their own initiative.

The activists as change agents

A broad group of people are prepared to work within the present educational system but want major changes or additions to it. This group might be called "institutional meliorists," to distinguish them from the anarchists. This group accepts the notion that the educational system must have a complex institutional structure and therefore differs from the anarchists on this major point. The activists want broad and fundamental changes in the educational system.

There is much disagreement among the activists. Many of them have just one program which they emphasize, such as:

- Pre-school programs for disadvantaged children starting as early as age 3.
- Decentralization of the public school system to place responsibility and decision making more in the hands of parents and local community leaders.
- Educational parks.
- Black teachers for black schools.
- Alternative educational systems to the public schools, supported with public funds.

The U.S. Office of Education has been promoting activist programs through its very large funds under Title III of the Elementary and Secondary Education Act. Several of the educational foundations have been supporting activist projects.

To this writer, who is an activist, it appears that there are some serious weaknesses in the activist approach, but that these weaknesses are being corrected.

A major weakness is a general lack of systematic reporting and evaluation of the results of experimental work. Several major big-city programs of compensatory education for disadvantaged children have been given wide publicity as successful on the basis of preliminary and inadequate evaluation, only to withdraw their claims after more systematic study of their outcomes.

But there have been some outstanding examples of careful research evaluation of innovative programs. For instance, the Higher Horizons Program in New York City elementary schools was evaluated by the Bureau of Reasearch, and its successor program, the More Effective Schools, has been carefully studied by the Center for Urban Education. The fact that these evaluations did not support some of the hopes and expectations of the sponsors of the programs is an unfortunate fact which the big city systems must learn to use constructively.

At present there are some serious and sophisticated evaluations of several types of pre-school programs for disadvantaged children supported by the U.S. Office of Education. This should go a long way toward helping the educational systems to make rational judgments about the practical wisdom of expanding pre-school programs at public expense as a regular part of the public school program.

After a period of uncritical spending on innovations designed to improve the education of disadvantaged children and youth, stretching from Head Start through Title I of ESEA to the Job Corps, the federal agencies are now going in for evaluation, under pressure from congressmen and the Bureau of the Budget. The USOE is engaged in cost-benefit studies of the Title I program, and here there is another kind of danger. The educational benefits of pre-school and other innovative programs may not be fully measurable in terms of gains of children on reading-readiness tests and ordinary standardized tests of school achievement, applied immediately after an experimental program lasting a year or so. Yet cost benefit studies are limited to assessing the costs of benefits that are measured. If the benefits of certain experimental programs cannot be measured simply after a short trial of the program, we should take the time and make the effort to measure the benefits in more complex ways over longer periods of time.

Working on motives rather than skills

Recently some of the activists appear to have discovered a principle that may produce much more effective ways of teaching disadvantaged children than the conventional way. The conventional way is to work directly on the mental skills of the child—his vocabulary, reading, writing, arithmetic. *Teach, teach, teach* with all the energy, time, patience, and techniques available. This has not worked very well. Hence, some experimental methods have been tried that work on *motives* rather than skills and drills. The aim is to help the pupil *want* to learn, to help him see himself as a learner in school, as he now may see himself as a basketball player, a fighter, an attractive person to the opposite sex, a helper in the home, etc.

The theory underlying this approach might be outlined as follows: When a person *wants* something, he *tries* to get it. For example; when a child wants to read, he tries to read, and will use whatever help he can get from teachers, parents, other pupils, television, street signs, books around the house. He will drill himself, or accept the teacher's drill methods.

The desire to learn may be conscious or unconscious. One may have an explicit desire to be a good basketball player, or a good dancer, or a good reader, or a good singer. In this case, one seeks opportunity to improve oneself. On the other hand, one may have only a generalized and vaguely felt desire to please somebody else, or to be like somebody. In this case one accepts opportunity to move in the desired direction, but does not actively seek it.

Programs aimed directly at improving mental skills have had remarkably little success with children beyond the age of 7 or 8. Only a few people, generally with highly personal methods, appear to have succeeded with classes in slum schools beyond the third grade. For example, Herbert Kohl taught a sixth-grade class in Harlem with a kind of freedom and spontaneity that seems to have motivated many of his pupils to care about their school work. Perhaps it is significant that he did relatively little drilling, and did not bother to correct spelling and grammar. In fact, he drew criticism from his supervisors because he did not emphasize the mental skills in the usual way. And Jonathan Kozol, in Boston, made friends with his pupils, took them on trips with him, visited their homes, but did not seem to stress the conventional training.

A rather common element of motivating situations is the presence of a model—a person who is accepted by the pupil as one he would like to be like. The habit of *modeling* one's behavior after that of others is learned very early in life, and becomes largely unconscious. A person forms the habit of imitating his parents and other persons in authority and persons who are visible to him and attractive to him. Teachers may or may not be effective models, depending on their behavior toward pupils and on the attitudes of pupils toward them.

Examples of motivating situations

There are a growing number of experiments with inner-city youth that seem to be successful and yet do not represent what we think of conventionally as good teaching. The methods are erratic; the teachers are not well-trained. These *experiments have in common a motivating element.*

Storefront academies and mini-schools.   Small, informal schools and classes springing up in the inner city appear to be accomplishing more than the conventional schools with disadvantaged youth. For example, the "street academies" of New York City appear to be working successfully with some dropouts and failing students from the high schools. These are described in an article by Chris Tree in *The Urban Review* for February, 1968, and are now a part of the Urban League's Education and Youth Incentives Program. The mini-school idea has already been presented.

Such projects must have methods, and the methods are being worked out pragmatically. It is too soon to say with any assurance what such a program would accomplish if it were expanded and made a part of the school system. Careful, empirical evaluation will have to be made to find out what kind of children and youth profit from this type of school and what kind do not.

Perhaps the essential factor in whatever success these schools have is that of acceptance by the teachers of the pupils as persons who want to learn, and the acceptance by the pupils of the teachers as people they want to be like.

Tutoring projects.   A few years ago there was a wave of tutoring projects which put college students and middle-class adults in the role of tutors to inner-city pupils of the intermediate and high school grades. These seem to have been largely discontinued, even though the tutors often reported that they got great personal satisfaction from their work and that it helped them to understand better the social structure of their society. Several careful evaluations of the effects of tutoring on mental skills of pupils throw some doubt on the value of the project from this point of view.

More recently there has been a development of tutoring by students only a little bit older and more skilled than the pupils being tutored. Some of these projects have shown surprising success. For example, Robert Cloward of Rhode Island University has evaluated a tutoring program in New York City in which teen-agers somewhat retarded in reading tutored middle-grade pupils in slum schools. Both tutees and tutors gained more in reading achievement tests than their controls did in a carefully designed experiment.

I have been told by several teachers of primary grades that they have occasionally asked an older or more advanced child to help a slow first-grader, with good results.

Whatever success these procedures have must be due more to motivation than to method. Getting *involved* with someone in a helping relationship apparently increases the desire to learn on the part of both the helper and the helped.

Games.   Games have an accepted place in schools, as activities for recess and sometimes physical education and even spelling lessons. Generally they have been used as a change from the serious business of the school. But now games are being used as part of the planned curriculum. The reason is that games are motivating to most players, and they try to learn in order to win the game. There are now a good many mathematical games available, as well as games in geography. James S. Coleman and his colleagues have been working out games for high school students. The Mecklenberg Academy in Charlotte, North Carolina, has a number of games available for high school students.

It is not clear to what extent games can be used in slum schools, though there seems to be no reason to suppose that inner-city children cannot be interested in games aimed at teaching geography and arithmetic.

Self-concept building.   Middle-class white Americans have difficulty understanding the demand for courses in African culture and history, for African languages such as Swahili, and for units on the Negro in American history in the elementary school. It is a waste of time if one is only interested in understanding the present world and in learning "useful" foreign languages.

But the need of a disadvantaged minority group to learn about its own cultural history in a positive way is related to the need for a positive self-concept—a self-concept of a person as a member of a social group that has a dignified and competent past. This need is hardly recognized by the white middle-class American, partly because he does not feel the need consciously and partly because his own competence and success as a person give him a positive self-concept which he can pass on to his children. Yet many children of Negro and other disadvantaged groups are told by their parents that they come from inferior stock, that they have "bad blood," that they suffer from their social past of slavery or of defeat by the white man.

While the best basis for a positive self-concept as a person who can learn in school and can succeed in American social and economic life is achievement—in school, in play, and in work—it may be that Negro children, in particular, would gain something from a study in school of the contributions of the Negro group to American life and culture, and of African history and culture.

When we find the good and effective ways to teach disadvantaged children and youth, we will still have to solve the problem of social integration of ethnic and poverty-plagued minority groups into the economic and political life of our large metropolitan areas. The solutions will go hand in hand. Big city and suburban governments as well as big city and suburban school systems will be remade in this process of social urban renewal.

I see the educational establishment reorganized and revitalized, together with the socio-political establishment. The work will largely be done by activists who learn to innovate creatively and to evaluate their innovations scientifically.

■   Discuss: Havighurst alleges that the schools have been victimized by a bad press. The media, with their proclivity for "bad news is good news," have tended to accept the critics at face value.

■   Enumerate some of the achievements of the public schools Havighurst claims are generally omitted in media reports.

*"...the advocates of free schools have
cared enough about human beings to try to
make education more humane and that is
to be prized. Where they have failed...is
at the point of theory: they have not asked
the right questions insistently enough, and
as a result they have tended to come up
with superficial and shopworn answers."*

Examine Cremin's position in relation to
Mortimer Smith's "The Reforms Most
Needed in Education" (Section One) and to
the Ford Foundation's "Matters of
Choice" (Section Two).

The Free School Movement: A Perspective

Lawrence A. Cremin

About a decade ago, I published a study of the progessive education movement of
John Dewey's time—the movement that began around 1890, peaked in the 1920's
and 1930's, and then collapsed in the years after World War II. I am often asked,
is there any relation between that movement and the free school movement
today? Is there anything to be learned from a comparison? And if so, what? My
answer is, we can learn a great deal.

In my study of the progressive education movement, which I titled *The
Transformation of the School,* I put forward a number of arguments:

First, that the movement was not an isloated phenomenon in American life, not
the invention of a few crackpots and eccentrics, but rather the educational side of
the broader progressive movement in American politics and social thought.

Lawrence A. Cremin, "The Free School Movement: A Perspective," *Notes on Education*
2 (October 1973). Published by the Institute of Philosophy and Politics of Education,
Teachers College, Columbia University, New York City. Reprinted by permission.

Lawrence A. Cremin is the author of *American Education: The Colonial Experience
1607–1783; The Transformation of the School;* and numerous journal and magazine
articles. He has been a Guggenheim Fellow and a fellow of the Center for Advanced Study
in the Behavioral Sciences. Professor of Education and Director of the Institute of
Philosophy and Politics of Education at Columbia University, he is also a member of the
board of trustees of the Children's Television Workshop.

Second, that the movement began in protest against the narrowness, the formalism, and the inequities of the late nineteenth-century public school.

Third, that as the movement shifted from protest to reform, it cast the school in a new mold, viewing it as (1) a lever of continuing social improvement, (2) an instrument of individual self-realization, (3) an agency for the popularization of culture, and (4) an institution for facilitating the adjustment of human beings to a society undergoing rapid transformation by the forces of democracy, science, and industrialism.

Fourth, that the movement was exceedingly diverse, enrolling men and women as different as Theodore Roosevelt, Jane Addams, Booker T. Washington, and Samuel Gompers, but that one could discern at least three major thrusts: a child-centered thrust, which peaked in the 1920's; a social-reform thrust, which peaked in the 1930's, and a scientific thrust, which peaked in the 1940's.

Fifth, that John Dewey saw the movement whole and served as the chief articulator of its aspirations—recall his little book *The School and Society* (1899), in which the first essay ("The School and Social Progress") reflected the social reform thrust, the second essay ("The School and the Life of the Child") reflected the child-centered thrust, and the third essay ("Waste in Education") reflected the scientific thrust.

Sixth, that the movement enjoyed its heyday during the 1920's and 1930's, that it began to decline during the 1940's, and that it collapsed during the 1950's for all the usual reasons—internal factionalism, the erosion of political support, the rise of an articulate opposition associated with post-World War II conservatism, and the sort of ideological inflexibility that made it unable to contend with its own success.

In the original plan of my study, I included a final section addressed to the question, "Where do we go from here?" But when the time came to write it, my thoughts were not clear, so I decided to end on a "phoenix-in-the-ashes" note: If and when liberalism in politics and public affairs had a resurgence, progressive education would rise again.

Now, I did manage to work out that last section in 1965. I had a chance to give it initially as the Horace Mann Lecture at the University of Pittsburgh, and then published it in a little book called *The Genius of American Education.* I argued there that the reason progressive education had collapsed was that the progressives had missed the central point of the American educational experience in the twentieth century, namely, that an educational revolution had been going on outside the schools far more fundamental than any changes that had taken place inside—the revolution implicit in the rise of cinema, radio, and television and the simultaneous transformation of the American family under the conditions of industrialism and urbanization. The progressives had bet on the school as the crucial lever of social reform and individual self-realization at precisely the time when the whole configuration of educational power was shifting radically.

And what was desperately needed, it seemed to me, was some new formulation that put the humane aspirations and social awareness of the progressive education movement together with a more realistic understanding of the fundamentally different situation in which all education was proceeding.

By the time I wrote *The Genius of American Education,* a new progressive education movement was already in the making. You are all familiar with it, so I shall describe it only in the roughest outline. I would date its beginning from precisely the time I was wrestling with that last section of *The Transformation of the School* that I found I could not write. I would date it from the publication of A. S. Neill's *Summerhill* in 1960. (Incidentally, the appearance of that book marked an extraordinary event in publishing. Nothing in it was new; Neill had published more than a dozen books on education; and most of what he recommended had been tried in the progressive schools of the 1920's and 1930's. When the original publisher, Harold H. Hart, first announced the title, not a single bookseller in the country ordered a single advance copy; ten years later, in 1970, the book was selling at over 200,000 copies a year.)

The new movement began slowly, with the organization of Summerhill societies and Summerhill schools in different parts of the country. It gathered momentum during the middle 1960's, fueled by the writings of John Holt, Herbert Kohl, George Dennison, James Herndon, and Jonathan Kozol (whose book *Death at an Early Age* won the National Book Award in 1968). And it manifested itself in the appearance of scores of new child-centered schools of every conceivable sort and variety.

Simultaneously, growing out of the civil rights movement, there arose the political programs of black and ethnic self-determination and the so-called community free schools associated with them—Harlem Prep in New York, the CAM Academy in Chicago, and the Nairobi Community School in East Palo Alto.

By the summer of 1971 Allen Graubard, whose book *Free the Children* (1972) is the most recent effort to state the history and theory of the movement, was able to identify some 350 such schools and in all likelihood there are more than 500 of them today. And these are what Graubard calls "outside-the-system" schools, so that we must add many more schools, schools within schools, and classrooms within schools that are part of the public school system and variously referred to as alternative schools or community schools or open schools.

Also, during the last five or six years, we have seen a fascinating interweaving of the child-centered and political-reform themes in the literature of the movement, so that open education is viewed as a lever of child liberation on the one hand and as a lever of radical social change on the other (the interweaving is beautifully illustrated in the early issues of the West coast quarterly *Socialist Revolution*).

At least two of the three themes of the first movement, then, the child-centered theme and the social-reform theme, have emerged full-blown in the present-day movement. Interestingly enough, however, the scientific theme of the first movement has been noticeably absent from the present version. In fact, there has been an active hostility on the part of many free school advocates toward present-day efforts to apply scientific principles to the techniques of instruction and evaluation. Whereas the progressive education movement reached a kind of culmination in the eight-year study, in which Ralph Tyler and his associates tried systematically to assess the outcomes of progressive methods, latter-day advocates of free schools have seemed on the whole uninterested in such assessment.

Interestingly, too, the radical side of the current movement has been much more sweeping in its radicalism than was earlier the case, culminating, I would suppose, in Ivan Illich's proposal that we deschool society completely. There were radicals in the 1890's who were fairly skeptical about educational roads to reform—one of them once told Jane Addams that using education to correct social injustice was about as effective as using rosewater to cure the plague. But I have yet to find a radical at that time who wanted to do away with schools entirely; it was rather the reactionaries of the 1890's who sought that.

What is most striking, perhaps, in any comparison of the two movements is the notoriously a-theoretical, a-historical character of the free school movement in our time. The present movement has been far less profound in the questions it has raised about the nature and character of education and in the debates it has pursued around those questions. The movement has produced no John Dewey, no Boyd Bode, no George Counts, no journal even approaching the quality of the old *Social Frontier.* And it has been far less willing to look to history for ideas. Those who have founded free schools have not read their Francis W. Parker or their Caroline Pratt or their Helen Parkhust, with the result that boundless energy has been spent in countless classrooms reinventing the pedagogical wheel.

Further, the movement has had immense difficulty going from protest to reform, to the kinds of detailed alternative strategies that will give us better educational programs than we now have. Even Jonathan Kozol's *Free Schools,* which was written explicitly to help people found alternative institutions, is egregiously thin in its programmatic suggestions; while Joseph Turner's *Making New Schools,* which pointedly proffered a rather well-developed reformist curriculum, has not even been noticed by the movement.

Finally, the current movement has remained as school-bound as the progressive education movement of an earlier time. Even Charles Silberman's *Crisis in the Classroom* (1970), surely the most learned and wide-ranging analysis to be associated with the present movement (though it did not emanate from the present movement), begins with a lengthy discussion of how television writers, filmmakers, priests, rabbis, librarians, and museum directors all educate but then goes on to propose the open classroom as the keystone in the arch of educational reform. Ironically, the one book to come out of the movement that appears to have comprehended the educational revolution of our time is Ivan Illich's *Deschooling Society.* But the appearance is deceptive. Illich would like to abandon schooling in favor of what he calls educational networks, but he does not deal with the inevitable impact of the media and the market on those networks.

Now, it is easy enough to criticize, and my remarks should not be taken as a defense of the educational status quo. At the very least, the advocates of free schools have cared enough about human beings to try to make education more humane and that is to be prized. Where they have failed, it seems to me, is at the point of theory: they have not asked the right questions insistently enough, and as a result they have tended to come up with superficial and shop-worn answers.

Let me then put my question once again: What would an educational movement look like today that combined the humane aspirations and social awareness of the progressive education movement with a more realistic understanding of the nature of present-day education? What if free schools (and all other schools for that matter) were to take seriously the radically new situation in which all education inescapably proceeds? What would they do differently?

Let me venture three suggestions. First, viewing the situation from the schools outward, they would begin to contend with the fact that youngsters in the schools have been taught and are being taught by many curricula and that if they want to influence those youngsters they must be aware of those curricula. The Children's Television Workshop has a curriculum. The advertising departments of the Ideal Toy Company and Love's Lemon Cosmetics have curricula. The *Encyclopaedia Britannica* and the *World Book Encyclopedia* have curricula.

The Time-Life Science Program has a curriculum. The Boy Scouts and the Girl Scouts have curricula. Our churches and synagogues have curricula—the Talmud has been a curriculum for centuries and so has the Book of Common Prayer. And each family has a curriculum, though in many instances that curriculum may do little more than leave youngsters to the fortunes of the other educators.

To understand this is to force educators to change fundamentally the way they think about education. It means, as James Coleman and Christopher Jencks—and one should probably add Plato—have pointed out, that the school never has *tabulae rasae* to begin with, that when children come to school they have already been educated and miseducated on the outside, and that the best the school can do in many realms is to complement, extend, accentuate, challenge, neutralize, or counter (though in so doing the school does crucially important work). It means that one of the most significant tasks any school can undertake is to try to develop in youngsters an awareness of these other curricula and an ability to criticize them. Young people desperately need the intellectual tools to deal critically with the values of a film like *The Clockwork Orange,* or with the human models in a television serial like *Marcus Welby, M.D.,* or with the aesthetic qualities of the music of Lawrence Welk. None of this can substitute for reading, writing, and arithmetic, to be sure; but reading, writing, and arithmetic are no longer enough.

Incidentally, if one accepts this line of argument, it is utter nonsense to think that by turning children loose in an unplanned and unstructured environment they can be freed in any significant way. Rather, they are thereby abandoned to the blind forces of the hucksters, whose primary concern is neither the children, nor the truth, nor the decent future of American society. Second, looking beyond the school, once educators took seriously the fact that we are all taught by radio and television, peer groups and advertising agencies, libraries and museums, they would necessarily become interested not only in alternative schools but in alternative education of every kind. It may well be, for example, that the most important educational battle now being fought in the United States is over who will control cable television, who will award the franchises, and what will be the public requirements associated with a franchise. Once forty to fifty channels are readily available to every American home—some of them with the capacity for responsive interchange—then what comes over those channels in the form of education or miseducation will profoundly affect *all* teaching, in schools and everywhere else. There is simply no avoiding it, and educators had best face it.

Further, if educators were to take seriously what Urie Bronfenbrenner has been saying about the extraordinary power of the adolescent peer group in American society and the need for a greater variety of adult models in the life of every child, they would press for a host of innovations, both inside the school and out. They would be more interested than they seem, for example, in peer-mediated instruction, or in summer camps, or in arrangements under which children spend time in factories, businesses, offices, or shops, with real adults doing real work, along the lines of the experiment Bronfenbrenner carried out with David Goslin at the *Detroit Free Press.* You are doubtless familiar with the recent publication called *Yellow Pages of Learning Resources,* in which a whole city is seen as a potential learning environment and successive pages indicate what can be learned at an airport, a bakery, a bank, a butcher, a courtroom, a department store, and so on, all the way to a zoo. Once again, I might note that it does not take less planning and less structure to pursue these sorts of learning, it takes different plans and different structures. And without such plans and structures, there is simply no freedom.

Finally, focusing on the learner himself, once educators took seriously the fact that we are living through a revolution in which opportunities for education and miseducation are burgeoning throughout the society, they would give far more attention to the need to equip each youngster as early as possible to make his way purposefully and intelligently through the various configurations of education, with a view to the kind of person he would like to become and the relation of education to becoming that kind of person. In other words, they would do all they could to nurture an educationally autonomous individual.

I happen to think that kind of individual was at the heart of John Dewey's theory of education and central to his conception of a democratic society. And I find it not at all strange to be ending on such a note, for as critical as I have been of the progressive education movement of yesterday and the free school movement of today, I find myself much more in sympathy with the authentic aspirations of both movements—at least as articulated by Dewey—than I am opposed to them. In the last analysis, my critique is simply an effort to call the free school movement to the service of its own best ideals, and it can only learn what those ideals are by studying its own history.

- How does Cremin delineate similarities and differences between the two major educational reform movements of this century: the progressive movement and the free-school movement?

- What projections does Cremin make for school reform?

- With which of the many people and book references in this article are you familiar? What steps can you take to become more knowledgeable about those unknown to you?

Annotated Bibliography

ACKERMAN, NATHAN W. *et al. Summerhill: For and Against.* New York: Hart, 1970.

The famous Summerhill school of A. S. Neill has produced passionate proponents and opponents. In this volume educators present a wide range of differing perceptions and evaluations. (271 pp.)

"Alternatives in Public Education: Movement or Fad?" *National Association of Secondary School Principals Bulletin* **57** (September 1973), whole issue.

A series of interesting reports on different kinds of secondary schools experimenting with alternative ways of organizing their programs, as well as some comment on the alternative-education movement.

EISNER, ELLIOTT W., ed. *Confronting Curriculum Reform.* Boston: Little, Brown, 1970.

Do you wonder if all the publicity about "new" curricula is based on fact or fancy? This volume includes some critical reviews of efforts to change the curriculum, presented by an individual responsible for the curriculum project, and this presentation in turn is criticized by an "outside" educator. (206 pp.)

GARTNER, ALAN, COLIN GREER, and FRANK RIESSMAN, eds. *After Deschooling, What?* New York: Harper & Row, 1973.

Most of the essays in this volume appeared in *Social Policy*. They are directed at critical analysis of Illich's proposal to do away with formal schooling. An interesting array of commentary ranging from those sympathetic to Illich to those who are highly critical of him. (162 pp.)

GINTIS, HERBERT. "Toward a Political Economy of Education: A Radical Critique of Ivan Illich's *Deschooling Society.*" *Harvard Educational Review* **42** (February 1972), pp. 70–96.

This analyst considers Illich's description of social ills significant, but his solution to be simplistic, nonpolitical, and economically impossible.

HAPGOOD, MARILYN. "The Open Classroom: Protect It from Its Friends." *The Saturday Review,* 18 September 1971, pp. 66 ff.

Concern is expressed that the effectiveness of British open classrooms has generated admirers whose haste to implement the approach in America will cause them to do a poor job, thereby generating public disapproval of the open-classroom style. The author's plea is essentially for patience and a transitional stage which will allow Americans to find their own "open" style.

LIFTON, WALTER M., ed. *Educating for Tomorrow: The Role of Media, Career Development and Society.* New York: Wiley, 1970.

A humanistic approach to solving the problem of how new media may be utilized and harnessed for individual instruction and career fulfillment. (242 pp.)

MILES, MATHEW B., ed. *Innovation in Education.* New York: Teachers College Press, 1964.

In "The Fate of Innovations," the editor sums up the failures and the successes of innovation. One of the most succinct and illuminating statements in the literature. (689 pp.)

SARASON, SEYMOUR B. *The Culture of the School and the Problem of Change.* Boston: Allyn and Bacon, 1971.

One of the outstanding books on the theoretical aspects of educational change. Particularly valuable for the social-cultural context in which the discussion is placed: the "real" school, here and now. Based in part on the author's experience in trying to introduce some changes in his own local schools. (241 pp.)

SMITH, MORTIMER *et al. A Consumer's Guide to Educational Innovations.* Washington, D. C.: Council for Basic Education, 1972.

The conservative view of the feasibility and educational value of the many innovations being proposed or tried. Brief descriptions of each practice are given, with a critical appraisal. (99 pp.)

SMITH, MORTIMER. "What Is Going On in the Social Studies?" *Council for Basic Education Bulletin* 16, no. 7 (March 1972), pp. 1–9.

Attacks the "new look" in social studies, which the author says causes teachers to try to do too many things and to eschew the learning of essential information. "Perhaps what the social studies suffer from the most is ambition. Instead of setting up all-inclusive aims in this field we ought to ask ourselves what essential learnings we can transmit to students in the limited time at the disposal of the schools."

WINSOR, CHARLOTTE, ed. *Experimental Schools Revisisted.* New York: Agathon Press, 1973.

The experimental schools described in this book were "revisted" in 1917–1924. As one reviewer noted, this book seems to have been lost in transit for fifty years; that is, the experiments of over fifty years ago have a very modern ring to them. Interesting to contrast the similarities and the differences from prescriptions for new programs today. (335 pp.)

Index of Names

The listings that follow are selective, confined to proper names. Classifications for alternative schools, names of schools and programs, and terms for philosophical positions are so numerous in this collection that listing them in an index would be confusing rather than helpful.